ONCE UPON A CORNER IN DETROIT

By Harlan Rector

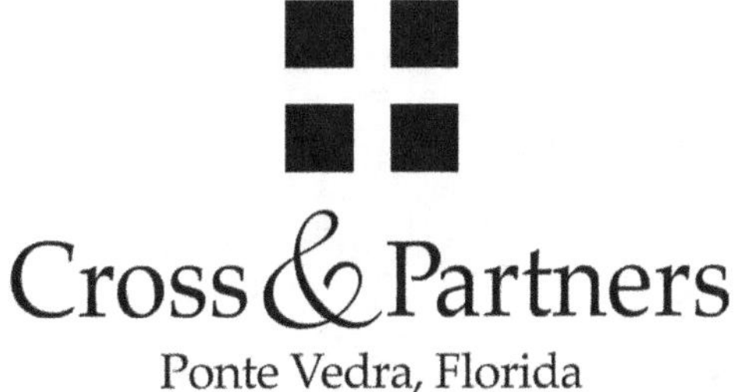

Cross & Partners
Ponte Vedra, Florida

Once Upon a Corner in Detroit

By Harlan Rector

First Edition June 2020

ISBN-13: 978-1-7350747-0-2

Published in the United States by Cross & Partners II, LLC

Cover Design by Robert Chester Design

Book Design and Typesetting by
Cynthia J. Kwitchoff (CJKCREATIVE.COM)

A TRIBUTE TO MY CARICATURE 'BOOKENDS'

J.P. McCARTHY

'THE VOICE OF DETROIT'.

HONORING THE MEMORY OF ONE

OF THE GREATEST VOICES IN BROADCASTING.

IN GRATITUDE FOR THE PRIVILEGE OF BEING A SMALL

PART OF HIS RADIO LIFE ON 'FOCUS'.

AND TO THE MEMORY OF

TOM ADAMS

CHAIRMAN OF THE BOARD

OF CAMPBELL EWALD ADVERTISING,

WHO ALLOWED ME THE LUXURY EACH DAY

OF HAVING 'LUNCH' WITH J.P. AND HIS FAMOUS FRIENDS.

TABLE OF CONTENTS

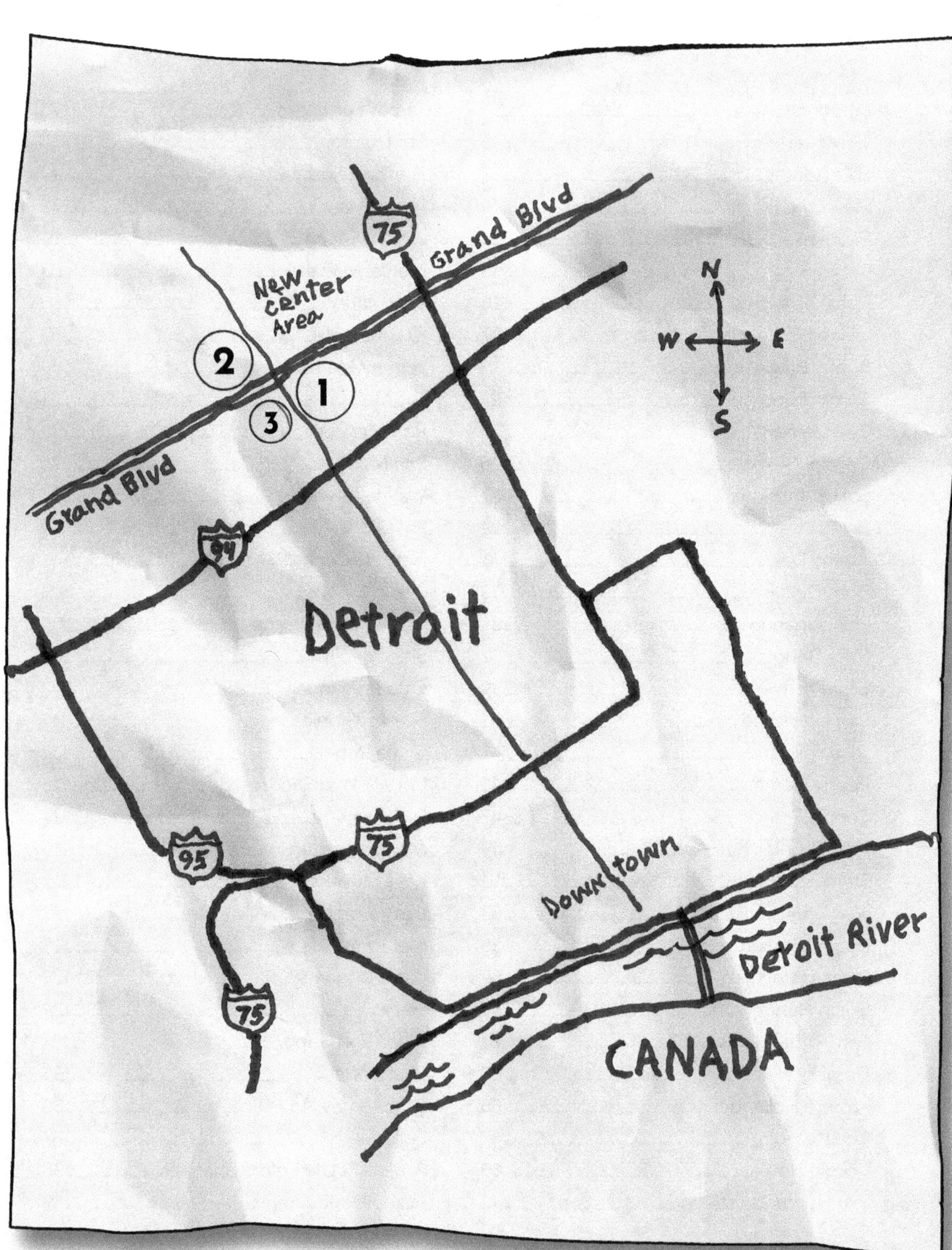

75
Grand Blvd
New Center Area
N
W   E
S
2
1
3
Grand Blvd
94
Detroit
95
75
75
Downtown
Detroit River
CANADA

Once Upon a Corner in Detroit

The General Motors Building (1), built in 1923, and the Fisher Building (2), built in 1928, were both designed by architect, Albert Kahn. The GM Building was the headquarters of General Motors, Chevrolet and Campbell Ewald Advertising.

My office window, as well as 156 other windows on the north facing fourth floor, had a view of Grand Boulevard.

Across the street, at the corner of Grand and Second, stood the 30-story Fisher Building, a beautiful example of art deco architecture. It was home for a competing ad agency, the Fisher Theatre, an upscale restaurant and WJR Radio.

Also across the street was the Steering Wheel Restaurant (3), where JP McCarthy invited Detroit to have lunch with him and his celebrity friends every day.

Three other notable areas of Detroit in 1971 were: Tiger Stadium, where Mickey Lolich won 28 games pitching for the Detroit Tigers, Olympia Stadium where Red Wing hockey icon Gordie Howe (included in this book), would retire after 25 years with the team, and Motown, a few blocks west of The Steering Wheel, where twenty-one-year-old Stevie Wonder was found re-negotiating a huge recording contract.

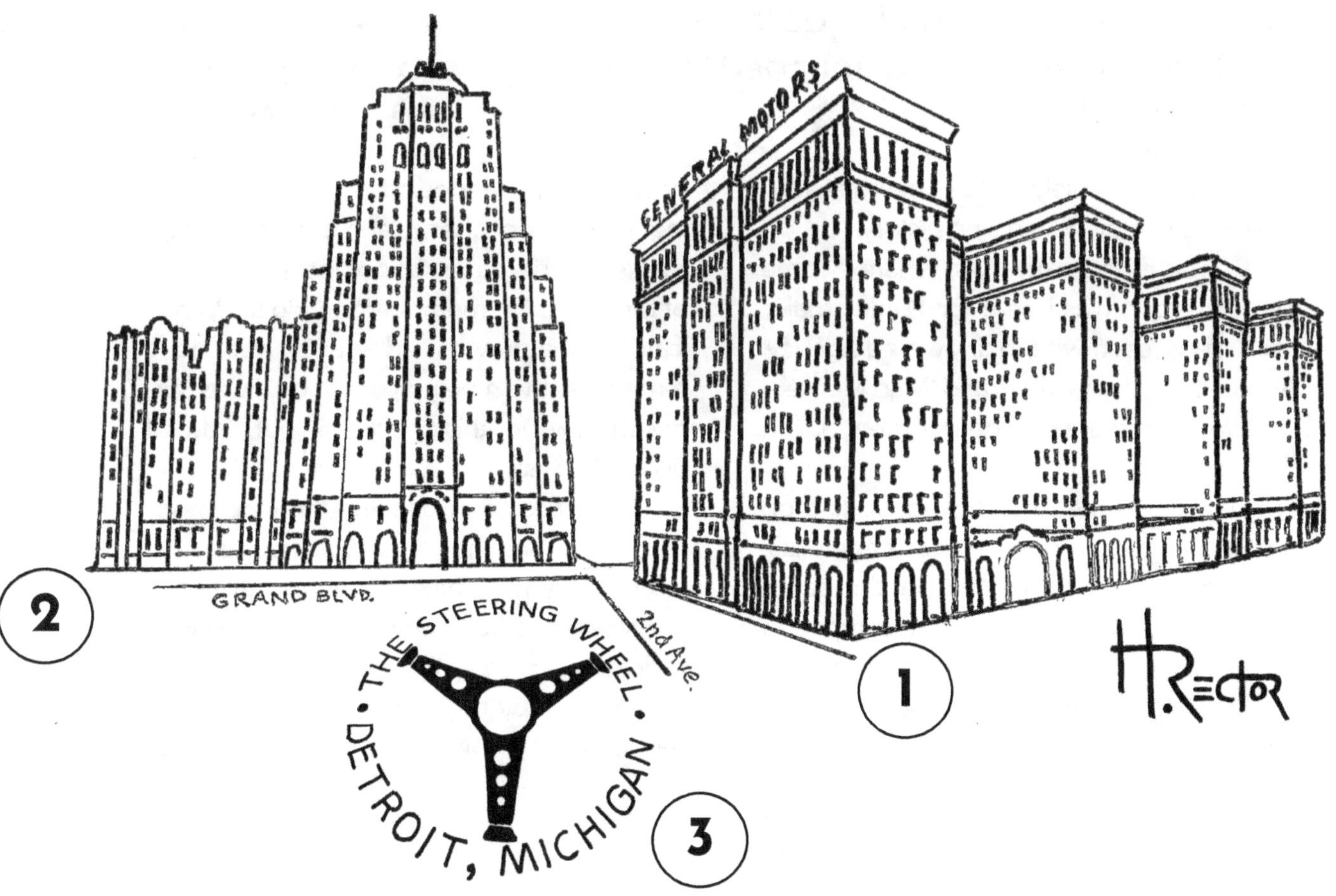

Once Upon a Corner

No other major city in the United States has been so utterly dependent on one product. Detroit's product is automotive, and its mouthpiece is advertising.

One advertising agency mentioned in this book, Campbell-Ewald, began in 1911 with six employees. Chevrolet became Campbell-Ewald's first major account in 1919.

In 1922, its owner Henry Ted Ewald was awarded all five automobile divisions of General Motors as clients. Cadillac, Oldsmobile, Buick, Pontiac, and Chevrolet made a handsome package until General Motors decided to break up the five using different advertising agencies to handle them. To placate the loss, General Motors let Ted Ewald have the first pick, suggesting the prestigious name of Cadillac as his new client. Ted wisely chose Chevrolet, and the rest is Detroit advertising history.

Detroit in the early 70's, where I come into this story, was home for 11 plus major car brands, each with their own ad agency. Art directors, copywriters and 'Mad Men' executive types were competing every day in the motor city.

Hats off to the people who worked on an automobile account at these agencies! They knew each other, ate in the same restaurants, maybe had a job at a competing agency before, but they were still expected to have exciting, fresh ads as their competition, doing the same thing right next door.

The word "detroit" is French for "strait." The French called the river running by, "Le detroit dulac Erie" meaning "the strait of Lake Erie."
In 1701, the French explorer Antoine de la Mothe Cadillac founded Detroit.

I was new to Detroit and my workday centered at the 'corner' of Grand Boulevard and Second Avenue—hence the title of this book.

I worked as an art director in Detroit, St. Louis, New York, and Los Angeles—totaling seven different ad agencies throughout my career. I quit four of the jobs and was fired from three, but the best job I ever had in my twenty years was at Campbell-Ewald, the largest agency in Detroit. I was hired to create advertising for Rockwell International, an exciting conglomerate of companies manufacturing products as varied as knitting machines for the fashion industry all the way to the space shuttle.

One day, in 1971, a copywriter and I sat in my office trying in vain to create a print ad for one of Rockwell's divisions. We were getting nowhere and needed a break. With a drawing pad in one hand and Sharpie magic marker in the other, I doodled a caricature of the writer. I remembered trying to do caricatures at a previous ad agency, but I don't remember them being very good. I was surprised how well this one turned out. I stuck it up on the wall.

My office soon became the most popular place in the agency. Anyone who stopped by my office was immortalized—the four walls decorated to the ceiling with caricatures.

Inspired by my new-found talent, I began taking a drawing pad and a Sharpie or two with me everywhere I went. For lunch one day, I wandered into a restaurant near my office. Everything in Detroit pertained to automobiles so the restaurant was aptly named The Steering Wheel. Off in the corner near the bar, WJR was remotely broadcasting. The 50,000 watt radio station was conducting their daily, hour-long interview show Focus.

Any celebrity on a publicity tour hawking a movie, book or just happened to be in town, was interviewed on Focus by JP McCarthy, the Voice of Detroit. Known by all as JP, he could talk on any subject and with such personal delivery his listeners felt they were sitting with him at their kitchen table for lunch. For a while, JP had both morning and evening drive-time shows, five times a week. That was unprecedented for Detroit radio. Later, he dropped his evening show to concentrate more on his morning show and the noontime "Focus" show.

Back to that day at The Steering Wheel, I was sitting at the bar, close to the radio show already in progress with an interview ending. I felt compelled so I grabbed my pad, uncapped my Sharpie, and drew a caricature of McCarthy. After the show, JP and his producer came over to the bar next to where I was sitting.

I introduced myself and showed JP his caricature. He laughed. "Nice to meet you Harlan, do you have a job or do you just hang around bars for a living?" I smiled. "I'm an art director at Campbell-Ewald across the street. I just happened to be here for lunch."

JP looked over at his nodding producer. "What do you think about coming to The Steering Wheel every day to draw caricatures of our guests on the show?" He asked.

What could I say? "Wow," I answered.

The very next day I was on the Focus show and for a couple of years I spent my lunch hour drawing more than 100 celebrities as they were being interviewed. When an interview was over, I'd meet the guest, ask them to autograph the caricature and Clarence Baker, the restaurant owner, would thumbtack it to the wall—the goal was to replicate the décor of Sardi's in New York.

When WJR decided to broadcast Focus from their own studio, I took the caricatures off the wall. I can tell which ones were done at The Steering Wheel by the tiny thumbtack holes in the corners of the paper.

The interviews were about 16 minutes so I had to draw fast to catch an expression or feature to produce their likeness. Every line or stroke had to be right because you can't erase a Sharpie magic marker.

In WJR's studio I decided to make two identical caricatures of every celebrity. I gave the guest their own and asked them to autograph the other for me. No one ever objected and some of them wrote messages. Only two celebrities were unhappy with their caricature but graciously signed them anyway. I've included 65 celebrity caricatures in this book. My favorite is on the next page.

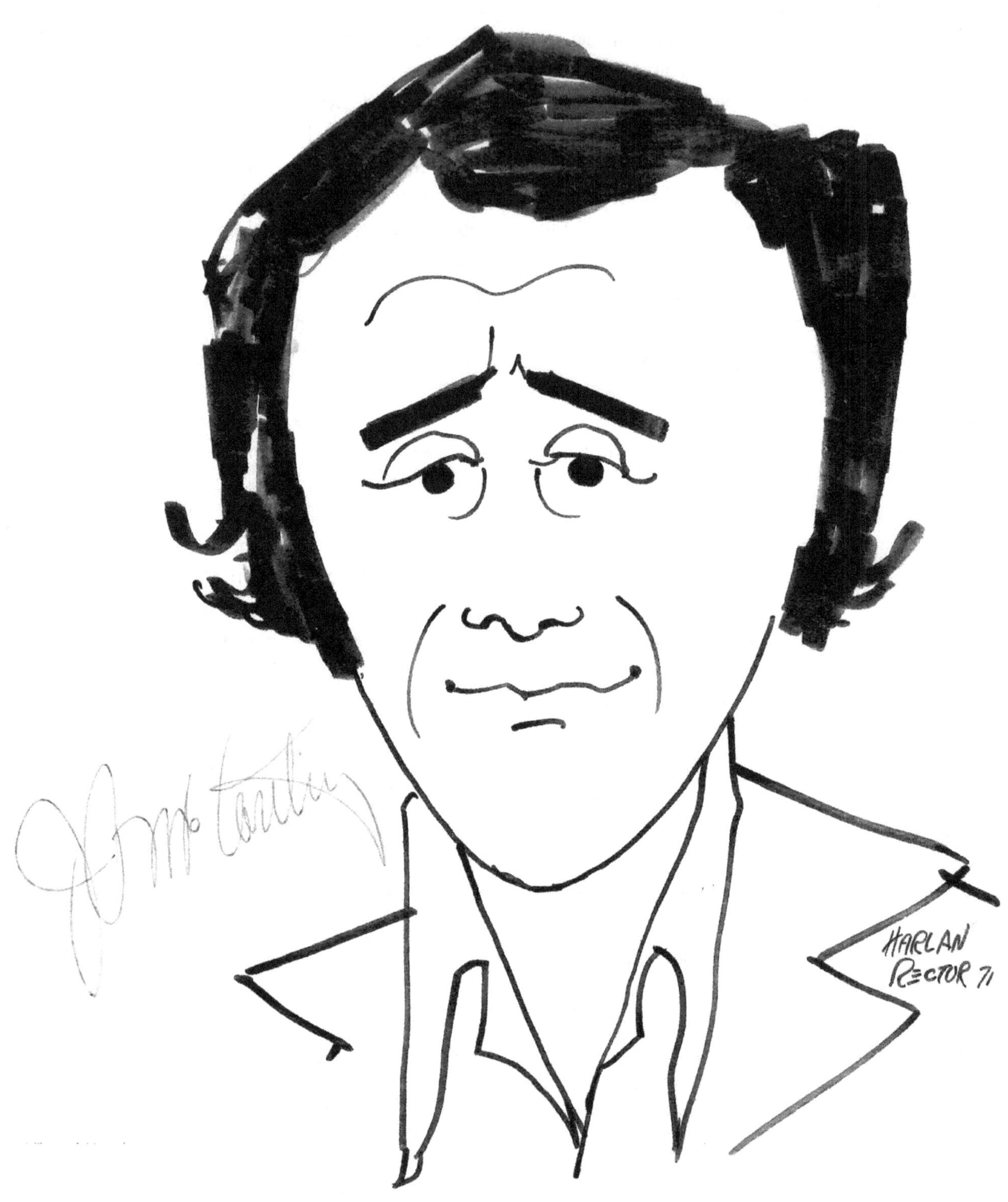

There's a saying, "He had a face for radio", so here it is.

J.P. McCarthy

Joseph Priestly McCarthy was born in New York City on March 22, 1933. The family later moved to Detroit when Joseph was in elementary school. He graduated from De La Salle Collegiate High School and went on to the University of Detroit, where he attended until he was drafted and stationed in Alaska.

Fairbanks seemed like the end of the world, but it was the beginning of JP's radio career. While still in the Army, he had a part time job on the air at radio station KFAR in Fairbanks. It was there that he met and married Sali Thompson, who mothered their five children.

Once discharged, JP returned to radio full time working at WTAC in Flint, Michigan, but he had his eyes set on the big prize in Detroit.

In 1956, he landed a staff announcer job at WJR. Two years later he became the host of WJR's *Morning Music Hall* show. As WJR's morning man, he soon became the #1 radio host in Detroit. His easy style was a welcome voice in the morning for commuters.

He was offered the opportunity to be the spokesman for Stroh's, the top brewery in Detroit, but radio personalities endorsing products were frowned upon at WJR. Despite the extra income benefiting JP, and saving WJR having to give him a raise, WJR still said no. Feeling he had no choice, he left Detroit to become the morning man at KGO in San Francisco.

WJR was sold in 1964 to Capital Cities Broadcasting and the new management was eager to bring JP back to Detroit. They made the change to allow radio personal-ities to be commercial spokesmen on the side and JP came back. He was host of the morning drive-time show as well as the evening drive-time show.

After a divorce in 1965, he married Judy Buttorf and had one son, James (Jamie). JP eventually dropped the evening show and began a noon interview show called *Focus*.

The celebrities I drew in this book represent some of the great people interviewed in 1971 and 1972. I left Detroit in 1975, but *Focus* stayed on the air for 23 additional years.

JP had interests outside of the studio like golf and sailing—he was an expert at both. A lover of sports, especially his beloved Detroit Tigers, he interviewed countless players and managers. He awed them all with his depth of knowledge about their game. In 1975, he even served as color commentator on WJR's Detroit Lions football broadcasts.

In the summer of 1995, he was diagnosed with myelodysplastic syndrome, a condition that frequently develops into leukemia. With his entire family at his bedside and thousands of prayers from his listeners, JP McCarthy died at only 62 from pneumonia in his sleep on August 16, 1995. ∎

HARLAN RECTOR

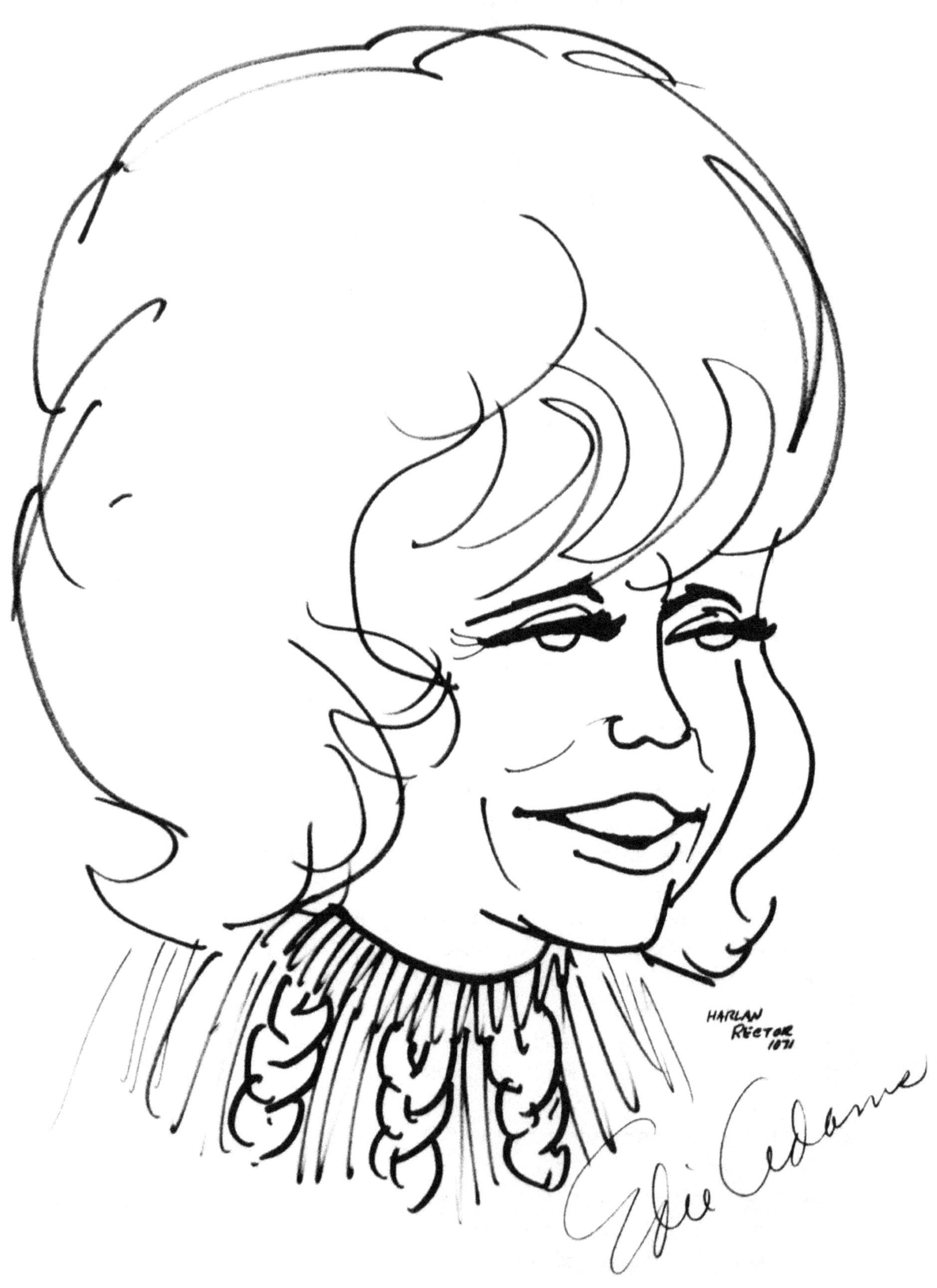

HARLAN
RECTOR
1971

Edie Adams

Edie Adams was born in Kingston, Pennsylvania on April 16, 1927, as Edith Elizabeth Enke. Her parents were Ada Dorothy Enke and Sheldon Alonzo Enke, members of the choir at Grove City Presbyterian Church. Ada instructed Edie in piano and singing.

Edie's grandmother was a seamstress who passed on the skill to Edie; in sixth grade, Edie was making her own dresses and later began Bonham, Inc., her own line of designer clothing.

Edie pursued her studies at Juilliard School in New York City, earning a vocal degree and graduated from the Columbia School of Drama. She tossed a coin to decide whether to follow a career in music or fashion design: music won.

From 1949 to 1950, Adams did live commercials. She won a beauty contest in 1950, which enabled her to appear on Milton Berle's television show. She auditioned for *The Ernie Kovacs Show,* where despite knowing only three popular songs, she soon became part of the show.

Adams worked regularly on television with Kovacs, who unexpectedly proposed. She accepted. It was his second marriage and it lasted until his tragic death—a car accident in 1962.

In 1957, they both were nominated for Emmy awards for their comedy series. Edie starred in multiple Broadway shows, even winning the 1956 Tony Award for Best Featured Actress in a Musical in *Li'l Abner.*

After Kovacs died, ABC gave Edie her own show, which lasted only one season. Adams did television commercials for Muriel Cigars and she made other occasional appearances. She played supporting roles in several films in the 1960s and was a successful nightclub performer.

After Kovacs died, Edie fought and won a "nasty custody battle" with Kovacs's ex-wife over her stepdaughters. There was another court battle with Ernie's mother over the debts in Kovacs's estate. Edie worked for years to pay off the IRS for his debts.

Adams began her own businesses and because of her 20 years of commercials for Muriel Cigars, as well as her success in business, she went from being in debt to becoming a millionaire in 1989.

Adams was married two more times, first to Martin Mills in 1964 and then Pete Candoli in 1972. She gave birth to Mia Susan Kovacs, who predeceased her, and son Joshua Mills.

Edie Adams died in Los Angeles, California, on October 15, 2008 at age 81 from cancer and pneumonia. She is buried alongside her first husband, Ernie, between her daughter Mia and stepdaughter, Kippie. ◼

EMILY MELENDEZ

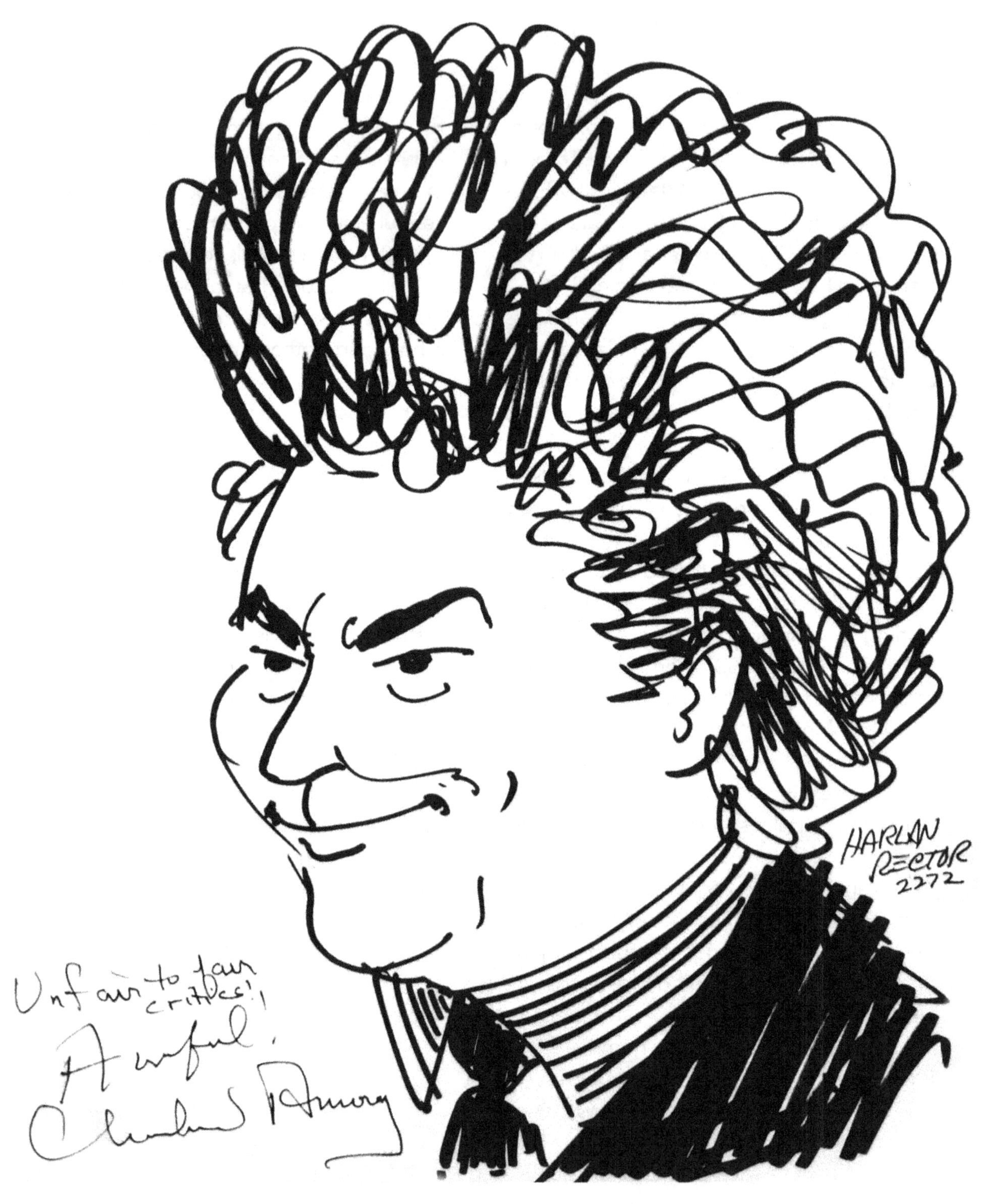
Unfair to fair
critics!
Awful!
HARLAN
RECTOR
2272

Cleveland Amory

Cleveland Amory was born on September 2, 1917, in Nahant, Massachusetts. His parents, Robert and Lenore Cobb Amory, were part of Boston's high society. His father was a manufacturer of textiles—a descendant in generations of well-to-do merchants and his mother was the daughter of Chicago's top architect Henry Ives Cobb.

But it was Cleveland's aunt Lucy and her affection for stray animals that influenced him most. It started the day she helped him get his first puppy—a childhood memory that shaped his life forever.

Cleveland attended the Milton Academy private school then went on to Harvard where he held the position of president for *The Harvard Crimson* paper. After graduation, he became a reporter for *The Nashua Telegraph,* moved to Arizona to become the managing editor of *The Prescott Evening Courier*, and in 1939, at only twenty-one years old, he became the youngest editor ever hired for *The Saturday Evening Post.*

Following his three years service working Army Intelligence, Cleveland witnessed an inhumane bullfight in Nogales, Mexico that rekindled his passion for animals. For the next fifteen years, he wrote books, with his first book published in 1947.

Amory became a regular columnist for *The Saturday Review* from 1952 to 1972. He was a commentator on Today and the NBC Morning News.

Despite his usual humor on air, ironically, he was fired in 1962 over an animal rights commentary. As the story goes, Amory traveled to Harmony, North Carolina where he learned a "bunny bop" was planned to kill the local wild rabbits. He debated with its planners, suggesting a "hunt club" be created instead—human hunters should be tracked down and killed for sport. All this was said on air and the shocked listeners response was negative. Amory was only reprimanded by NBC president Julian Goodman but when Amory expressed his controversial opinions again, and only a few months later, he was fired.

Amory was a television critic from 1963 to 1976 drawing negative attention from hunters for his biting comments about sports hunting. His writings focused on animal rights more and more. His book *Man Kind? Our Incredible War on Wildlife* (1974) talked about the inhumane hunting practices, precipitating a CBS documentary and New York Times editorial. Curmudgeon at Large was a daily radio essay he aired and he wrote a column called Animail. From 1980 to 1998 Amory was the senior contributing editor of Parade.

Cleveland Amory wrote another series of nonfiction, best-selling books about a stray white cat named Polar Bear that he rescued from a street in New York City on Christmas Eve, 1977. *The Cat Who Came for Christmas* (1987) was a New York Times bestseller for twelve weeks. The sequels were bestsellers as well—*The Cat and the Curmudgeon* (1990) and *The Best Cat Ever* (1993).

Amory died in 1998 of an abdominal aortic aneurysm. His ashes were spread across Cleveland Amory Black Beauty Ranch in Murchison, Texas. ∎

EMILY MELENDEZ

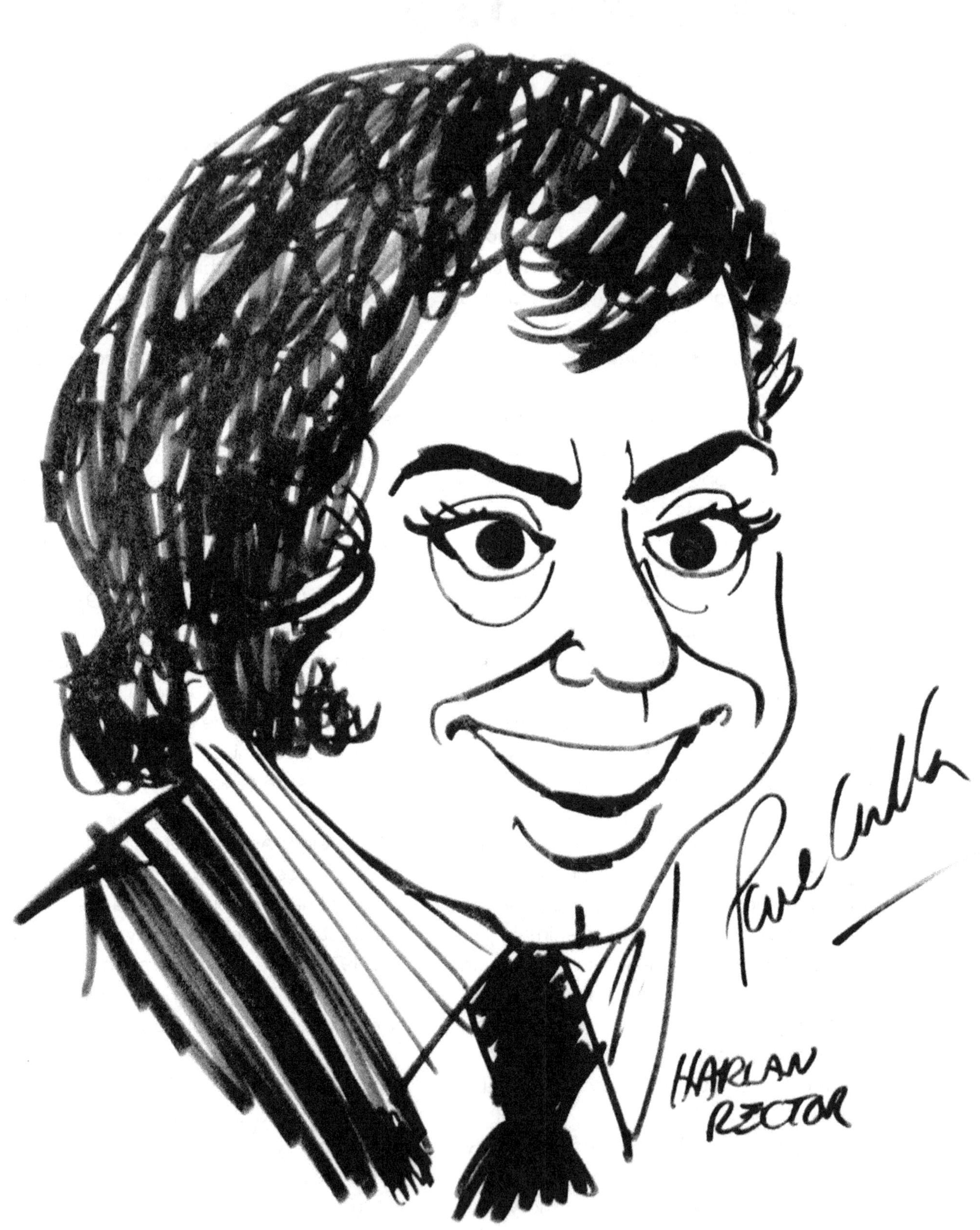
HARLAN
RECTOR

Paul Anka

Paul Albert Anka was born on July 30, 1941, in Ottawa, Ontario, Canada to parents of Syrian and Lebanese descent. Camelia (Tannis) Anka and Andrew Emile "Andy" Anka, Sr. owned the Locanda Restaurant. Camelia died when Paul was just 18.

Paul was a member of the St. Elias Antiochian Orthodox Cathedral choir, directed by Frederick Karam, who taught him music theory while Winnifred Rees taught him piano. He attended Fisher Park High School and sang with the vocal trio the Bobby Soxers.

Paul's early success began with I Confess, which he recorded at age 14. In 1957, Paul went to NYC and auditioned for Don Costa at ABC. When *Diana* flew to No. 1 on the US and Canadian music charts, Anka achieved stardom.

Four songs, including *It's Time to Cry* and *My Heart Sings*, rose to the Top 20 in 1958. At 17, Paul became one of the greatest teen idols of his time. He toured Britain and Australia with Buddy Holly.

Anka wrote the theme for The Tonight Show starring Johnny Carson. He wrote *Teddy* for Connie Francis in 1950. Anka composed *She's a Lady* for Tom Jones, which went on to become Jones's biggest hit record. Paul also wrote the English lyrics to *My Way*, which became Frank Sinatra's signature song.

Anka began his acting career in motion pictures alongside composing songs for them; he wrote the theme song for *The Longest Day*, in which he made a cameo appearance. He also wrote and recorded *Lonely Boy* for his film work—was one of his greatest hits. Anka performed in Las Vegas casinos and signed with RCA Victor in 1960. His career was stymied in the 1960s by the British Invasion of rock groups coming to the US.

In the 1970s, Paul Anka made a comeback as he signed with United Artists and teamed up with Odia Coates to record *(You're) Having My Baby*. This proved his versatility and power to stay popular with fans. He wrote and sang many more hit songs, such as *Hold Me Til the Morning Comes* in the summer of 1983.

Paul's 1998 album, *A Body of Work*, became his first new release since 1983, and he included many guest vocalists and performers on that album. Anka also found success in Italy as a singer / song writer in the 1960s.

He became a naturalized US citizen in 1990.

Anka married Anne de Zogheb on February 6, 1963, and they had five daughters together, though eventually they divorced in 2001. In 2008, Anka married Anna Aberg, then divorced two years later; he has custody of their only son. He most recently married Lisa Pemberton in California, October 2016.

Paul Anka won the Juno Award for songwriting in 1975 and was inducted into the Canadian Music Hall of Fame in 1980. ∎

EMILY MELENDEZ

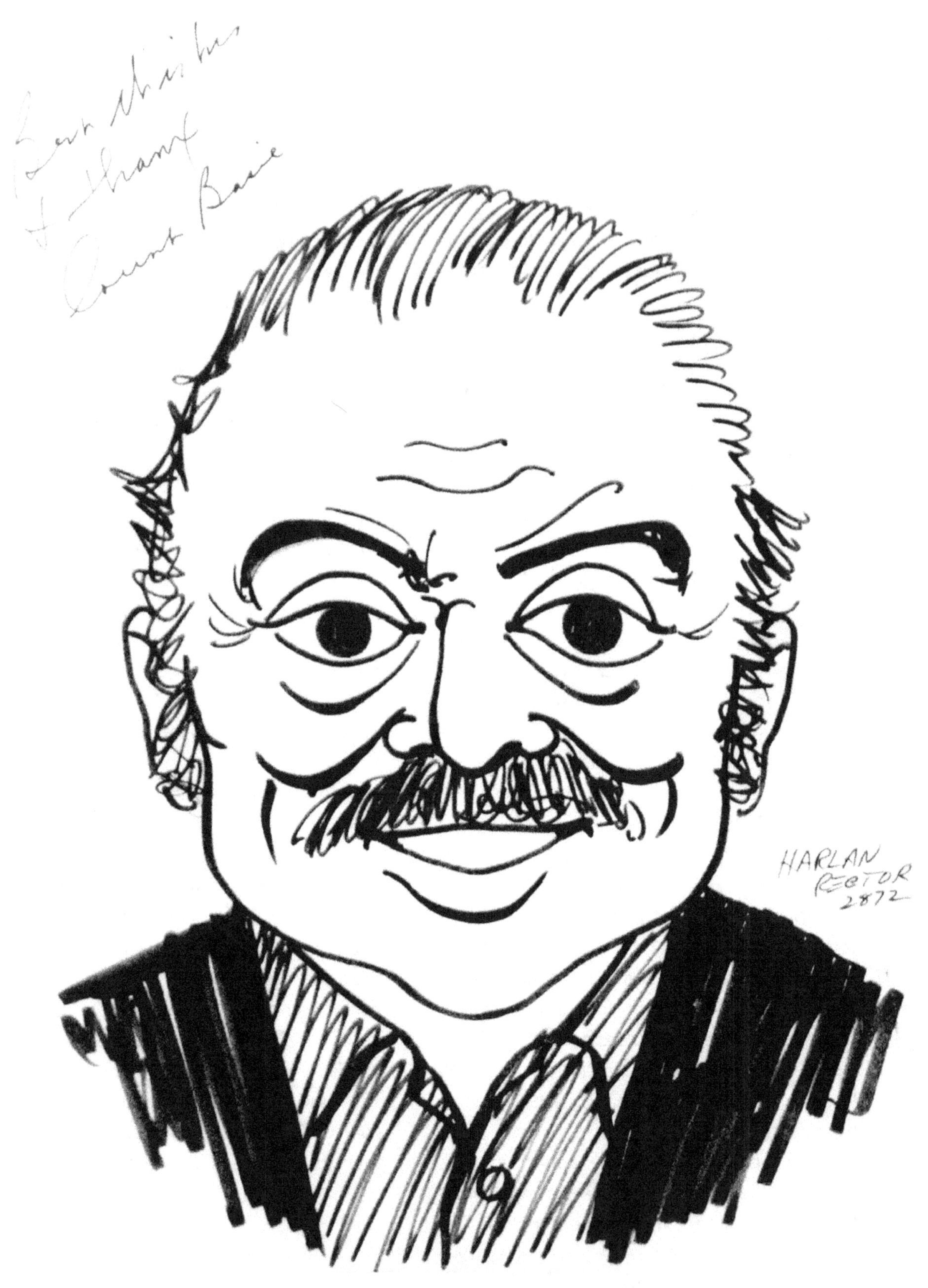

Count Basie

By the time he was interviewed at WJR, Count Basie was well-recognized as a musical giant. He was an influential musical composer, band leader, jazz pianist, and organist.

Count Basie's talent crossed genres, including jazz, swing, big band, and piano blues. He led the Count Basie Orchestra for nearly 50 years. Many musicians came into their own under his tutelage, including Lester Young, Herschel Evens, Freddie Green, and trumpeters Buck Clayton and Harry "Sweets" Edison.

William James Basie was born in Red Bank, New Jersey, in 1904. His father was a coachman and his mother took in laundry. Young William felt fortunate that his mother could pay 25 cents per lesson for him to learn to play the piano.

As a teenager, Basie got his start playing at the Palace Theater in Red Bank, quickly learning to keep time accompanying a variety of stage acts and silent movies. Shortly thereafter, he arrived in Harlem, which was brimming with jazz innovators including Sonny Greer, James P. Johnson, and Willie "The Lion" Smith.

By the mid-1920s, known at the time as Bill Basie, he had hooked up with several area bands before joining touring bands accompanying Katie Crippen and Gonzelle White, among others. Touring took Basie to Kansas City, St. Louis, New Orleans, and Chicago, where he met many well-known jazz musicians, including Louie Armstrong. He acknowledged that those experiences influenced how he played music for the rest of his life.

Basie branched out into swing, blues, and the increasingly popular big band sound in the 1930s. He put together a nine-piece band named the Barons of Rhythm.

While he was on tour, Bill Basie was given his nickname. Prior to introducing the band one evening, the announcer of the venue called Basie over to the booth. He told him that introducing him as Bill Basie sounded boring and that he should have a nickname like his contemporaries "Earl" Hines and "Duke" Ellington. He told him he would introduce him as "Count" Basie. He did, and the name stuck.

For many years, Count Basie and his band used the Woodside Hotel in Harlem as their base of operations, often using its basement as a rehearsal space. While at the hotel, they recorded hits including *Pennies from Heaven* and *Honeysuckle Rose*.

Post-war musical tastes were changing. Basie began adding bebop components to his sound "so long as it made sense." He wanted the songs he played "to have feeling." He began sharing the stage with accomplished bebop artists, including Charlie Parker, Dizzy Gillespie, and Miles Davis.

By the early 1960s and for the next two decades, Count Basie got more involved with TV specials, cruises, festivals, and Las Vegas shows. He made special appearances in films including *Cinderfella*, with Jerry Lewis and *Blazing Saddles* with Mel Brooks.

Basie was a musical innovator with a vast library of popular tunes spanning the better part of the 20th century. On April 26, 1984, Count Basie died at the age of 79 of pancreatic cancer in Hollywood, Florida. ■

GREG BARRY

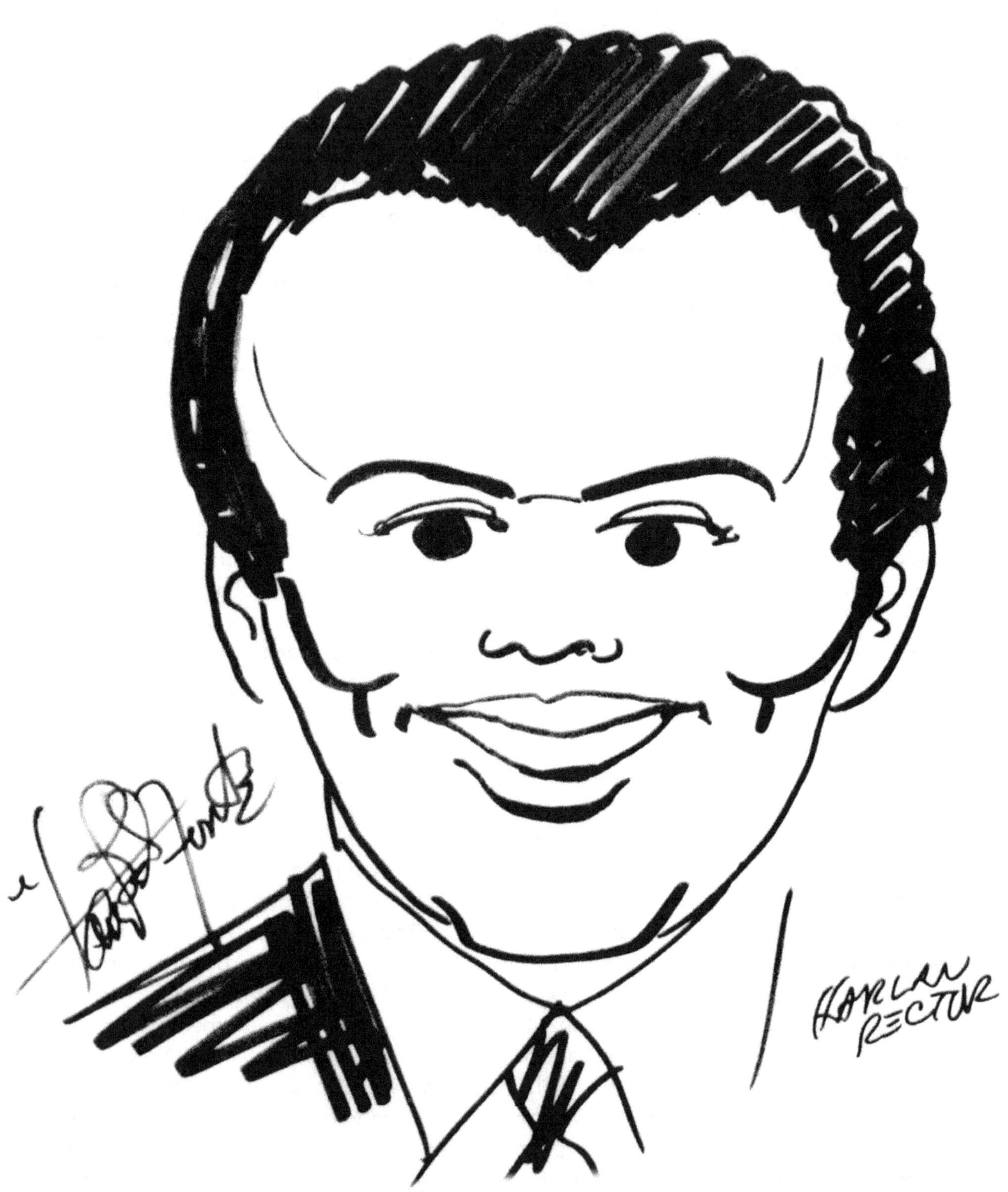
HARLAN
RECTOR

Harry Belafonte

Harry George Belafonte, Jr. was born in Harlem, NY, on March 1, 1927. Harry's parents were emigrants from the Caribbean Islands of Martinique and Jamaica. Harry's father, Harry George, was a chef on merchant ships and eventually left their family when Harry was still a young boy. After becoming a single parent, Harry's mother, Melvine, often left the children to fend for themselves as she worked mending dresses and cleaning homes. The family was nomadic, traveling between New York and the Caribbean, which meant Harry never experienced lasting friendships while growing up.

Harry dropped out of high school in 1944 and enlisted in the US Navy. After being discharged, he returned home and took his first job as an assistant janitor. He never intended to become a singer. In his words, "Being a janitor was not an artistic job, but it paid the bills." Belafonte states in an NPR interview conducted when he was 84, "One day I did a repair at a tenant's apartment —they gave me tickets to the theater. So, I went to this place, the American Negro Theater, and it was there the universe opened up to me."

"I was touched by the silence in the audience. Everybody seemed so reverential. I took my cue from that—something's coming. When the curtain opened, the actors walked onstage, the evening overwhelmed me. I decided with any device I could possibly find, I wanted to stay in this place. What I discovered in the theater was power: power to influence, power to know others, and know other things."

Harry took a job as a stage hand and from there, his acting career took off. He acted in many films, including Otto Preminger's, *Carmen Jones* (1954), *Island in the Sun* (1957), and Robert Wise's *Odds Against Tomorrow* (1959).

Despite his success with acting, Harry was better known for his singing. His mother once told him, 'Don't ever let injustice go by unchallenged.' Belafonte took his mother's words to heart in a "Rosebud moment," that would change his songs and start an awareness to injustice. His lyrics speak of hardships but put with such an upbeat, vacationing rhythm, one might not perceive what they're hearing while sipping a margarita.

The *Banana Boat Song (Day-O)* depicts men singing out as they carry their wares on their heads. Their songs told people what they were selling. They would wait for the tallyman to pay them, sometimes in rum.

In 1956, Belafonte's album *Calypso* became the first LP to hit one million dollars by a single artist. Although known for Caribbean music, he also sings the blues, show tunes, gospel, and American standards. Harry Belafonte's ten most famous songs remain *Brown Skinned Girl, Monkey, Turn Around, Angelina, Man Smart (Woman Smarter), Jamaica Farewell, Jump in Line, Matilda,* and *Day-O (The Banana Boat Song).*

Belafonte received a Grammy Lifetime Achievement Award, two other Grammy Awards, a Tony, an Emmy, the Kennedy Center Honors in 1989, the National Medal of Arts in 1994, and the Jean Hersholt Humanitarian Award in 2014. Harry Belafonte lived out his passions and helped others to want change as well. ■

TRACY TRIPP

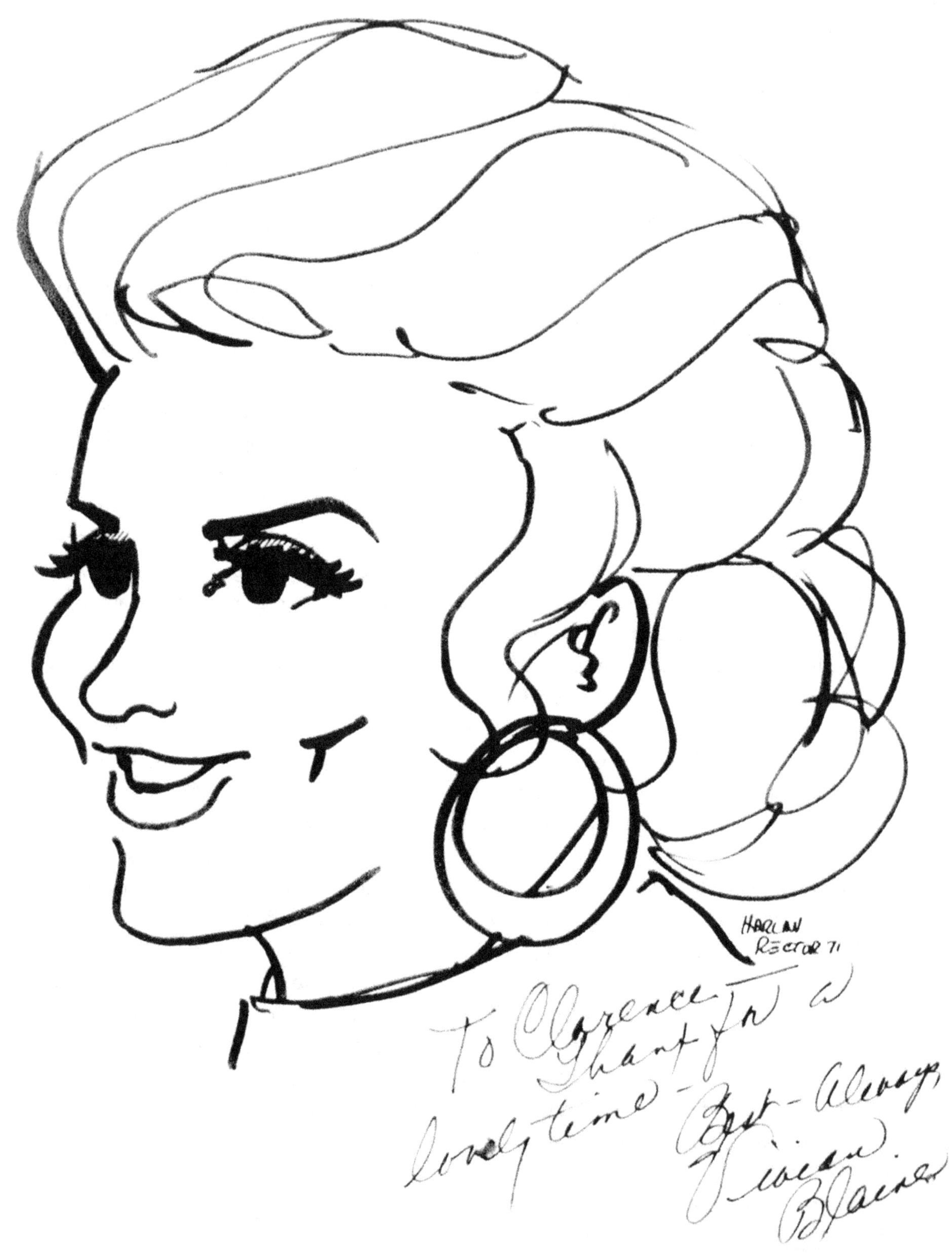

HARLAN
RECTOR 71
To Clarence —
Thank you for a
lovely time —
Best — Always,
Vivian
Blaine

16

Vivian Blaine

Vivian Blaine is best remembered for portraying Miss Adelaide in the stage musical *Guys and Dolls*. In her career she became an accomplished stage, film, and television actress and singer.

Blaine was born on December 21, 1921, in Newark, New Jersey. As a high school student, she was already performing in local playhouses. After graduating from South Side High School, she began her singing career touring with several dance bands.

By 1940, she was in high demand as a singer, becoming the top-billed act at the popular Copacabana nightclub in New York City.

Restless for a new challenge, Blaine left New York for Hollywood to take her skill from the stage to the screen. In 1942, she signed a contract with 20th Century Fox and for the next eight years was featured in a string of musicals and comedies including *Jitterbugs* with Stan Laurel and Oliver Hardy. She was also featured in *Greenwich Village*, *Nob Hill*, *State Fair*, and *Something for the Boys* with Carmen Miranda.

In 1950, Blaine was ready for the lights of Broadway. She originated the role of Miss Adelaide in Broadway's *Guys and Dolls*, playing a chorus girl engaged for 14 years to gambler Nathan Detroit. Because of their unreasonably long engagement, her character blamed Nathan for causing her bad cold. A highlight of the show was when Adelaide expressed her frustration through the song *Adelaide's Lament*, showing off her humor, memorable accent, and emotional range.

When the 1,200-show run ended on Broadway, the production company took the show to Great Britain for another 553 performances, including a command performance before Queen Elizabeth II in 1953.

Blaine performed in other Broadway shows, notably *Say, Darling*, *Enter Laughing*, *Company*, and *Zorba*, based on Zorba the Greek.

Blaine was also given the opportunity to join touring companies showcasing musicals and dramas, including *Gypsy*, which was loosely based on the memoirs of Gypsy Rose Lee. She also had a role in the touring version of *A Streetcar Named Desire*.

In 1955, Blaine reprised her role as Miss Adelaide in the film version of *Guys and Dolls*, which also starred Frank Sinatra and Marlon Brando. The film was a massive success at the box office.

By the 1970s, Blaine began doing television work, including a recurring role in *Mary Hartman, Mary Hartman*. She also guest-starred in episodes of *Fantasy Island*, *The Love Boat*, and *Murder She Wrote*.

Vivian Blaine was married three times. She died from congestive heart failure on December 9, 1995. She was survived by her husband, Stuart Clark. ∎

GREG BARRY

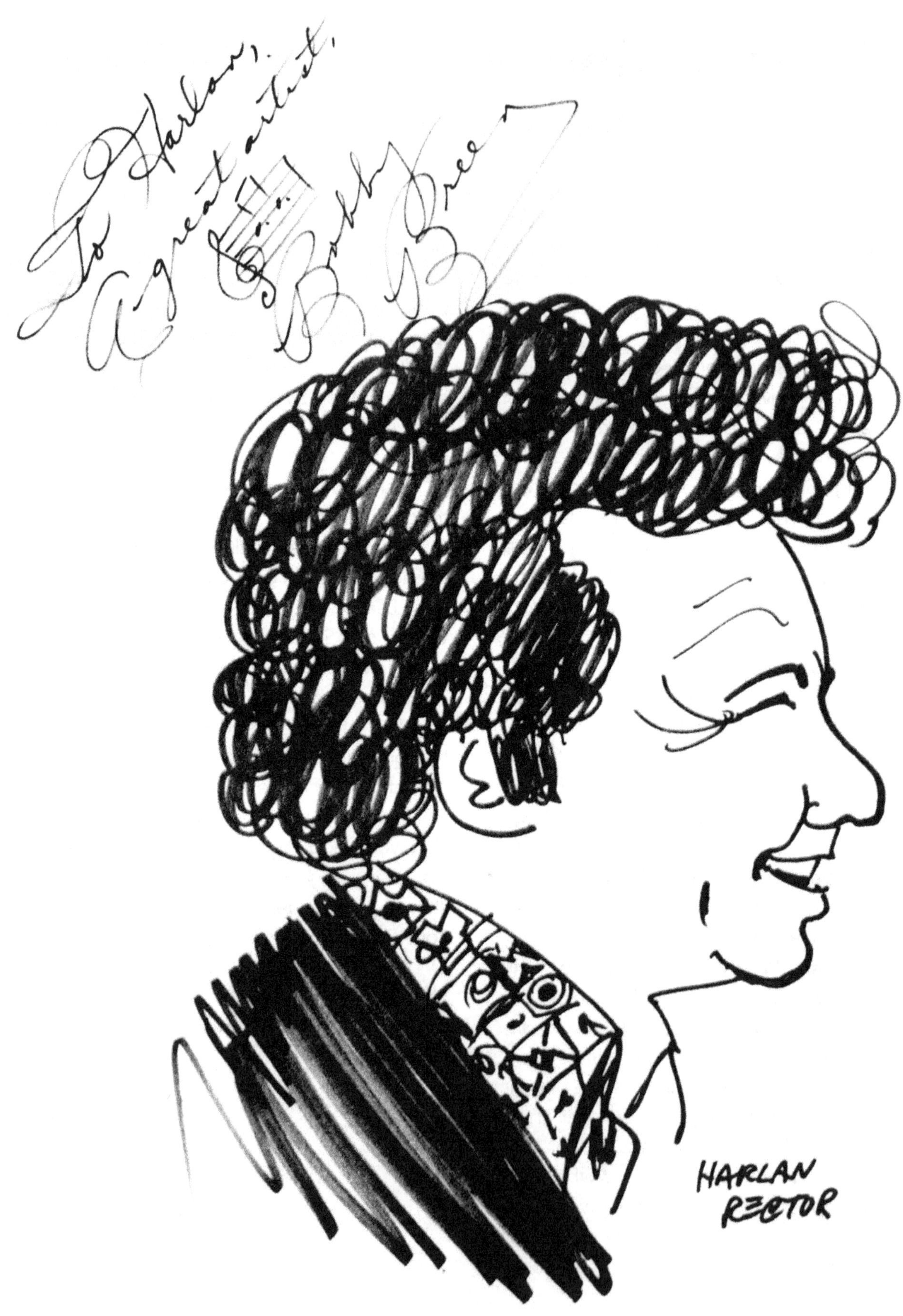

HARLAN
RECTOR

Bobby Breen

Canadian-born, American singer and actor Bobby Breen, formerly "the boy Shirley Temple," was a major child star in the 1930s, with numerous movie and radio appearances.

He later shifted his career to representing other once-famous celebrities, such as Debbie Reynolds, Anne Blyth, and Mickey Rooney, with the *Where Are They Now* fond memory clips for listeners every time he visited WJR Radio Station in the early 1970s.

Bobby was born Isadore Borsuk on November 4, 1927, in Montreal, Quebec, Canada to poor Jewish immigrants from Ukraine. After the family moved to Toronto, his sister discovered that her 3-year-old brother had a great singing talent. At her urging, he performed at a nightclub and won monetary prizes in theater competitions.

The siblings sought stardom in the United States, taking the bus to Chicago in 1934. He worked with Gloria Swanson and Milton Berle in local theater productions before Breen hopscotched to New York City then Hollywood. He portrayed Bob Hope's newsboy son in the Broadway musical *Say When* in 1934. RKO Radio signed him, and he became a regular on Eddie Cantor's weekly show.

His first movie *Let's Sing Again*, which he received top billing, was leading to comparable Freddie Bartholomew, Shirley Temple, Nelson Eddy, and Al Jolson. At just 8 years old, the young soprano sang his next movie title *Rainbow* on the River in 1936. He co-starred with Basil Rathbone in *Make a Wish* in 1937.

Four of his films received Oscar nominations for their musical scores. He issued two albums and 19 singles, which sold moderately well.

After completing his 8th film in 1939, Escape to Paradise, puberty changed his voice so he retired from the movie industry to attend Beverly Hills High School. He lamented, "There's a darker side to Hollywood's golden era. My fall from grace came quicker and was harder than my meteoric rise to stardom." He returned to film in 1942, playing himself in *Johnny Doughboy* and sang with former child stars Carl "Alfalfa" Switzer and George "Spanky" McFarland.

He served in the US Army during WWII, entertaining the troops with Mickey Rooney. He was hospitalized in France in 1945 and earned the Bronze Star Medal.

Finding postwar entertainment work was tough—limited to some theater and radio appearances in New York, he took singing lessons to adapt to his new tenor voice. He explained his struggle to return to relevance in the 1953 ABC reality show The Comeback Story.

He sang in nightclubs and in stock theater throughout the 1950s and 1960s, also playing as a guest pianist for the NBC Symphony Orchestra. Berry Gordy recorded him for Motown, but decided that Breen did not suit the Motown style and dropped the album *Better Late Than Never.*

Breen died at age 87 of natural causes in Pompano Beach, Florida on September 19, 2016, three days after his wife passed away. Fun fact: To Breen's surprise, he was on the Beatles' *Sergeant Pepper's Lonely Hearts Club Band* album cover. ∎

EDWARD MICKOLUS

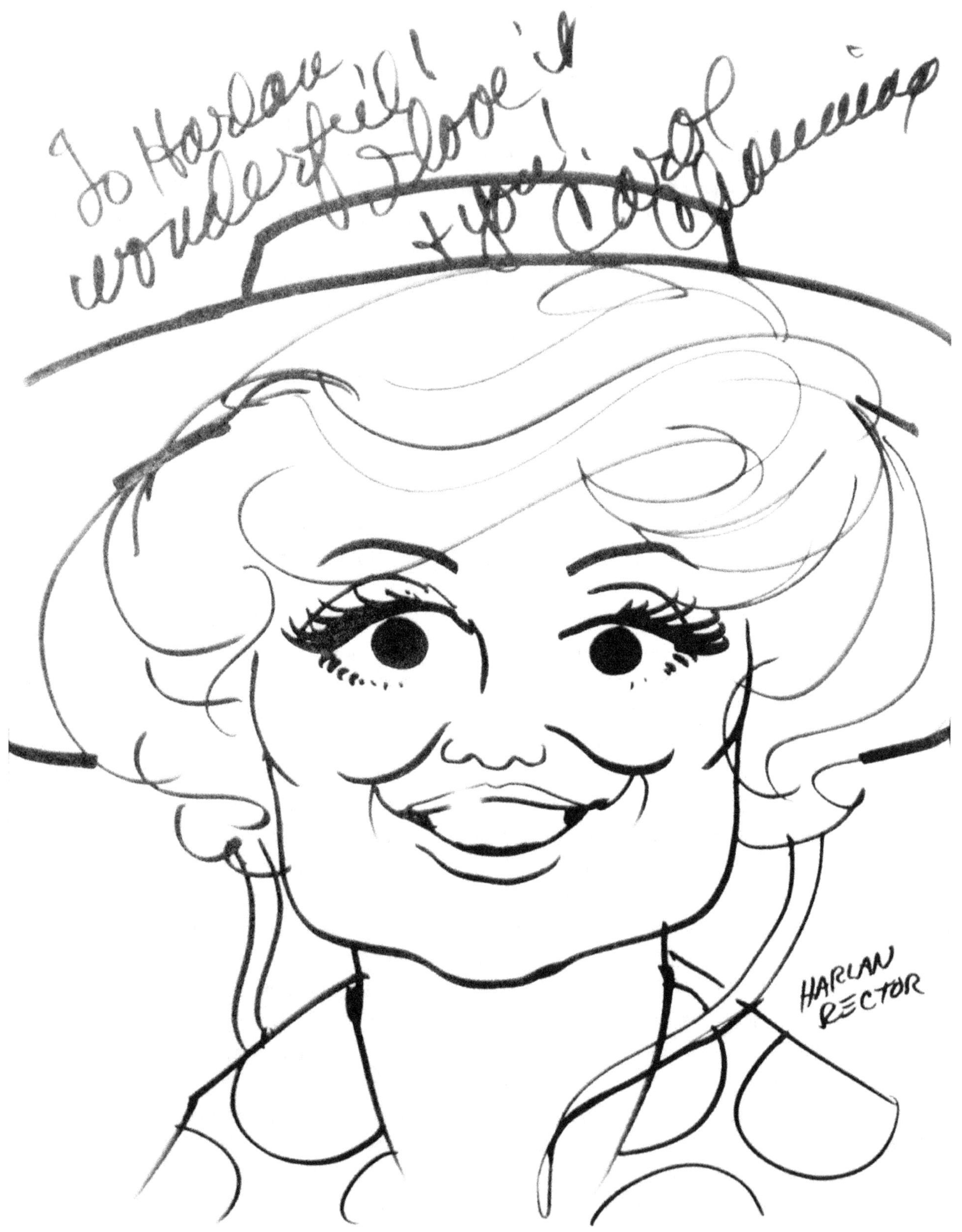

Carol Channing

Not unlike a doll herself, Carol Channing was born with huge eyes and a Broadway smile that could mesmerize any audience she performed for. Born in Seattle, Washington on January 31, 1921, she was the only child of Adelaide and George Channing. Her father's ancestry was multi-racial. George's mother, Clara, was African-American and George's father was the son of German immigrants.

The family moved to San Francisco when Carol was two years old. She was first introduced to the stage while helping her mother deliver newspapers to theaters backstage. At 17, Carol left for Bennington College in Vermont. Carol publicly revealed her African-American ancestry in 2002.

Although she excelled in speech and some drama in college, her first real stage appearance happened two years later in 1941. Carol's rise to stardom began when she landed the lead in *Gentlemen Prefer Blondes* — she belted out the hit song *Diamonds Are a Girl's Best Friend*.

In January 1950, *Time* magazine ran a cover story about her becoming a new Broadway star. Her hits included—*The Matchmaker, The Skin of Our Teeth, Lorelei,* and *Thoroughly Modern Millie,* but she'll always be remembered for *Hello Dolly,* the longest-running musical in Broadway history with nearly 3,000 performances.

She was a triple threat performer. In addition to a fabulous stage career, many film roles followed and she was a regular guest on a host of television shows. Channing won the Sarah Siddons Award, Theater World Award, and was nominated for a Tony as well as nominated for Best Actress in a Musical.

Along the way, Carol was married four times. She wed her first husband, Theadore Naidish, in 1941 at the young age of twenty. Her second love, Alexander "Axe" F. Carson, was a center for the Ottawa Rough Riders Canadian Football team and a private investigator. They were married for six years and had one son, Channing Carson. She divorced in 1956 to marry her manager/publicist, Charles Lowe, who died before their divorce was final. She later re-kindled a long lost romance with her junior high sweetheart, Harry Kullijian and were married in 2003 but 8 years later, he too died.

Carol had unique dietary habits and for 15 years she avoided restaurants. When she finally began eating in restaurants, she brought sealed containers of prepared organic food and asked the waiter to bring her a plate and empty glass. She ate seeds for dessert and never drank alcohol.

Carol was an ovarian cancer survivor and lived a vibrant, charismatic life. She died of natural causes on January 15, 2019, six days before her 98th birthday. The lights on Broadway dimmed in her memory. ■

HARLAN RECTOR

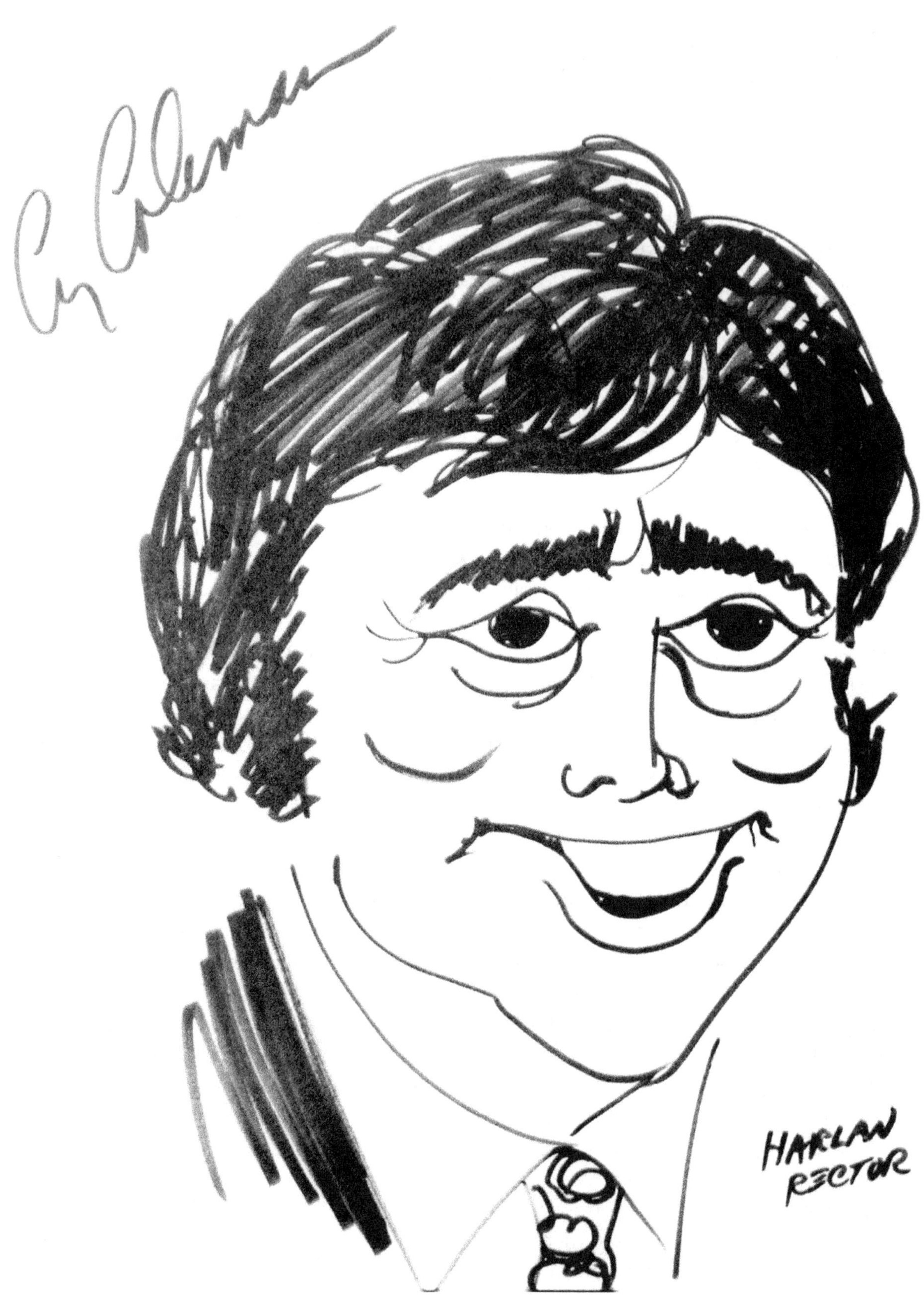

HARLAN
RECTOR

Cy Coleman

Some child prodigies flare out, others build on their fame and go on to long-lasting successful careers. The star of former child pianist Cy Coleman, last and youngest of the Great American Songbook composers, continued to rise when he visited WJR.

Cy Coleman, born as Seymour Kaufman on June 14, 1929, in the Bronx, performed at Carnegie Hall at the very young age of only 7 years old. He attended the High School of Music and Art and the New York College of Music.

Capitol Records signed his jazz trio in the early 1950s. In addition to songwriting, he issued 31 albums, 17 singles, and four compilations.

He wrote standards for Frank Sinatra, Nat King Cole, Tony Bennett, Louis Armstrong, and Peggy Lee with hit titles like *The Best is Yet to Come*, *Big Spender*, and *Hey Look Me Over*.

He scored major Broadway hits spanning from the 1960s to the 1990s with titles like *Wildcat*, *Little Me*, *Sweet Charity*, *Seesaw*, *I Love My Wife*, *On the Twentieth Century*, *Barnum*, *City of Angels*, *Will Rogers Follies*, and *The Life*.

While Coleman was a frequent contributor to the movies, his television credits also include *Midsomer Murders*, *The Tonight Show Starring Johnny Carson*, *The Girls Next Door*, and *Great Performances*.

He composed scores for such films as *Hocus Pocus*, *Father Goose*, *Sweet Charity*, *Family Business*, *Power*, *Ride to Hangman's Tree*, *Garbo Talks*, *The Art of Love*, and *The Troublemaker*.

Coleman collaborated with Carolyn Leigh to write the hit pop song *Witchcraft*, made famous by Frank Sinatra, with its first recording in 1957. It experienced many hit recordings thereafter by various artists including Elvis.

A vibrant career garnered Coleman three Emmys, five Tony's (among 19 nominations), two Grammy's, an Academy Award nomination for Best Score and seven Drama Desk Awards.

He was inducted into the Songwriters Hall of Fame in 1981 and the American Theatre Hall of Fame a decade later. The American Society of Composers, Authors and Publishers presented him with its ASCAP Foundation Richard Rodgers Award for Lifetime Achievement in American Musical Theatre. He served on ASCAP's Board of Directors for 30 years and Hofstra University awarded him an Honorary Doctorate.

Coleman was writing until the day he died of cardiac arrest at age 75 on November 18, 2004, in New York City after attending the premiere of a Broadway play earlier that day. The Broadway theatre marquees dimmed their lights to honor a great American composer. ∎

EDWARD MICKOLUS

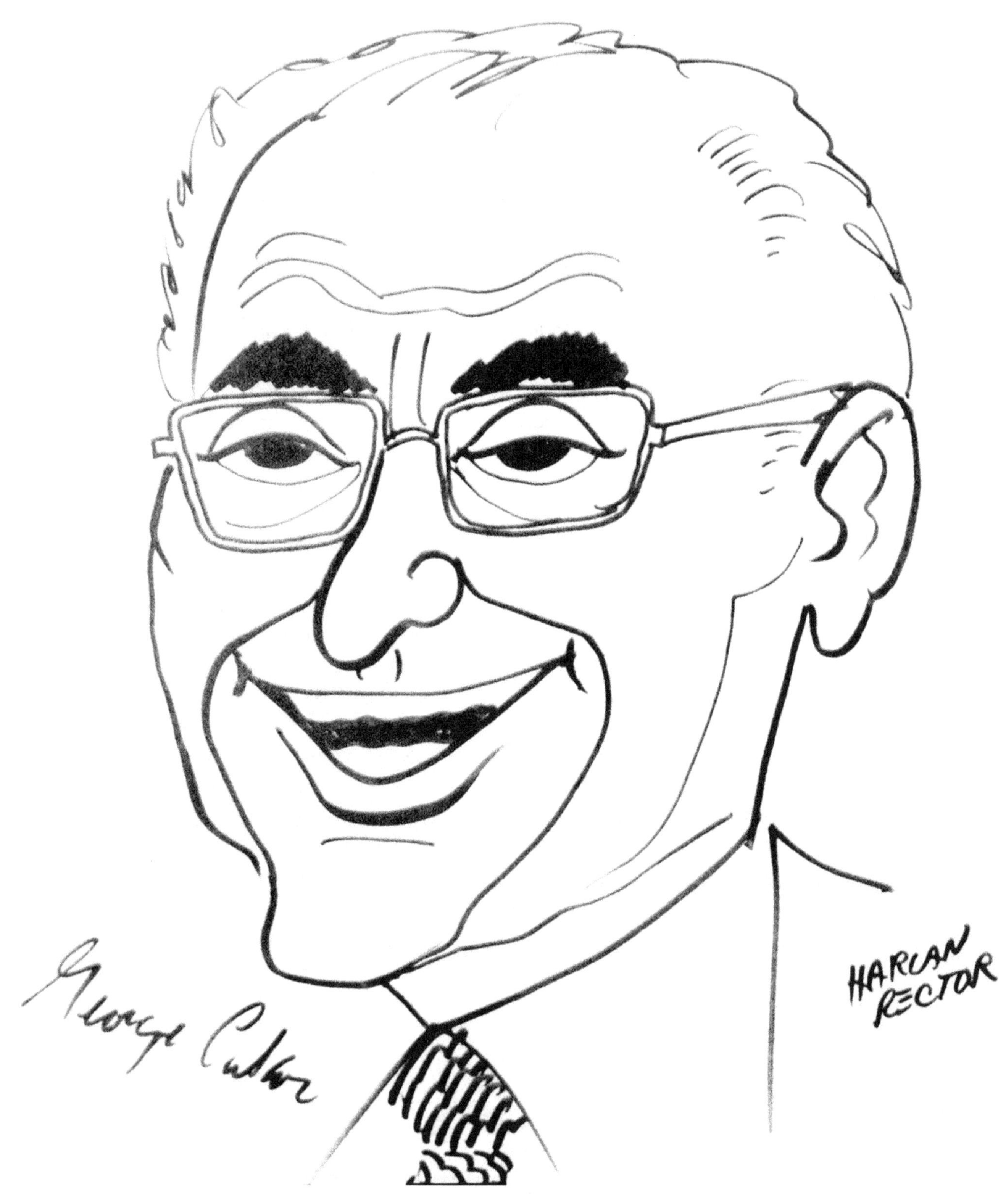

George Cukor
HARLAN
RECTOR

George Cukor

George Cukor was a highly successful film director during the golden age of movie making and worked with some of the finest actors of his time. In 1964, he won an Academy Award and a Golden Globe Award as Best Director for *My Fair Lady*.

George Dewey Cukor was born on July 7, 1899, in New York City. He was the only son of Hungarian-Jewish immigrant parents. As a child, Cukor became enamored with acting and set design.

In the 1920s, Cukor worked in New York theater productions, progressing from stage manager to general manager, eventually becoming a director of Broadway plays, including an adaptation of *The Great Gatsby*, which got him favorable reviews from theater critics.

By 1928, as Hollywood was converting to talkies, Cukor had become well-connected with New York's acting community, including actors ready to try their hand at film. Cukor signed a contract to become an apprentice with Paramount Pictures in Hollywood.

Within a few years, Cukor was making his directorial debut in *Tarnished Lady*, starring Tallulah Bankhead. Several years later, Cukor left Paramount to direct films for David O. Selznick at RKO Studios.

Cukor achieved success at RKO, directing films including *Bill of Divorcement, Little Women,* and *Holiday*. Cukor was the first director assigned to *Gone with the Wind*. However, due to problems on the set, Cukor's disappointment with the final script, and Selznick's frustrations with Cukor's work pace, Cukor was replaced as director by Victor Fleming.

Despite his acrimonious departure from RKO, Cukor had developed a reputation for being adept at expertly preparing actors for their roles. Cukor had the ability to sense the finest qualities from individual actors and would allow them to display them naturally on screen. Among his favorite actors were Greta Garbo, Judy Holliday, and Katharine Hepburn, who he directed in 10 films.

Cukor moved on to direct films for MGM Studios, where he thrived. He directed Philadelphia Story, starring Katherine Hepburn, and *The Women*, starring Joan Crawford. Several years later Cukor directed *Gaslight*, starring Ingrid Bergman and Charles Boyer. In the late 1940s and early 1950s, Cukor directed more commercially and critically acclaimed films, including *A Double Life*, starring Ronald Coleman; *Adam's Rib*, starring Katharine Hepburn and Spencer Tracy; *Born Yesterday*, starring Judy Holliday and William Holden; and *It Should Happen to You*, starring Judy Holliday and Jack Lemmon.

In 1964, George Cukor experienced his greatest success as a film director with the release of *My Fair Lady*, starring Audrey Hepburn and Rex Harrison. The film won eight Academy Awards, including Best Picture, Best Actor, and Best Director. It is ranked by the American Film Institute as the 91st best American film of all time, and the 8th best Movie Musical.

Cukor enjoyed the Hollywood lifestyle. A bachelor for life, he hosted many parties at his palatial estate in the Hollywood hills. For many years Cukor's events were the place to be among the Hollywood elite.

Never married, George Cukor died of a heart attack on January 24, 1983. ∎

GREG BARRY

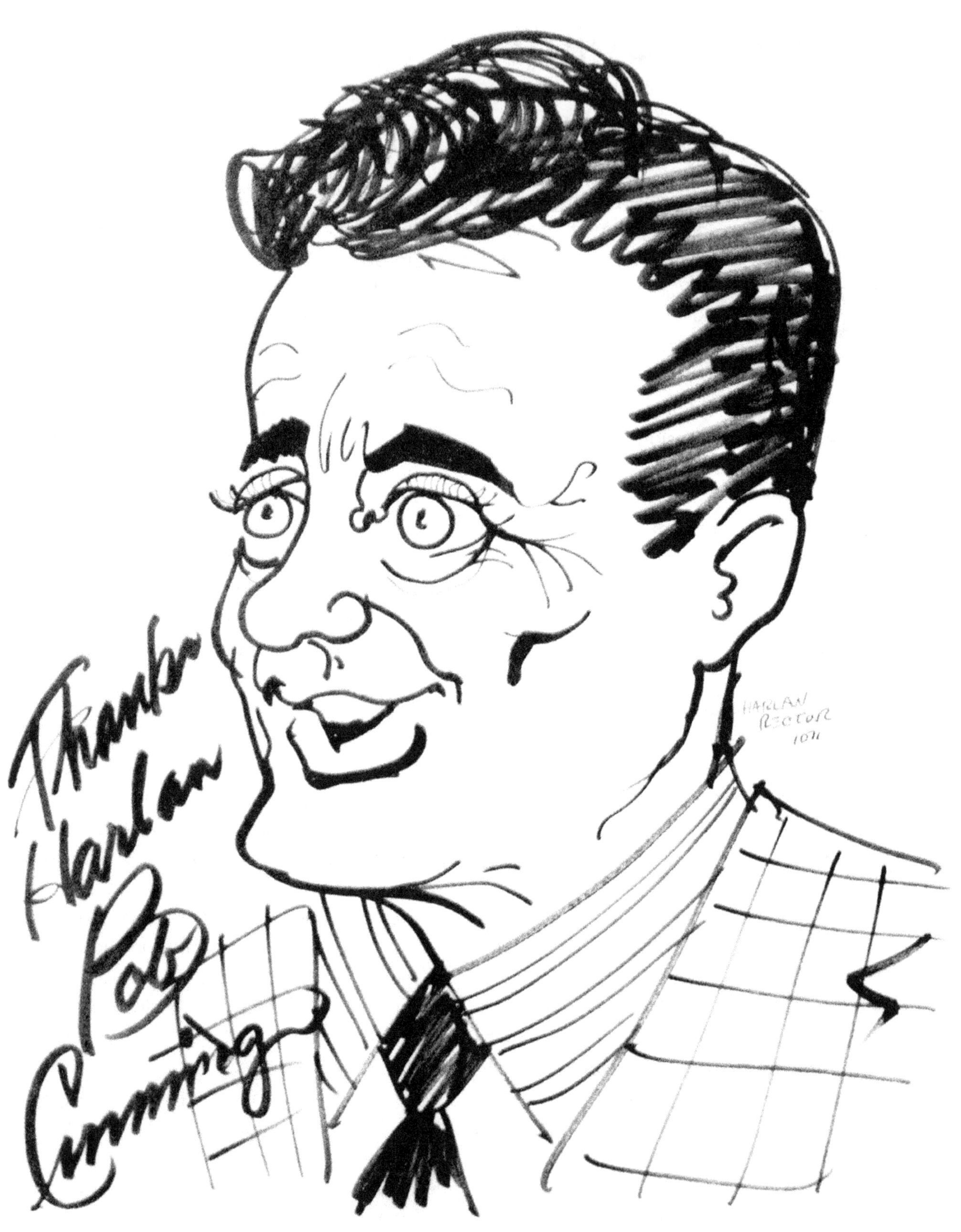
Thanks
Harlan
Bob
Cummings
HARLAN
RECTOR
1971

Bob Cummings

Charles Clarence Robert Orville Cummings was born June 9, 1910, in Joplin, Missouri. His father, Dr. Charles Clarence Cummings, a surgeon, and mother, Ruth Annabelle (Kraft), an ordained minister of the Science of Mind, gave their son a good, affluent life but they experienced financial hardship when they lost heavily in the 1929 stock market crash.

While Cummings was in high school, his godfather, Orville Wright, taught him to fly. Once licensed, Cummings charged $5 to Joplin residents for rides in his aircraft. When the government began licensing flight instructors, Cummings became the first official flight instructor with the first issued certificate in the United States. He attended Carnegie Institute of Technology in Pittsburgh to study aeronautical engineering but dropped out due to the family's financial loss.

He refocused his interests while performing in plays at Carnegie Tech and changed his career to acting. He studied at the American Academy of Dramatic Arts in New York City because they paid their actors $14 per week. A steady road of opportunities and several name changes from "Blade Stanhope Conway" to "Bryce Hutchens," it was Cummings, as himself, who landed a long-term contract with Paramount but it would take a dizzying two years before the name, Bob Cummings, found its way into Hollywood jargon.

Several B rated motion pictures were released from 1935 to 1937 such as: *The Virginia Judge, Millions in the Air, Desert Gold, Forgotten Faces, Three Cheers for Love, Beyond Flight, Hollywood Boulevard, The Accusing Finger, Hideaway Girl, Arizona Mahoney,* and *The Last Train to Madrid.* About the same time, Cummings and his mother received $1 million from a mining stock left by his father, which afforded Cummings to 'live' the part of a real Hollywood star despite the B ratings.

Cummings secured a seven-year contract in the late 1930s which Universal eventually increased to $3,000 per week (equivalent to $55,000 per week today). Universal featured Cummings for their projects, renting Cummings and his contract out to MGM, RKO, 20th Century Fox and other studios.

During WWII, Cummings joined the Civil Air Patrol, and later the United States Army Air Force, as a flight instructor. After the war, he continued his movie career into the 1950s.

Cummings starred in, sometimes wrote and directed his first regular television series in 1952, *My Hero.* The series ran for 33 episodes. In 1954 he played Juror Number Eight in the original television production Twelve Angry Men. From 1955 to 1959, he starred in the successful NBC sitcom, *The Bob Cummings Show* and was nominated for an Emmy Award for his role.

It was October 1971. I had the pleasure of meeting and sketching Charles Clarence Robert Orville Cummings, aka Bob Cummings, caricature. I never thought I would run into him several times thereafter in Hollywood. He was like the guy next door — fun loving and down to earth.

Robert Cummings died on December 2, 1990, of kidney failure and complications from pneumonia. ∎

HARLAN RECTOR

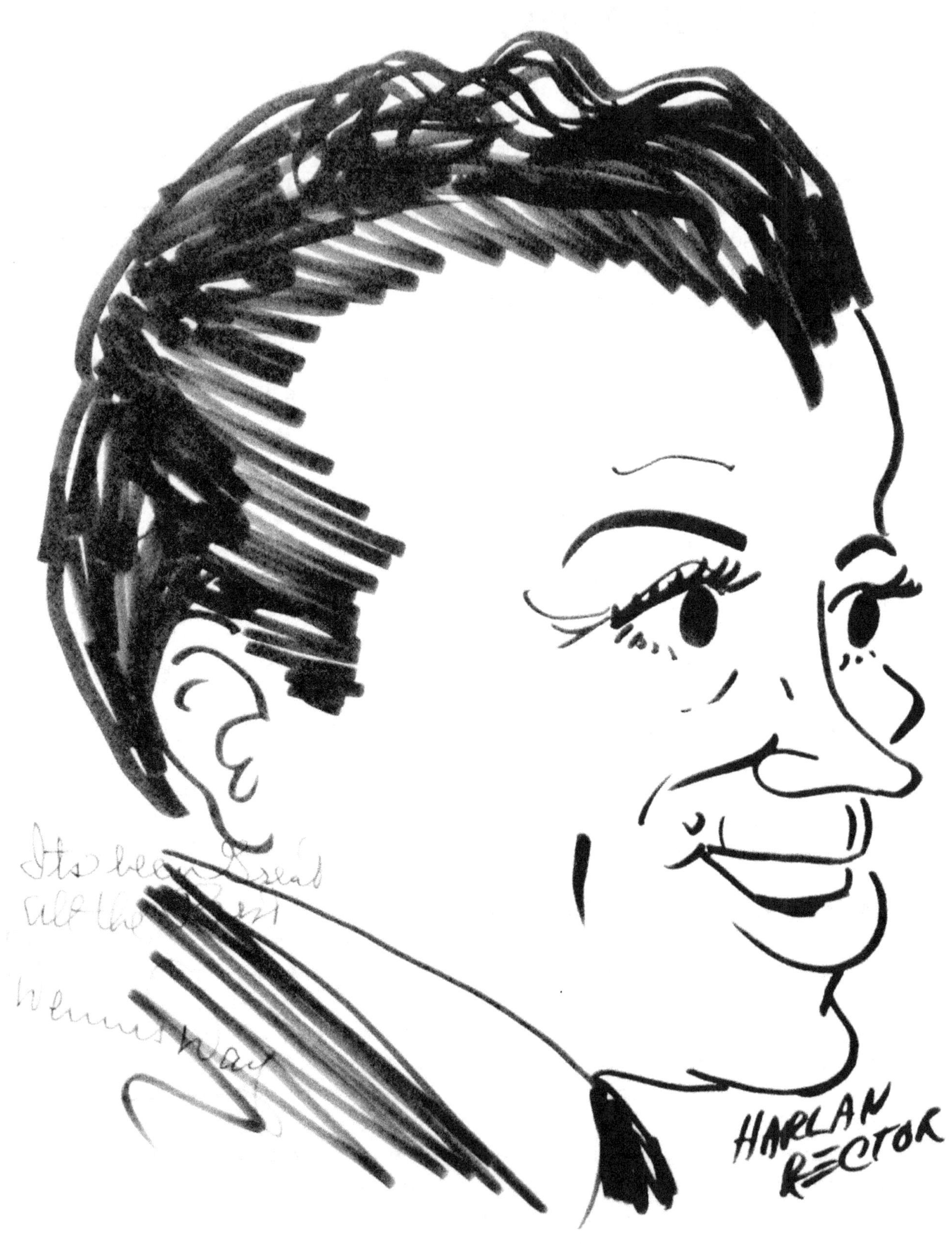
HARLAN
RECTOR

Dennis Day

Dennis Day was a major radio star as Jack Benny's comic foil and talented singer when he appeared on WJR.

"America's Favorite Irish Tenor" was born May 21, 1916, as Owen Patrick Eugene McNulty in the Throggs Neck of the Bronx. He graduated from the Cathedral Preparatory Seminary in New York City, and presided over the glee club while attending Manhattan College. By 1939, he was singing on network radio broadcasts aimed at college audiences who voted him favorite vocalist. His voice was heard in the St. Patrick's Cathedral choir.

Law school was expensive and Day needed money to fund his lofty goals. October 8, 1939, he found more than he hoped entertaining on Jack Benny's radio show and changed his focus forever. Day remained with the show until Benny's death in 1974.

He was introduced as the naive, wide-eyed character, a 19-year-old singer who never aged the entire time he was with Benny on radio or television. His tag line "Gee, Mr. Benny" drew immediate applause. Day was a natural. Doing wonderful, comedic impressions of stars like Ronald Coleman, Jimmy Durante, and James Stewart on the show.

With the Benny show platform, Day began his recording career starting with Goodnight My Beautiful and eventually released 15 albums.

World War II interrupted his career from 1944-1946. Day served as Lieutenant in the US Navy and upon discharge, he rejoined Benny, but also starred on NBC's radio sit-com *A Day in the Life of Dennis Day*, which ran from 1946 through 1951. Day's two shows to Benny's one was a running gag on Benny's show.

Day also had a TV series, *The Dennis Day Show* for a season—a comedy and variety show on NBC Radio in 1954-1955. From 1952 through 1978, he was a guest singer and actor on a variety of shows—*The Gisele MacKenzie Show*, *The Bing Crosby Show*, *Alfred Hitchcock Presents*, *Hour Glass*, *All Star Revue*, *Max Liebman Presents*, and Disney film features.

He was a voice actor for several animated shows. He acted in the movies—*Buck Benny Rides Again*, *One Sunday Afternoon*, *Music in Manhattan*, *Sleepy Lagoon*, *I'll Get By*, *Golden Girl*, *The Girl Next Door*, and *Won Ton Ton: The Dog Who Saved Hollywood*.

He has two stars on the Hollywood Walk of Fame for radio and television.

Day died at age 71 on June 22, 1988, of amyotrophic lateral sclerosis in Los Angeles. He and his wife of 40 years had ten children, none of whom followed him into show business. ■

EDWARD MICKOLUS

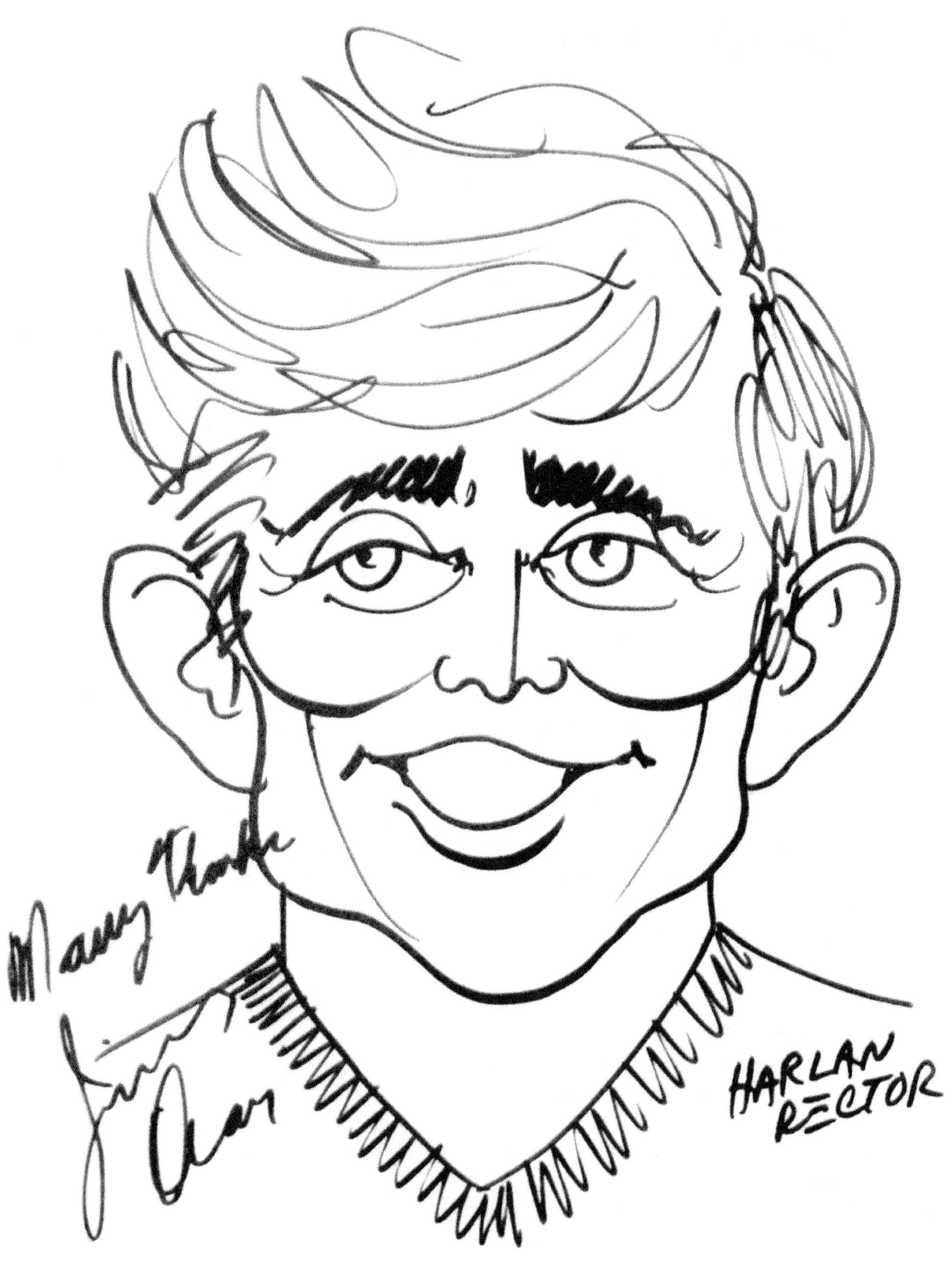

HARLAN
RECTOR

Jimmy Dean

Jimmy Ray Dean was born in Plainview, Texas, in 1928, to George Otto Dean and Ruth Taylor. They taught Jimmy how to play the piano at a young age, attributing his interest in music to the Seth Ward Baptist Church. He dropped out of high school in 1946 and became a professional entertainer after serving in the United States Air Force in the late 1940s.

Dean was 22 and just starting in show business in 1950 when he married his first wife, Mary Sue, with whom he had three children.

Dean had his first hit, Bumming Around, in 1953 on the Four Star label. Dean signed with Columbia Records in 1957 and had small pop hits, such as *Little Sandy Sleighfoot* (a Christmas novelty song) and *Sing Along*, which was later used as the theme for TV's *Sing Along with Mitch*, hosted by conductor Mitch Miller.

In 1954, Dean hosted the popular Washington DC radio program *Town and Country Time* on WARL with his Texas Wildcats, which became popular in the Mid-Atlantic region. Future stars such as Patsy Cline and Roy Clark got their start on his show. In 1955, the show moved to WMAL (now WJLA-TV).

While he lived in Arlington, Virginia, Dean hosted *Country Style* on WTOP-TV (now WUSA-TV). CBS picked up the show nationally from Washington for eight months in 1957 under the name *The Morning Show*.

From September 1958 to June 1959, CBS carried *The Jimmy Dean Show* on weekdays and Saturday afternoons.

Dean became best known for *Big Bad John*, his 1961 recitation song about a heroic miner. Recorded in Nashville, the record hit number one on the Billboard pop chart and inspired many imitations and parodies. The track peaked at number two on the UK Singles Chart. The song won Dean the 1962 Grammy Award for Best Country & Western Recording.

He had a top 10 that year with *PT-109*, a song honoring John F. Kennedy's bravery in World War II with the sinking of his PT boat in the South Pacific by the Japanese.

Dean was the first guest host on *The Tonight Show* during Johnny Carson's tenure, hosting for the first time on January 14, 1963.

In 1969, Jimmy founded the Jimmy Dean Sausage Company with his brother Don. The company did well in part because of Jimmy's extemporized, humorous commercials. Mary Sue divorced him in 1990 because of his affair with Donna Meade, who later became his second wife.

Jimmy Dean died on June 13, 2010, and was inducted posthumously into the Country Music Hall of Fame in October 2010. ■

DANA (RECTOR) GROVES

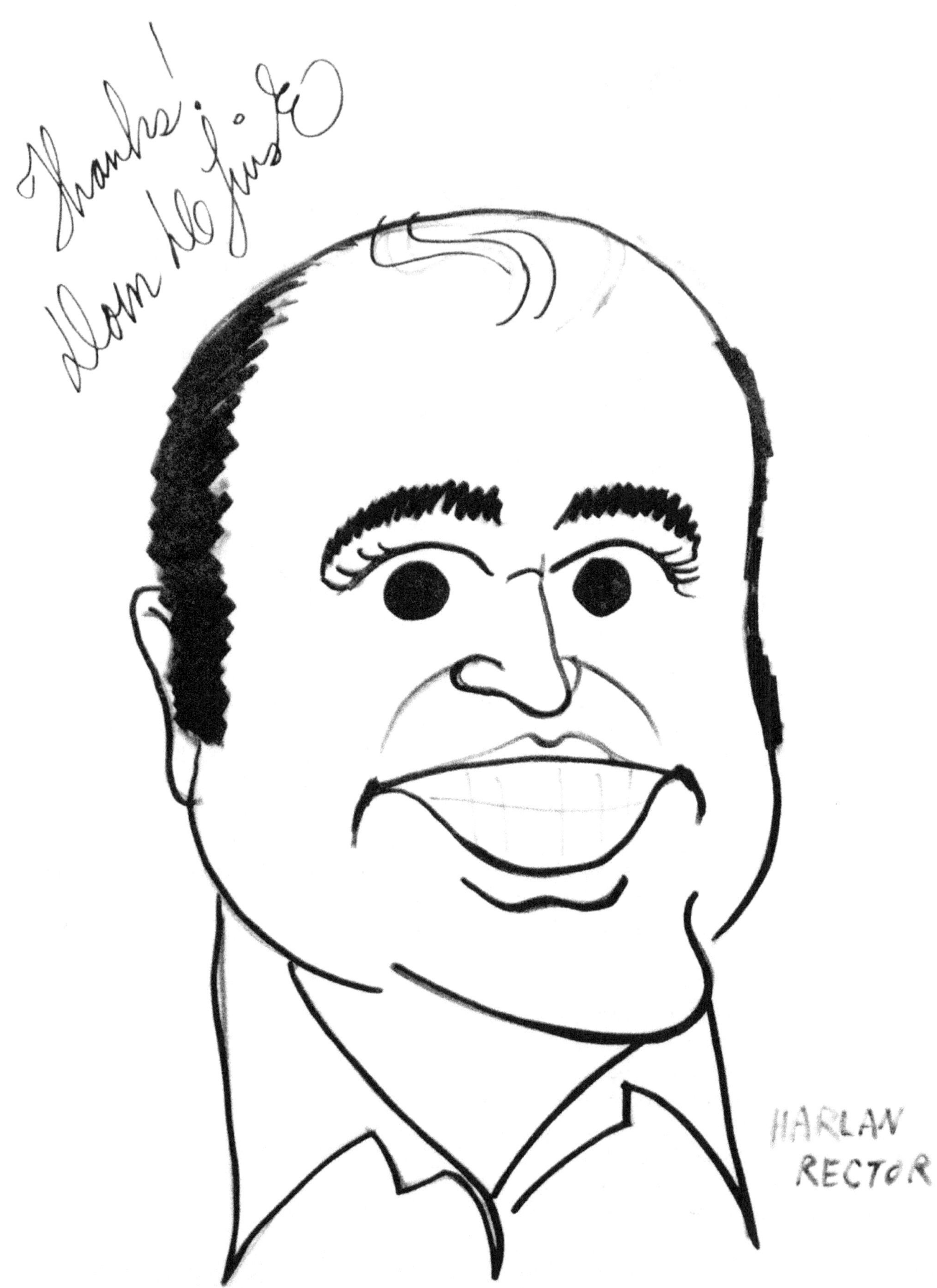

Thanks!
Dom DeLuise
HARLAN
RECTOR

Dom DeLuise

Dominick DeLuise was born on August 1, 1933, in Brooklyn, New York to Italian-American parents Vicenza "nee" DeStefano and John DeLuise. Dom was the last of three children. His older brother and sister, Nicholas and Antoinette, didn't have the gift of laughter like their brother nor the need for it as younger, attention seeking siblings often do. Dom loved to elicit a smile from anyone he could.

DeLuise graduated from Manhattan's High School of Performing Arts which jump-started his career. When he was 28 he landed a part in an off-Broadway revue titled *Another Evening with Harry Stoons*. It lasted for nine previews plus one performance. Another member of the cast was 19-year-old Barbra Streisand. That same year, 1961, he was in the off-Broadway play *All in Love*, which opened at the Martinique Theater and ran for 141 performances.

In 1964, while working the summer theater in Massachusetts, DeLuise met Carol Arthur. They married in 1965 and eventually had three sons—Peter, Michael and David, all became actors too.

DeLuise's career in film, television and as a voiceover talent included frequent collaborations with Dean Martin, Burt Reynolds and Mel Brooks. Dom co-starred with Burt Reynolds in six movies—*Cannon Ball Run*, *Cannon Ball Run II*, *Smokey and the Bandit II*, *The End*, *All Dogs Go to Heaven*, and *The Best Little Whorehouse in Texas*.

He was a regular on the Dean Martin television show, appeared in Dean Martin's Celebrity Roasts, and was in six different Mel Brooks films—*Twelve Chairs*, *Blazing Saddles*, *Silent Movie*, *History of the World Part 1*, *Spaceballs*, and *Robin Hood Men in Tights*.

Brooks always scheduled at least two extra filming days whenever he hired DeLuise because once the camera started rolling, and Dom started going, the laughter never stopped.

Known as the lovable, butterball comedian, Dom was also a celebrity gourmet chef, so it was no surprise when the director, shooting commercials for a California super market chain, came up with the idea to hire DeLuise to host a series of television spots.

He was perfect for the role but a challenge to draw. During a break in the shooting, I drew two caricatures of Dom; one with his tall chef's toque and one without. It was challenging. Try drawing a ball of playful energy. He was like a kid you couldn't contain but no one wanted to. That was his charm! He was an incredible ad-libber.

Though he was given a script, it was his unscripted comments 'playing with food' that were his most hilarious moments. We had the hardest time editing down for :60 and :30 commercials. What comedic footage do you cut when every second is great?"

Various physical ailments, chronic obesity, and diabetes exacerbated his health, but it was after battling cancer for a year that Dom DeLuise died of kidney failure on May 4, 2009, at 75 years old. He left his wife, three children, three grandchildren and a lifetime of happy memories for us to remember. ∎

HARLAN RECTOR

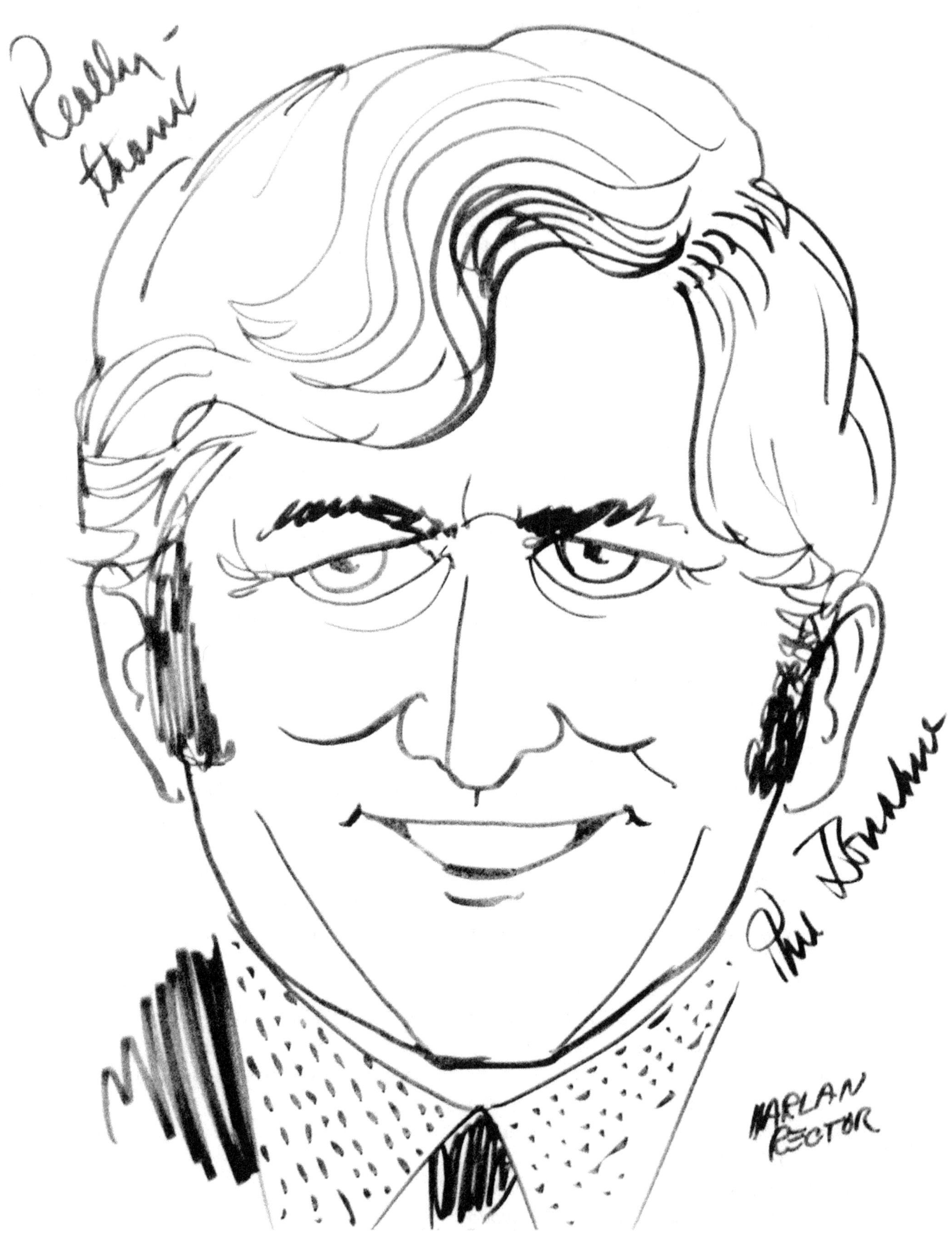

Really - thanks
Phil Donahue
HARLAN RECTOR

Phil Donahue

Phil Donahue created and hosted *The Phil Donahue Show*. His eponymous daytime television program ran for 29 years, beginning in Dayton, Ohio and finishing in New York City.

Phillip John Donahue was born in Cleveland, Ohio on December 21, 1935. He was raised Irish Catholic in a middle-class family. As a child, Donahue lived across the street from humorist Erma Bombeck in Centerville, Ohio. He graduated from St. Edward Catholic High School in Lakeland and went on to graduate from the University of Notre Dame with a Bachelor of Business Administration degree in 1957.

Donahue was hired as a production assistant at KYW television and radio station in Cleveland. Later, he became a freelance journalist for CBS Evening News. From 1963-1967, Donahue hosted an afternoon call-in radio show on WHIO titled *Conversation Piece*.

In 1967, Donahue switched his program format, moving from radio to television on WLWD in Dayton. His new program, *The Phil Donahue Show*, was sometimes controversial, covering topics such as civil rights, abortion, women's rights, homosexuality, and war issues.

His blend of discussing hot topic issues, engaging the studio audience, and permitting anyone to ask tough questions of a guest was revolutionary for the time. Donahue developed an interview style of trotting across the aisles of his studio with a microphone moving from one questioner to another. This technique created a more exciting exchange between guests and audience members.

By 1971, Donahue's syndicated program reached 40 markets. He moved from Dayton to Chicago in 1974, renaming the show simply *Donahue*. Combining controversial topics with controversial guests made him a household name. Guests included Jane Fonda, Ronald Reagan, Ralph Nader, and Nelson Mandela.

Donahue was awarded his first daytime Emmy for Outstanding Talk Show Host and by 1979 he was broadcast in 200 markets.

In 1985, Donahue moved his show again, this time to WNBC-TV in New York City. He arranged for the first simultaneous pairing of an American talk show with a Soviet Union talk show in 1987. It was the first time an American television program had been broadcast to a Soviet audience.

Donahue's interactive hosting approach paved the way for many other television hosts, including Geraldo Rivera, Sally Jesse Rafael, Jerry Springer, and Oprah Winfrey. Oprah once said, "If there hadn't been a Phil, there wouldn't have been a me."

Over the course of his career, Donahue won 20 Emmy Awards: 10 for Outstanding Talk Show Host and 10 for *The Phil Donahue Show*. In 1996, he was awarded a Lifetime Achievement Emmy. He won a Peabody Award in 1980, and on November 20, 1993, he was inducted into the Academy of Television Arts & Sciences Hall of Fame.

Phil Donahue has been married twice. His first marriage produced five children. In 1980, Donahue married Marlo Thomas, Danny Thomas's daughter and star of the 1960s television program *That Girl*. They live in New York City. ■

GREG BARRY

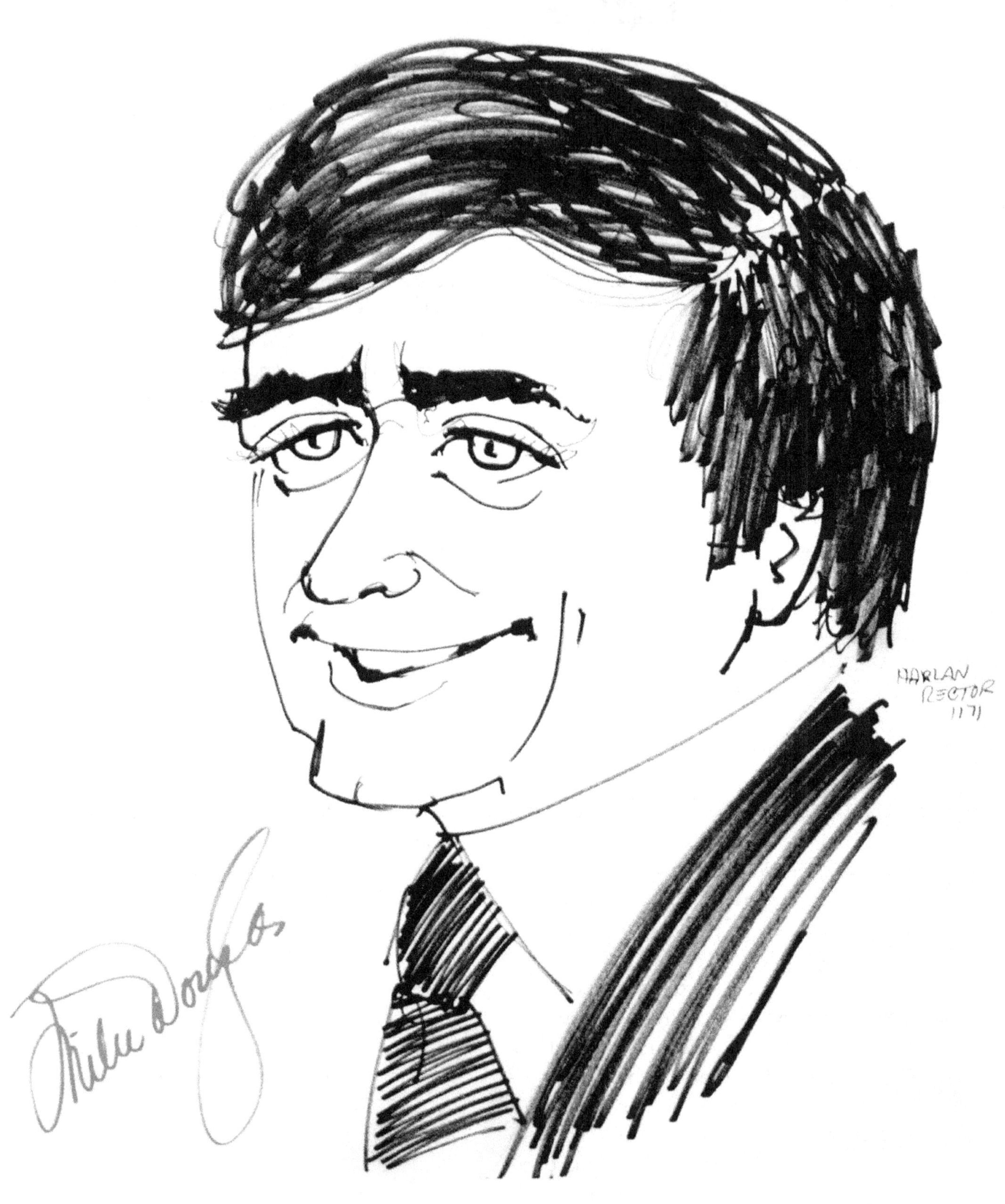

HARLAN
RECTOR
1171

Mike Douglas

Every afternoon for two decades, millions of Americans tuned into *The Mike Douglas Show* for entertaining music, as well as interviews with celebrities and political figures. The host, Mike Douglas himself, was enjoying enormous success on his nationally syndicated talk show when WJR in Detroit interviewed him.

Michael Delaney Dowd, Jr., was born in 1925 in Chicago, Illinois. Showing an affinity for singing, he left school at age 15 to pursue it professionally. Mike started singing in nightclubs before getting work as a singer on a cruise ship on Lake Michigan.

During World War II, he served in the Navy on a munitions ship. Following the war, Mike signed with Kay Kyser's Kollege of Musical Knowledge. Without his knowledge, he was introduced one night as Mike Douglas, and he became known by this stage name for the rest of his career. During this time, Mike married Genevieve Purnell, whom he met and fell in love with during his teenage years. They had three daughters. Mike scored a few hits with Kyser, including *Ole Buttermilk Sky* in 1946, and *The Old Lamplighter*.

In 1950, Mike was the voice of Prince Charming in the Disney animated classic *Cinderella*. His stint with Kyser's band lasted until 1951, when Kyser retired. At this time, rock 'n' roll was taking over the pop charts and the old standards faded from popularity. During his leaner times, Mike and his wife survived by "flipping" Los Angeles homes.

The year 1961 sparked a new beginning for Douglas when he was summoned to Cleveland by the Westinghouse Broadcasting Company to host a talk show. *The Mike Douglas Show* quickly gained popularity and was nationally syndicated in August 1963. Westinghouse returned to Philadelphia, and *The Mike Douglas Show* aired its first show from there on August 30, 1965. In 1967, it earned the first Emmy Award for Individual Achievement in Daytime Television.

During the turbulent 60s and 70s, while America was undergoing much change, one constant was *The Mike Douglas Show*. Americans tuned into his show every day to see an opening musical number and a different celebrity cohost each week. Viewers saw musicians ranging from Frank Sinatra to John Lennon. There was the unforgettable appearance of three-year-old golf Tiger Woods, putting on air while guest Bob Hope looked amazed. Some of the world's most iconic entertainers had their start on *The Mike Douglas Show*.

Mike was comfortable stepping back and putting his guests in the spotlight. He served up questions that would enhance them and entertain everyone. One shocking moment came when future NBC national correspondent John Dancy walked onto the set in the middle of the show. He announced the shooting of President Kennedy in Dallas. In that unscripted moment, Douglas followed his instinct, which was to lead everyone in a prayer.

The show's run ended in 1981. Next, Douglas hosted a celebrity interview show on CNN until 1983. On August 11, 2006, on his 81st birthday, Mike Douglas passed away suddenly in Palm Beach Gardens, Florida. His memory lives on through his wife, three daughters, several grandchildren, and great-grandchildren. ∎

DORRI HALL

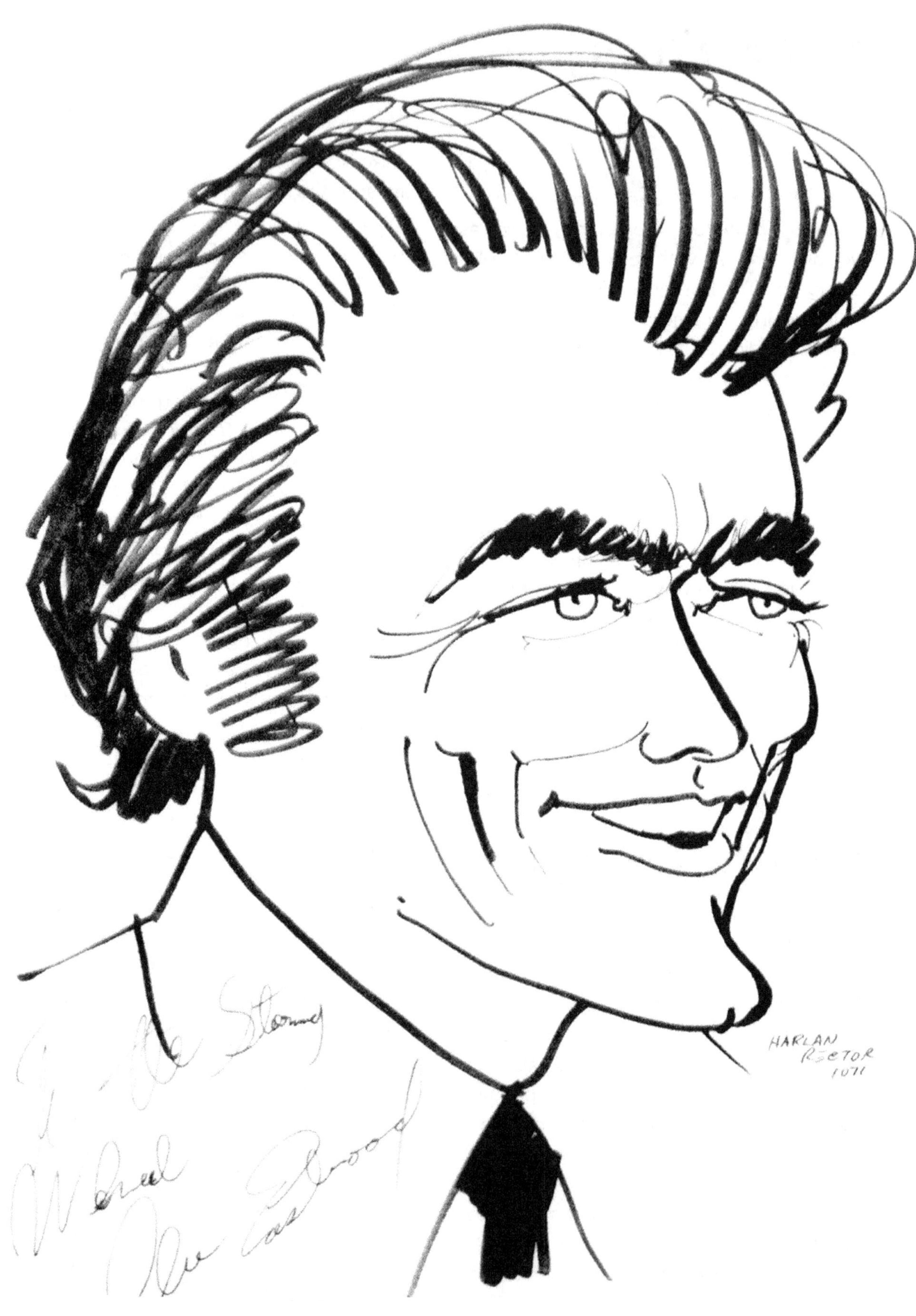
HARLAN
RECTOR
1971

Clint Eastwood

When I drew the caricature on the opposite page, Clint Eastwood was being interviewed on WJR radio. Eastwood was on a publicity tour for his latest movie, *Dirty Harry*, which was to be released in December 1971. That year was a turning point in Eastwood's career, as his directorial debut, *Play Misty For Me*, which he also starred in, was released. J.P. McCarthy, the host of the radio show, loved having a guest like Clint Eastwood. He had a lot to talk about and his soft-spoken delivery made the interview seem intimate and personal.

Clinton Eastwood Jr. was born on May 31, 1930, in San Francisco, California, the son of Clinton Eastwood and Ruth (Runner) Wood. Eastwood was nicknamed "Samson" by the hospital nurses because he weighed 11 pounds, 6 ounces at birth. He was held back in middle school and while no one is absolutely sure if he ever graduated from high school, he went on to hold jobs as a lifeguard, paper carrier, grocery clerk, forest fighter, and golf caddy.

In 1951 during the Korean War, Eastwood was drafted into the Army and served as a lifeguard at Fort Ord, California. After his service, Eastwood went to Hollywood and reconnected with a friend from Fort Ord who was instrumental in getting him an audition with film director Arthur Lubin. After the audition, Lubin urged Eastwood to attend drama classes. In 1954, Eastwood signed his first acting contract for $100 a week.

From 1954 until 1958, Eastwood played minor roles in a dozen or more films. His big break came in 1958, when he was cast as Rowdy Yates for the CBS hour-long western series *Rawhide*, for which he earned $750 an episode. After only three weeks on the air, *Rawhide* entered the top 20 in TV ratings. As the ratings went up, so did Eastwood's salary. Seven years later, *Rawhide* was cancelled in the middle of a television season but Eastwood received $119,000/episode as severance pay.

It is said that when one door closes another one opens. For Eastwood, the opening came with *A Fistful of Dollars*, the first in a trilogy of spaghetti Westerns filmed in Spain. In 1965, he was signed to star in the second film in the trilogy, *For a Few Dollars More*. In 1966, *The Good, The Bad and the Ugly* completed the trilogy. Eastwood developed a vigilante persona that brought him through *Hang 'Em High* and *Coogan's Bluff*, both released in 1968.

Proving that there was more to his skills than just talking through clenched teeth in a sombrero, he starred in the war epic *Where Eagles Dare*, and rounded out his change of character by starring in the only musical of his entire career, *Paint Your Wagon*, singing with Lee Marvin.

From 1971 to 2020, Eastwood starred and/or directed in *Play Misty for Me*, *Breezy*, *The Outlaw Josie Wales*, *Heartbreak Ridge*, *Bird*, *Unforgiven*, *The Bridges of Madison County*, *Space Cowboys*, *Mystic River*, *Million Dollar Baby*, *Flags of Our Fathers*, *Letters from Iwo Jima*, *Changeling*, *Gran Torino*, *Invictus*, *Hereafter*, *J. Edgar*, *American Sniper*, *Sully* and *Richard Jewell*, garnering 41 Academy Award nominations and winning 13 Oscars. ■

HARLAN RECTOR

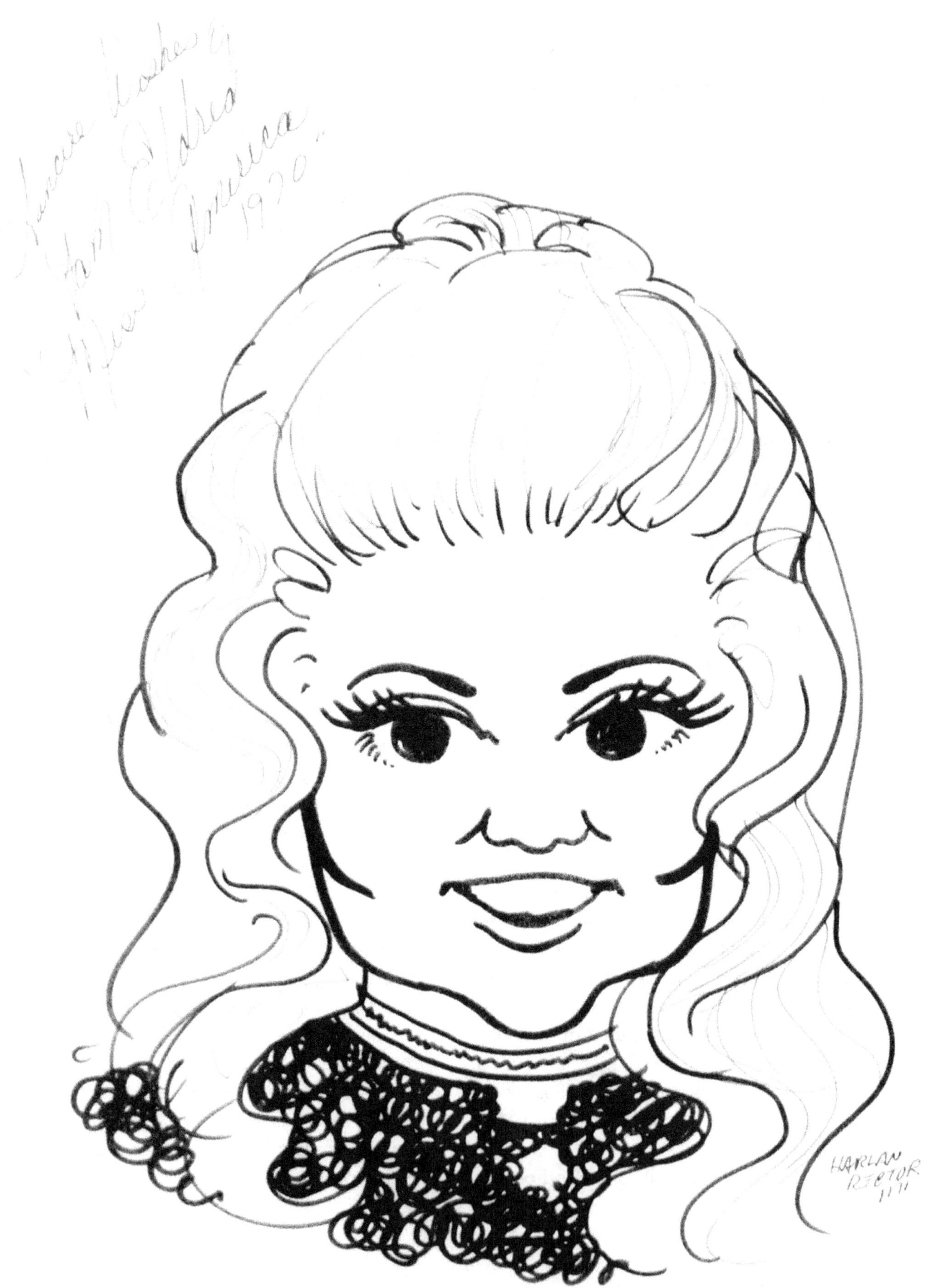
HARLAN
RECTOR
1171

Pamela Eldred

"There she is, Miss America." Pamela Anne Eldred took the title on September 6, 1969, at the age of 21. She was the third Miss Michigan to win the Miss America title. She traveled the country during her reign, logging thousands of miles, including time in Detroit when WJR interviewed her.

Eldred was born on April 21, 1948, in West Bloomfield, Michigan. When she entered the Miss America pageant, she was a student at Mercy College, now known as the University of Detroit Mercy. For the talent competition, Pamela performed a ballet dance number to music from Shakespeare's Romeo and Juliet. When asked what advice she would offer her younger sister, she shocked the judges with her honesty, revealing her younger sister, Melanie, was mentally disabled — something usually not discussed openly during that period of time. But she acknowledged how having a sibling with a disability gave her great perspective.

Pamela commented on the most important lesson she learned during that busy year as Miss America. She learned about the imperfection of life and how with everything, there is "give and take." She also enjoyed learning about her state and felt a sense of pride to be representing Michigan when she won the title.

Following her year as Miss America 1970, Pamela returned to school and earned her degree in speech and drama from the University of Detroit Mercy in 1971. She married Dr. Jules F. Levey and had a daughter, Hilary. After graduation, Pamela traveled the country as a dancer, spokesperson, model, and lecturer. Later in life, she even became a professional aesthetician. She said she enjoyed the profession because it allowed her to meet interesting people. Then she launched a career as an image consultant to help professional women build self-esteem and positive self-images. Pamela also wrote a bi-weekly self-improvement column for the *Oakland Press* for 11 years.

The four points of the Miss America crown stand for style, success, scholarship, and service—the four pillars of the Miss America Organization. Pamela used this platform to serve as an advocate for people with disabilities, serving as an ambassador for volunteers with the National Association of Retarded Citizens (ARC). Her sister, Melanie, died in 2008, and in her honor, Pamela founded the Pam Eldred Community Health Scholarship. It benefited students who were interested in working with people with special needs. She also recruited members of Congress to support the Development Disabilities Service and Construction Act, which provided funds for the mentally handicapped. In 1998, Pamela remarried to a lawyer named Norman Robbins.

She has continued working with various charities like March of Dimes, Easter Seals, and Michigan Cancer Foundation. She was awarded the Meritorious Service Award for Humanitarian services for the developmentally disabled.

Pamela is retired. She and her husband divide their time between Bloomfield, Michigan, and Boca Raton, Florida. ■

DORRI HALL

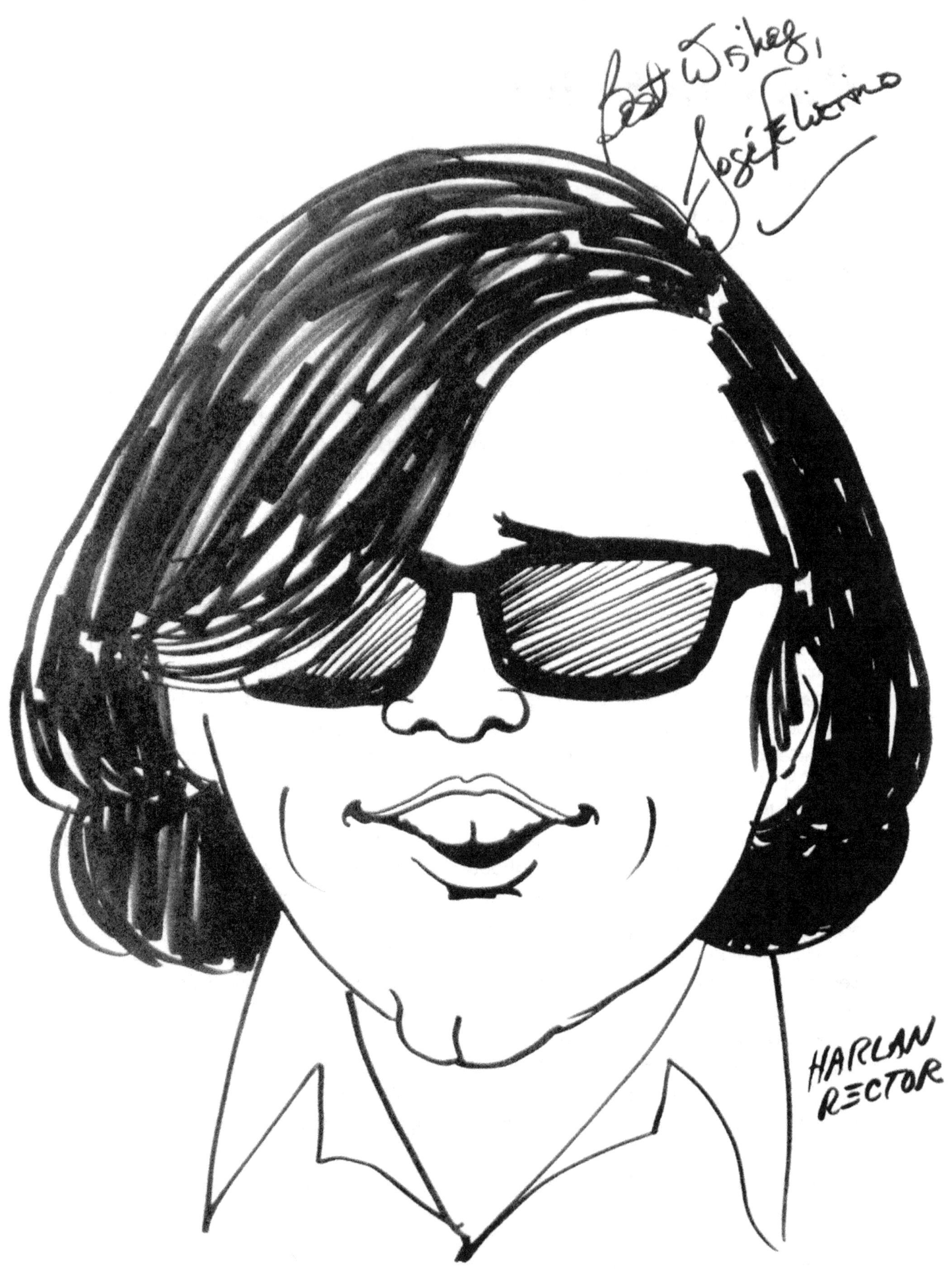
Best Wishes,
José Litrino
HARLAN
RECTOR

Jose Feliciano

Jose Monserrate Feliciano Garcia was born in Lares, Puerto Rico, on September 10, 1945. The fourth child of eleven sons, Jose was born blind as a result of congenital glaucoma. He began performing at age 3, playing on a tin cracker can while accompanying his uncle, who played the cuatro, a Latin American string instrument.

When Feliciano was five, his family moved to Spanish Harlem, in the Bronx section of New York City, where he made his first musical appearance at the age of nine. He taught himself the accordion but it was the guitar his father gave him two years later that he dedicated 14 hours daily, listening to 1950s rock and roll, classical guitarists, and jazz, playing along with the greats. Andres Segovia and Wes Montgomery were among his favorites. As a teenager, Feliciano took classical guitar lessons with Harold Morris, a staff music teacher at The Light House School for the Blind. Morris had once been a student of Segovia. Ray Charles and Sam Cook influenced his singing.

At 17, to help support his family, Jose quit high school and started frequenting the coffee houses of Greenwich Village, 'passing the hat' for his salary. His first professional performance was in 1961 at a coffee house in Detroit, Michigan. Ten years later, he came back to Detroit where he met his future wife, Susan Omillion, and was interviewed on WJR radio while my father drew his caricature shown on the previous page.

In 1963, Jose was discovered while performing at Gerde's Folk City in the Village and immediately signed by Jack Somer, an RCA Victor executive. In 1964, Jose released his first single, *Everybody Do the Click*. In 1965 and 1966, he released his first albums: *The Voice Guitar of Jose Feliciano* and *A Bag of Soul*, folk-pop-soul albums that showcased his talent on radios across the US.

Victor wanted him to record an album for them in Spanish. Jose suggested he record some of the bolero music of his parents with his added blues and folk influences while playing in the village. The result was two smash hit singles and the beginning of a series of successful singles, albums, and gold records throughout Latin America. One of his most beloved interpretations was *Extranos en la Noche*, the Spanish version of Frank Sinatra's *Strangers in the Night*.

In 1968, at the height of the Vietnam War protests, Detroit Tigers broadcaster Ernie Harwell invited Feliciano to perform the *Star-Spangled Banner* at Tiger Stadium. His rendition was highly controversial and damaged his career in the years that followed. But in 1970, Feliciano released an album of Christmas music, *Feliz Navidad*, which has become a traditional part of the music landscape around the world.

In 2018, Jose Feliciano celebrated the golden anniversary of his iconic rendition of the *Star Spangled Banner* by releasing his RCA album *Feliciano*, which featured *Light My Fire*, and performed at concerts in Australia, Europe, North America, and South America.

Jose Feliciano was honored in 2019 with a Lifetime Achievement Award for his contributions to the world of music during the 62nd Puerto Rican Day Parade in New York. ■

DANA (RECTOR) GROVES

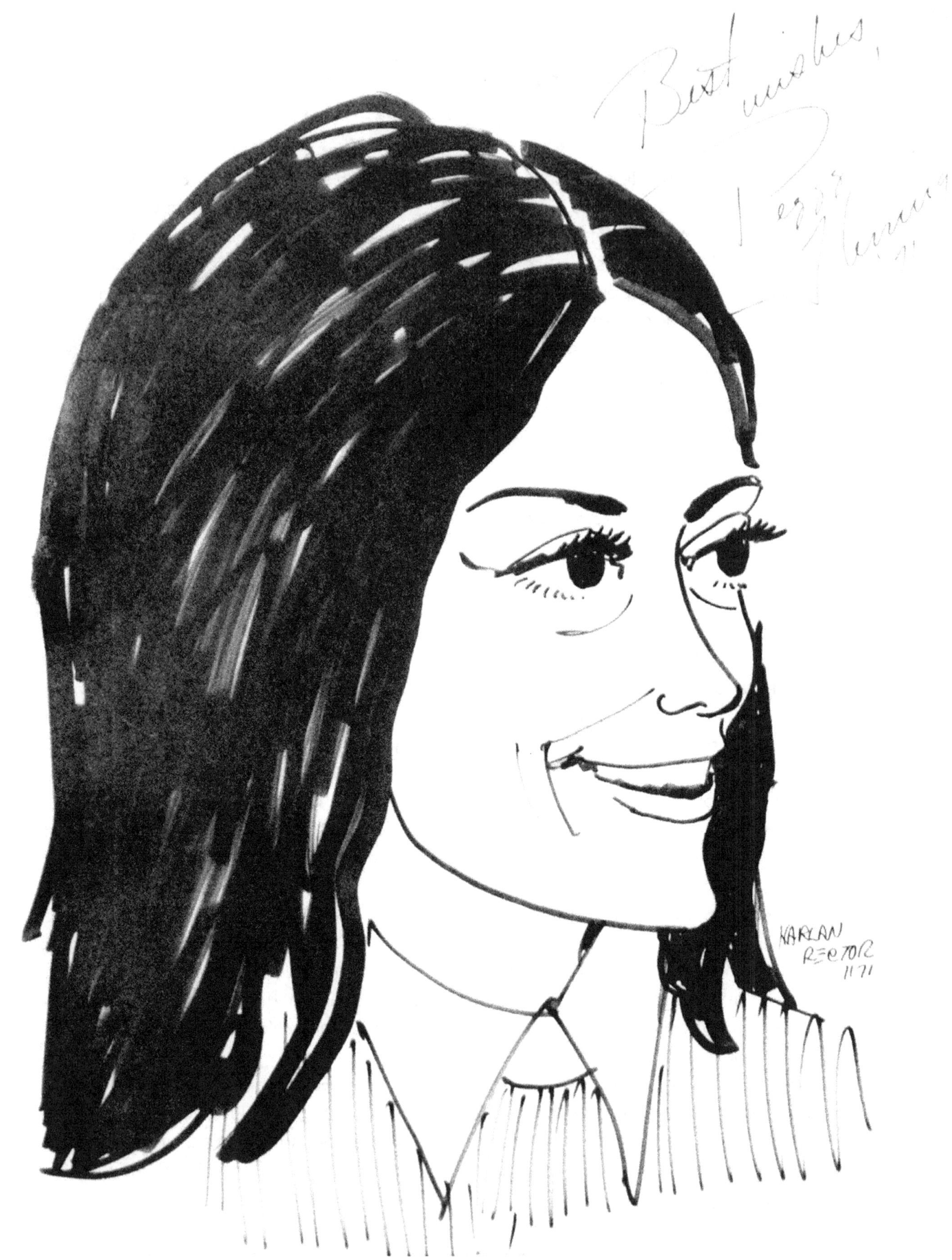

44

Peggy Fleming

When Peggy Fleming interviewed with WJR in 1972, she had accomplished what no other American athlete had in the 1968 Winter Olympics in Grenoble, France—she won the gold.

Peggy's inspirational figure skating performance earned her the title "Olympic Charmer" on the cover of *Life Magazine* on February 23, 1968. The nineteen-year-old appeared with her arm raised in victory, the gold medal around her neck, wearing a chartreuse skating dress. Her mother, Doris, made Peggy's costume and intentionally chose that shade once she heard that monks in that region of France produced chartreuse liquor. Doris hoped it would have a beneficial subliminal effect on the judges, cause the audience to cheer louder, and be inspiring.

Peggy was born in San Jose, California, on July 27, 1948, to parents Doris and Eugene. Her father was a newspaper journalist and former US Marine. At age 9, she had her first taste of skating, instantly feeling it was something she could be good at so she started taking lessons.

William Kipp, her first skating coach, was killed in a plane crash in Belgium along with the entire US Figure Skating Team in 1961. After this tragedy, her family moved to Colorado Springs so that Peggy could train with renowned coach Carlo Fassi. This partnership proved quite advantageous, as she went on to win three consecutive gold medals at the World Championships from 1966-1968, on her way to Olympic glory in 1968.

After the Olympics, Peggy turned professional and performed with the Ice Capades, Holiday on Ice, Ice Follies, and on other skating shows. She also performed on many TV specials and won two Emmy awards for her programs.

On June 13, 1970, Peggy married Greg Jenkins, a former amateur figure skater who later became a dermatologist. Together they had two sons: Andy (born in 1977), and Todd (born in 1988). From 1981 Peggy had been an expert commentator on figure skating for ABC Sports and later, ESPN. She participated in the broadcast of many skating competitions, including the Olympic Winter Games.

Arguably, her greatest challenge came in 1998 when she learned she had early stage breast cancer. Fortunately, following surgery and radiation, she was cancer-free. Peggy handled herself with the same strength, determination, and elegance we watched in her many skating performances. Peggy became a spokesperson for breast cancer awareness and the importance of early detection.

In 2005, Peggy and Greg created the Fleming Jenkins Vineyards & Winery. They donated proceeds from the sale of their Victories Rose wine to breast cancer research and treatment. In 2007, she joined the Art of the Olympians, where she has several paintings on exhibit.

Today, Peggy lives with her husband in Colorado, where she is close to her grandchildren. Fitness is still a vital part of her daily routine, and when she isn't at the gym, she and her husband enjoy playing tennis with their family ∎

Dorri Hall

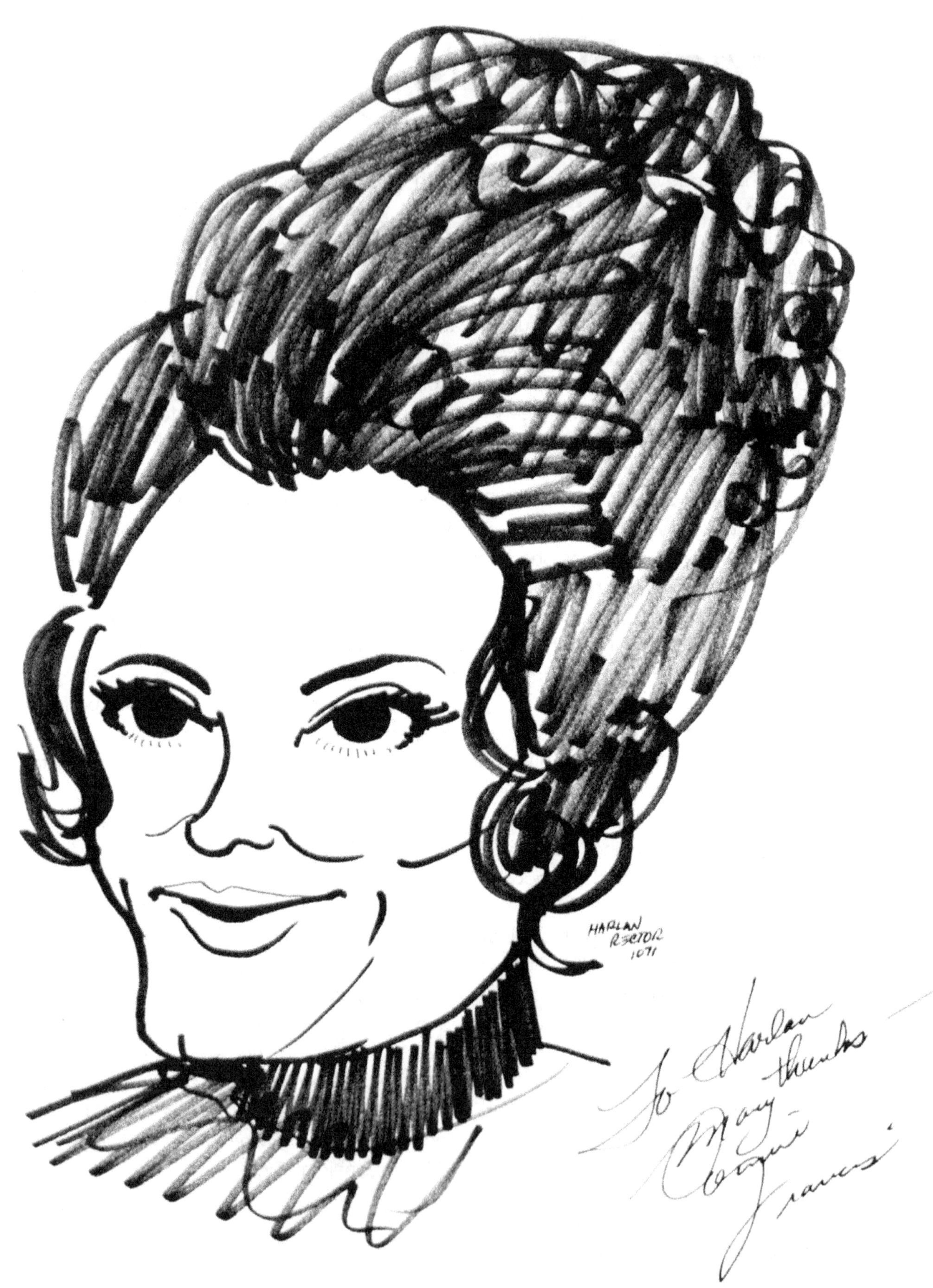
HARLAN
RECTOR
1971
To Harlan
Many thanks
Connie
Francis

Connie Francis

Concetta Maria Franconero was born in 1938 to first-generation Italian-American parents living in the Italian section of Newark, New Jersey. She changed her name to Connie Francis at age 10, when she appeared on NBC's *The Startime Kids* with host Arthur Godfrey. He couldn't pronounce her name, and suggested something "easy and Irish." Despite worrying about upsetting her dad, she accepted her new name.

Her father, an impoverished roofer, encouraged his daughter to perform by playing her accordion and singing in both English and Italian. But when advised to dump the accordion and only sing, Francis performed as a singer every week on *Startime* for four years. In June 1955, her first single, *Freddy*, was released.

At the same time, Connie was also a member of the National Honor Society with a goal of becoming a physician. In 1957, she was admitted to New York University on a pre-med scholarship. However, after obeying her father's request to sing the 1923 song, *Who's Sorry Now*, medicine was clearly not to be her path to success. After this song was played on Dick Clark's *American Bandstand*, her singing career took off. Connie wrote, "Without my friend and mentor Dick Clark, there simply would have been no Connie Francis."

Throughout the 1960s, she was "America's Sweetheart of Song." By 1967, Connie Francis had sold thirty-five million recordings worldwide. Thirty-five songs were top hits, including *Everybody's Somebody's Fool, My Heart Has A Mind of Its Own, Don't Break the Heart That Loves You*, and million-selling rock and roll song *Stupid Cupid*.

In 1963, after President John F. Kennedy was assassinated, Connie released, *In the Summer of His Years*. Donations from the sale of this recording went to dependents of the policemen shot during that incident.

A lover of languages, Connie sang the title song of the movie *Where the Boys Are* in six different languages, thereby internationalizing American music. In her unwavering support of American troops, Connie traveled 13,000 miles to Vietnam to entertain them. She was also on the *Voice of America, Radio Free Europe,* and the *Armed Forces Network*.

Connie Francis continues to sing to sold-out audiences. ◼

PATRICIA DALY-LIPE

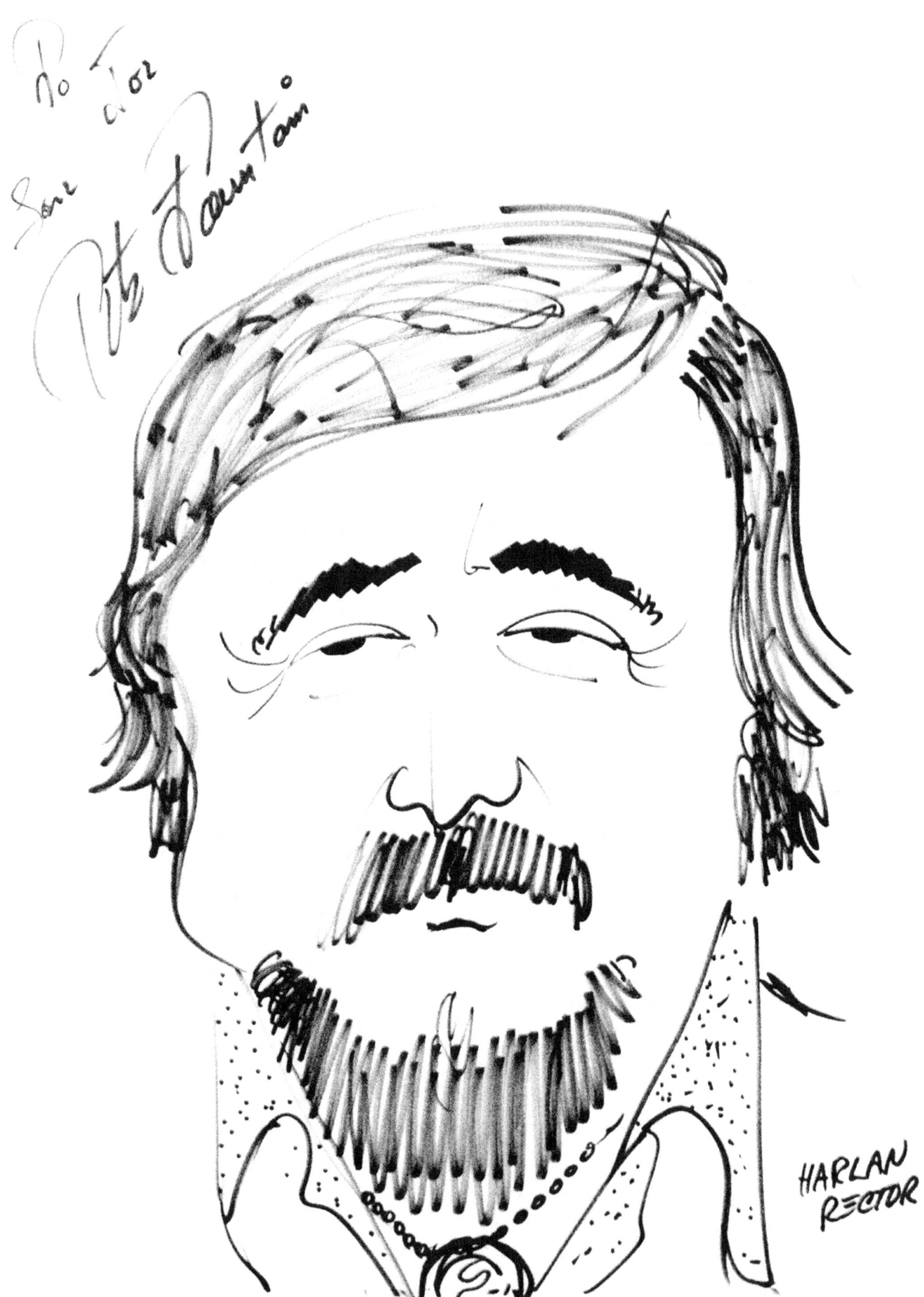
HARLAN
RECTOR

Pete Fountain

Pierre Dewey LaFontaine, Jr., later known as Pete Fountain, was born on July 3, 1930, in New Orleans, Louisiana. He was continually battling respiratory infections for which the expensive medications were prescribed but proved to not be very effective. Pete's father talked with a neighborhood doctor one day while at the local pharmacy and that doctor agreed to see Pete the next day. The diagnosis didn't change but this time, the doctor advised his father try a rather unorthodox treatment as therapy to strengthen his weak lungs. "Purchase a musical instrument, anything he has to blow into." Young Pete was introduced to the clarinet that same day.

At first, Pete produced little more than a weak sound, but he continued to practice and eventually he was able to produce smooth sounds and music as he successfully improved the health of his lungs. He took private lessons but also learned by playing along with jazz phonograph records.

The treatment not only worked but helped make Pete Fountain into a legend in a most unexpected way. In high school, Pete out-earned his teachers by playing the clarinet in the evenings on Bourbon Street. Pete bounced around to different cities and played with many different bands.

A talent scout signed him with Welk's Orchestra on the *Lawrence Welk Show* in Los Angeles. After two years on the show, Pete headed back to New Orleans to jam with one of his old bands, the Dukes of Dixieland. He became well-known enough that he formed a band under his name and opened up his own nightclub, where he could show off his talents anytime he chose.

Pete put together a quintet with double bass drummer Jack Sperling, pianist Merle Koch, vibist Godfrey Hirsch, and bassist Don Bagley. The gang often travelled to Los Angeles to play in Hollywood, including 56 appearances on *The Johnny Carson Show*.

In his nightclub, many talents came in to see and often perform with Pete. They included Frank Sinatra, Carol Lawrence, Phil Harris, and even Robert Mitchum. Brenda Lee enjoyed performing so much with Pete that they ended up recording together.

Pete Fountain recorded more than 100 albums. As a man who prospered from unusual situations, the unique sounds from his instrument also came about from what should have been debilitating circumstances. Most mouthpieces were rubber, but a crystal mouthpiece gifted from clarinetist Irving Fazola's mother gave Pete a more distinctive, sweet woody sound. Serendipitously, one night George Girard dropped his trumpet on the mouthpiece of Pete's clarinet and shattered it. He had to use George's crystal mouthpiece as a replacement and used it from 1949 until his final performance in 2014.

Pete married Beverly Lang in 1951 and stayed together until his death 65 years later. They raised two boys and a girl. Pete died age 86 in 2016. ■

JOHNNY DALY

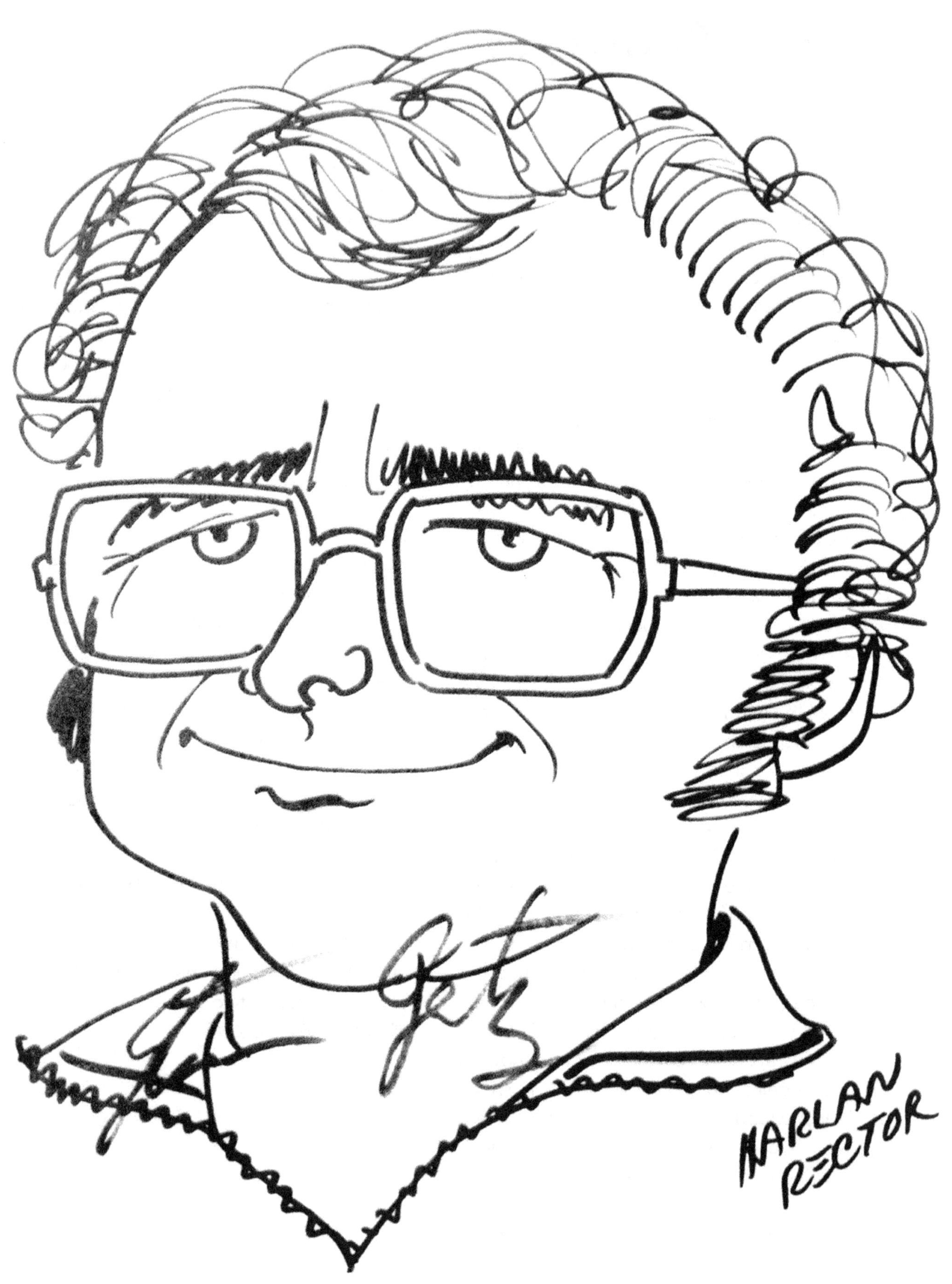

MARLAN
RECTOR

Stan Getz

Remember the 1964 hit *The Girl from Ipanema*? That song featured Stan Getz, one of the greatest saxophonists who ever lived.

Before Stan was born, his paternal grandparents fled to Whitechapel, London in 1913 from Kyiv to escape the anti-Jewish pogroms of the Russian Empire, which ruled the Ukraine at the time. They owned the Harris Tailor Shop for more than 13 years before emigrating to the United States with their three sons, Al, Phil and Ben.

Born Stanley Gayetski at the St. Vincent's Hospital in Philadelphia, Pennsylvania on February 2, 1927, the Getz family first settled in Philadelphia but the Great Depression forced the family to seek better opportunities so they moved to New York City.

Getz did very well in school, working hard to earn straight As and finish top of his class. His interest was music and he played any instruments he could get his hands on until his father finally bought him his first saxophone at the age of 13. Even though his father also got him a clarinet, Getz practiced eight hours a day on the instrument he loved most, the sax.

Stan loved jazz and played his saxophone constantly. In 1943, he was accepted into Jack Teagarden's band. Stan was known as the "Sound" because of his warm, wispy timbre. Later in the 1940s, Getz also accompanied Nat King Cole and Lionel Hampton. In the mid-fifties, he played cool jazz in Scandinavia. A 1953 line-up of the Dizzy Gillespie/Stan Getz Sextet featured Oscar Peterson, Herb Ellis, Ray Brown, and Max Roach.

In 1961, Getz returned to the United States, now playing music he called bossa nova. In 1962, teaming with guitarist Charlie Byrd, Getz recorded *Jazz Samba*. It quickly became a hit and Getz won the Grammy for Best Jazz Performance of 1963 for *Desafinado*. That album sold over one million copies. As a followup, Getz recorded the album *Jazz Samba Encore*, with one of the originators of bossa nova, Brazilian guitarist Luiz Bonfá. It also sold more than a million copies. In 1972, Getz recorded the jazz fusion album *Captain Marvel* with Chick Corea, Tony Williams, and Stanley Clarke. He also had a cameo in the 1980 film *The Exterminator*.

In the mid-1980s, Getz worked in the San Francisco Bay area and taught at Stanford University as an artist-in-residence. In 1986, he was inducted into the Down Beat Jazz Hall of Fame.

Stan married three times, fathering five children. On June 6, 1991, Getz died of liver cancer. His ashes were poured from his saxophone case six miles off the coast of Marina del Rey, California.

"My life is music, and in some vague, mysterious and subconscious way, I have always been driven by a taut inner spring which has propelled me to almost compulsively reach for perfection in music, often —in fact, mostly—at the expense of everything else in my life." – Stan Getz ■

Patricia Daly-Lipe

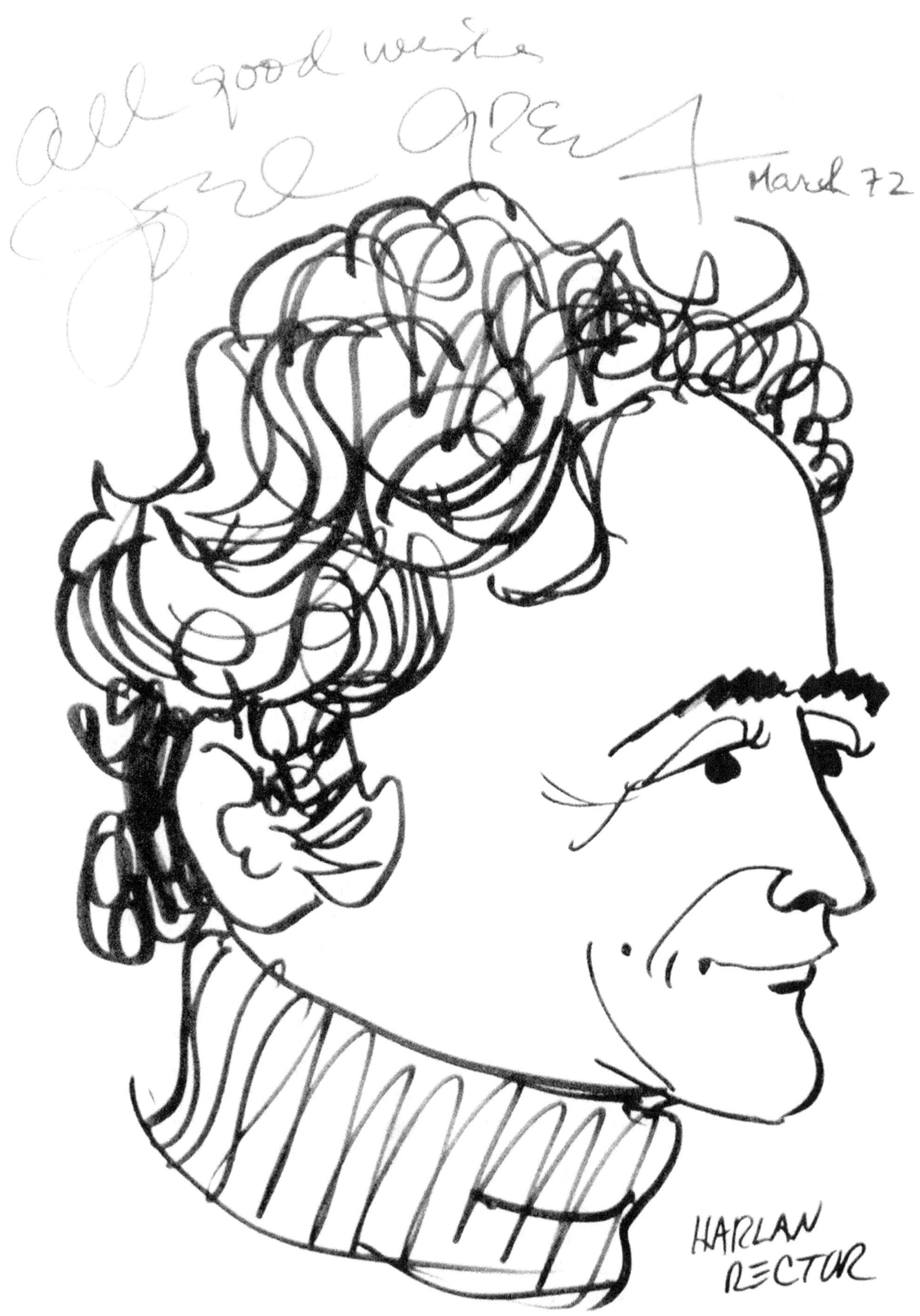

All good wishes
March 72
HARLAN
RECTOR

Joel Grey

Joel David Katz, born in Cleveland, Ohio, in 1932, transformed into the great performer we all know as Joel Grey. His talent came naturally as the son of performers Goldie "Grace" Epstein and Mickey Katz, both hard-working actors, comedians, and musicians.

Joel leapt onto the stage as a young man in the Curtain Pullers Children's Program at the Cleveland Play House in the 1940s and quickly found himself in lead roles. He easily transitioned to the big stage after outgrowing the children's theatre.

In 1966, he became a superstar, receiving the coveted Tony Award for Best Performance by an Actor in a Musical, as the Master of Ceremonies in the production of *Cabaret*. Over the next 30 years, Joel was nominated for numerous other awards for his performances in musicals.

In 1951, Joel's television and film career began as a Young Talent Guest on the *Colgate Comedy Hour*, followed by his film debut as Bender in the musical *About Face* starring Gordon MacRae.

From 1952 until 2008, Joel was cast in a film nearly every year but in 1972, he was in a unique position. After his great success with *Cabaret* on the stage, he returned to *Cabaret* but this time in a film adaptation and again receiving great recognition for his performance, accumulating numerous awards for his role as The Master Of Ceremonies, including Academy Award for Best Supporting Actor and the Golden Globe for Best Supporting Actor in a Motion Picture.

In 1985 he was nominated for another Golden Globe as Chiun "Master of Sinanju" in the film *Remo Williams: The Adventure Begins*.

Although his film career has slowed down in the past 20 years, his television appearances kept him busy as recently as 2014 with a performance in the hit show *CSI: Crime Scene Investigation* alongside Ted Danson and Elisabeth Shue. His television career has outpaced his film career, yet neither kept up with his passion for the stage.

In 2018, Joel was back in the theatre, performing *Fiddler on the Roof* in Yiddish.

Joel married Jo Wilder in 1958. After 24 years the marriage dissolved. He fathered two children with Jo, one of whom, Jennifer Grey, became a big star with her performance in the film *Ferris Bueller's Day Off*, followed by a Golden Globe nomination in the hit film *Dirty Dancing* alongside Patrick Swayze.

Joel, always the artist, spends much of his time these days working on books of photographs. His first book, *Pictures I Had to Take*, was printed in 2003. He has continued to publish further books, on average, every three years since. ∎

JOHNNY DALY

Thanks,
Bobby Hackett
HARLAN
RECTOR

Bobby Hackett

Call him Bobby—the most beautiful horn in the world! Robert Leo Hackett was born on January 31, 1915, and raised in Providence, Rhode Island. Bobby, one of nine children, played the ukulele, guitar and violin at a very young age and eventually saved enough money for his real passion—by age twelve he owned his first cornet.

Bobby left high school during his freshman year for a steady-paying job playing with a band performing seven days a week in Port Arthur at the local Chinese restaurant. When he wasn't strumming his guitar at the Rhodes and Arcadia ballrooms broadcasting on Providence radio, he was lovingly blowing his preferred cornet at the Megansett Tea Room in North Falmouth with Payson Re's Band. It was there Bobby got his first reputation when the manager said, "If that kid picks up the horn again, the whole band is fired."

Nearly two years passed before Bobby and Johnny Crandon formed The Harvard Gold Coast Orchestra. Their band consisted of four professional musicians and medical students. From 1935 to early 1936, he traveled to Boston and Providence for gigs primarily with Ted Roy.

Form a dixieland band! Play at The Theatrical Club in Boston! Who could turn down such exciting requests? With recommendations from Herbie Marsh, Bobby took Teddy Roy, Roger Malencourt from the Crescent Club, Russ Isaacs from Meyer Davis's band, and recruited Pat Barbara, Billy Wiles and Brad Gowans to create the Hackett band. Noted Boston music critic George Frazier drew widespread attention to the group and the band's one year stay at the Theatrical Club grossed more than a million dollars.

The band fell on hard times after leaving for New York but fast forward a few years and Bobby formed yet another big band, playing at New York's World Fair, the Ben Franklin Hotel in Philadelphia, the Famous Door and several other NYC clubs, with tours and several recordings. Recordings included two Hackett favorites: *Embraceable You* (his theme song) and *Ja-Da* but the honeymoon died six months later when the band was forced to disband owing MCA nearly $3,000. Taking leave from the Heidt band, Bobby recorded for the film *Second Chorus* starring Fred Astaire.

Dental problems prevented Bobby from playing the cornet regularly so his close friend Glenn Miller hired him in July of 1941 to play guitar. Bobby faithfully carried an amplifier with him, intending to switch to electric guitar, but he never plugged it in. Nevertheless, despite his medical circumstances, Bobby finally recorded his most admired cornet solos, *A String of Pearls* and *Rhapsody in Blue*. He even appeared in the movie *Orchestra Wives* after Glenn Miller negotiated the MCA debt down to $1,000.

From *What a Wonderful World* to *Strike Up the Band*, Bobby Hackett filled the hearts of so many generations with his smooth jazz. The most beautiful horn in the world stopped playing when Bobby passed away from a heart attack June 7, 1976, but his memory and sweet sounds play on in the Rhode Island Music Hall of Fame. ■

LINDA FIELDS

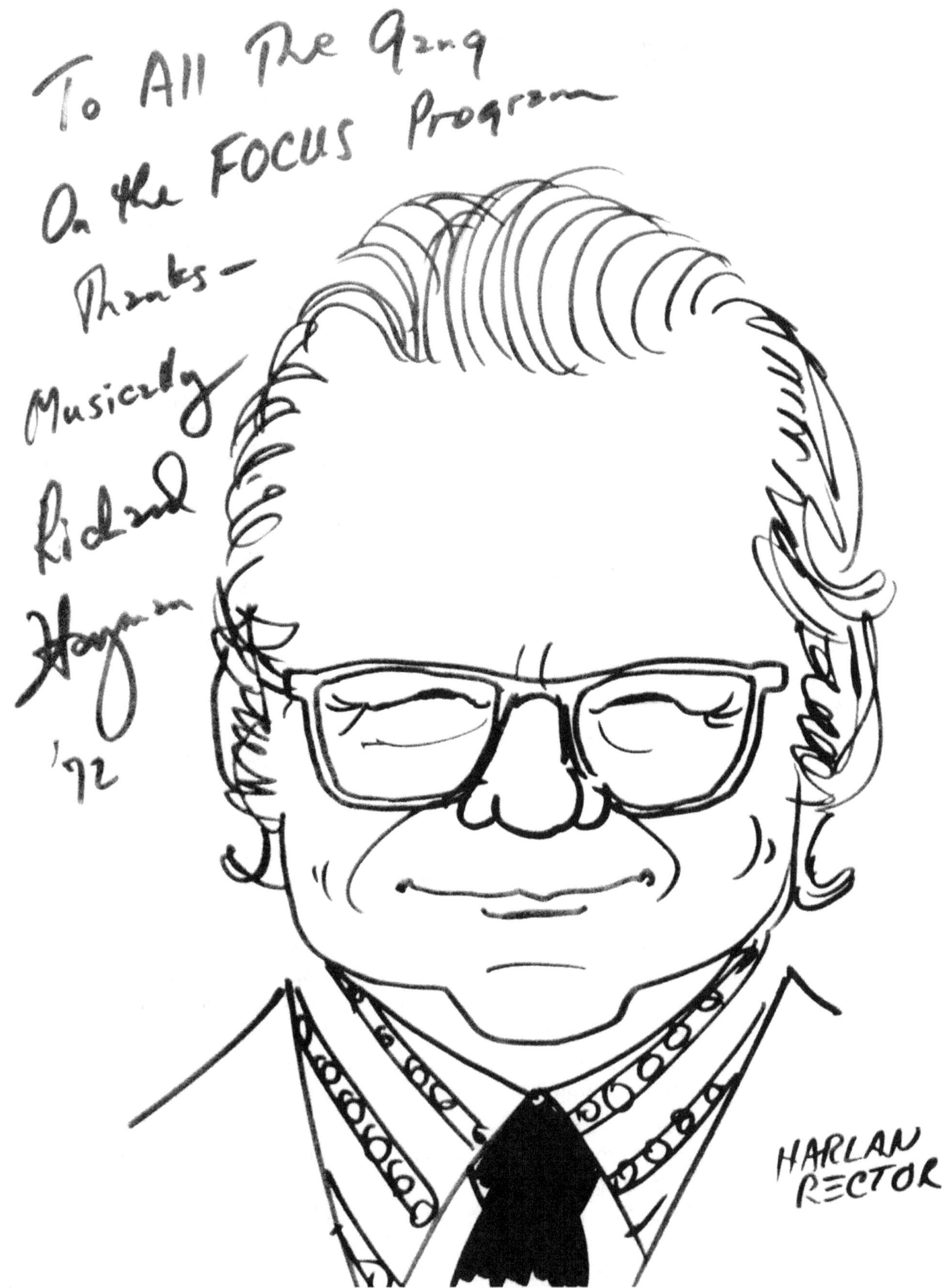

To All The Gang
On the FOCUS Program
Thanks—
Musically
Richard
Hayman
'92
HARLAN
RECTOR

Richard Hayman

One of America's premier conductors, Richard Hayman was well-known to Michigan radio audiences during his career. He served for 30 years as the chief arranger and backup conductor for the Boston Pops Orchestra during Arthur Fiedler's tenure, and conducted the Detroit and Grand Rapids Symphony Orchestras. He also was Principal "Pops" Conductor of the St. Louis and Hartford Symphony Orchestra, Florida's Sunshine Pops, the Orchestra London Canada, and the Calgary Philharmonic Orchestra.

Richard Warren Joseph Hayman was born on March 27, 1920, in Cambridge, Massachusetts. After attending Winthrop High School, he toured and made dozens of recordings for Mercury Records playing the harmonica under the name "Richard Hayman and His Orchestra." His biggest hit was the single *Ruby* from the 1952 film *Ruby Gentry*, starring Jennifer Jones and Charlton Heston. Hayman's arrangement featured himself as the harmonica soloist.

Hayman's career took off, encompassing much more to include conducting, composing, songwriting, and arranging, primarily for film. He created musical arrangements for more than 50 artists and entertainers including Barbra Streisand, Bob Hope, Liza Minnelli, and Olivia Newton-John.

Naxos credits him with 109 albums. Hayman and his orchestra worked on 23 albums and 27 hit singles for Mercury Records, for which he served as music director for 12 years.

He worked on film soundtracks and often performed in Hollywood productions, including *The Romanoffs*, *First Man*, *Exfrun*, *Monte Carlo*, *The OC*, *Girl Interrupted*, *Escape to Witch Mountain*, *Perry Como's Kraft Music Hall*, *Mysterious Stranger*, *Son of Lassie*, *Girl Crazy*, and *The Vaughn Monroe Show*. He was composer for the TV movies *Aladdin*, *The Emperor's New Clothes*, *Jack and the Beanstalk*, and *Pinocchio*.

While he was primarily involved with symphony orchestras, he was musical director and/or MC for tours with Kenny Rogers, Johnny Cash, Olivia Newton-John, Tom Jones, Engelbert Humperdinck, the Carpenters, the Osmond's, Al Hirt, and Andy Williams. He also scored numerous Broadway shows and movies.

In 1960, he got a star on Hollywood's Walk of Fame. With the St. Louis Symphony Orchestra, he became noted for his sequined jackets, harmonica solos, and corny jokes, influencing the styles of many conductors who followed him.

In 1985 he was named Principal Pops Conductor of the Grand Rapids Symphony, then in 2006 he was named Pops Conductor Laureate and finally, at the age of 90, he earned the title of Pops Conductor Emeritus after his last event with the St. Louis Symphony Orchestra on his birthday June 27, 2010. He passed away at age 93 on February 5, 2014, in a hospice facility in New York. ■

EDWARD MICKOLUS

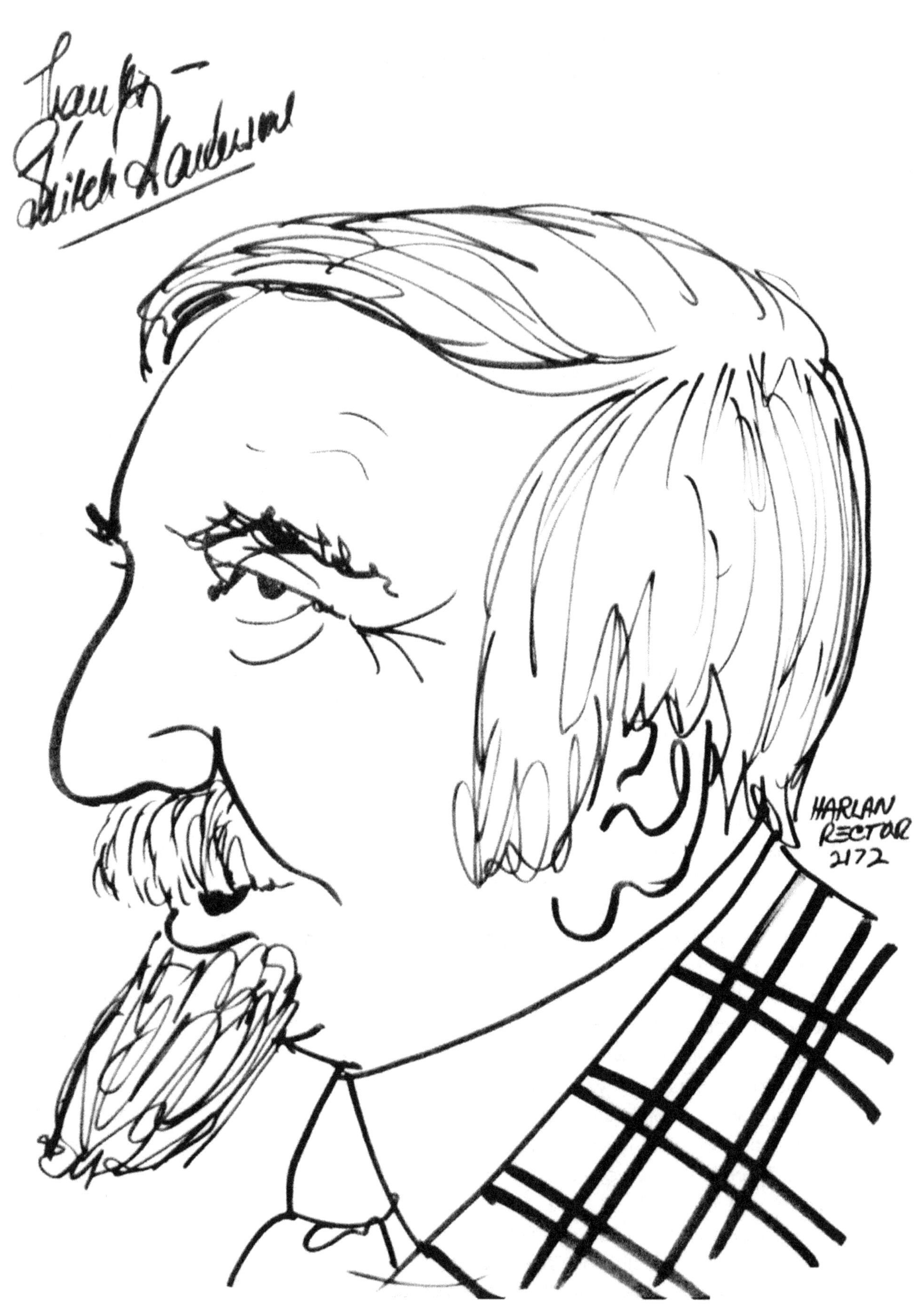

HARLAN
RECTOR
2172

Skitch Henderson

Lyle Russell Cedric Henderson, better known as "Skitch," was born on January 27, 1918, on a farm in Halstad, Minnesota. He was of Norwegian descent. His mother died when he was two years old, so he was raised by his aunt Hattie and uncle Frank Gift. They taught him to play piano at only four years old.

Though he did not receive formal musical training, he learned from his mentors Fritz Reiner, Albert Coates, Arnold Schoenberg, Ernst Toch, and Arturo Toscanini. Henderson said it was a combination of learning from masters and playing popular music with singers in taverns that rounded out his musical abilities.

While performing in roadhouses throughout the Midwest, Henderson received his first big break when he was hired in the MGM music department. He recalls working with Judy Garland on *Over the Rainbow*—he was the first musician to accompany her on piano prior to the film being completed. After World War II, Henderson formed his own orchestra, recording hundreds of compositions over the years. Some of his most notable instrumental recordings included *Skitch's Blues*, *Minuet on the Rocks*, *Skitch in Time*, *Come Thursday*, and *Curacao*.

In the late 1940s, Henderson worked at NBC Radio as musical director on Frank Sinatra's *Lucky Strike Show*. He also was an accompanist on *Philco Radio Time* with Bing Crosby on ABC. In addition, he found time to provide accompaniment on Bob Hope's *The Pepsodent Show*.

Bing Crosby anointed Henderson with the nickname "Skitch." Crosby was impressed with the way Henderson could quickly transcribe music to a written score. He was at first dubbed the "Sketch Kid," which was later shortened to "Skitch."

From 1951 to 1966, Henderson served at NBC as conductor and orchestra leader for both *The Tonight Show* and *The Today Show*. He was the original bandleader for Steve Allen, the original host of *The Tonight Show*. He was also Allen's band leader for his Sunday night variety show.

Henderson left *The Tonight Show* when Jack Paar became the host but returned as bandleader when Johnny Carson became host in 1962. Henderson left *The Tonight Show* for good in 1966.

In 1983, Henderson founded the New York Pops Orchestra. It was created to generate greater public awareness and appreciation of America's rich musical heritage through concerts and educational programs. The orchestra has toured internationally and provides a venue for families to enjoy American music to this day.

Henderson was also a guest conductor for several symphony orchestras, including The New York Philharmonic and the London Philharmonic.

In 1997, Henderson received the Handel Medallion for the important role he played in the cultural life of New York City. In 2005, the Smithsonian Institution awarded him the James Smithson Bicentennial Medal in recognition of his contributions to American culture.

In retirement, Henderson and his wife Ruth founded the Hunt Hill Farm Trust in an effort to preserve and protect their farm's land and holdings to celebrate Americana in music, art, and literature through the creation of a living museum.

Skitch Henderson was married twice and raised two children. He died on November 1, 2005. ◼

GREG BARRY

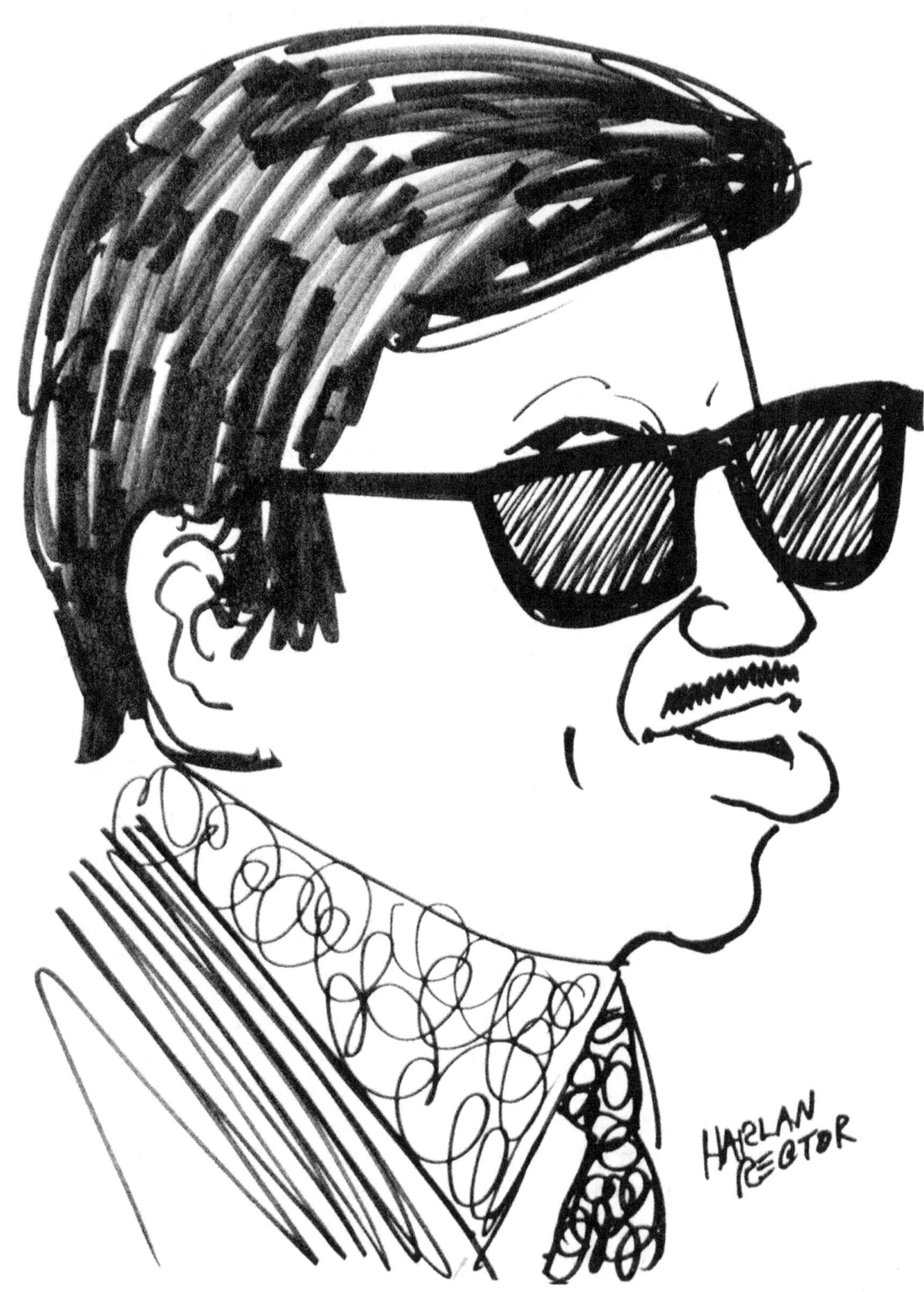

Earl 'Fatha' Hines

Earl 'Fatha' Hines, famed jazz pianist, composer and band leader, had lots to talk about during his visit with WJR, having released five albums in 1971 alone.

Earl Kenneth Hines was born on December 28, 1903, in Duquesne, Pennsylvania. He was raised by his father and stepmother after his mother died when he was three. His cornet-playing father taught him trumpet, his stepmother the piano, and his sister was a pianist who led bands in the 1930s.

Hines played the organ in church and learned piano tunes by ear. He played in trios while in high school, then branched out to various bands throughout the Midwest. He and band leader Louis Deppe became the first African-Americans to perform on radio in 1921. Hines joined Louis Armstrong's band in 1927 as pianist and musical director. He was part of Armstrong's Hot Five, recording jazz classics such as *West End Blues, Muggles, Skip the Gutter,* and *Weather Bird.*

In the late 1920s, Hines formed his own big band, which became the house band at Chicago's Grand Terrace Ballroom (owned by Al Capone), broadcasting his performances on radio to millions of fans. During one show, a putatively drunken announcer slurred his name as Fatha Hines; the nickname stuck.

Hines created a "trumpet style" of piano improv, focusing on speedy, single-note solo lines akin to a brass player. The style influenced such stars as Oscar Peterson and Herbie Hancock. Duke Ellington observed that his style became the roots of bebop, a transition from the more traditional swing.

In the early 1940s, Hines formed a West Coast band, attracting such legends as trumpeter Dizzy Gillespie, sax player Charlie "Bird" Parker, bassist Charles Mingus, and singers Sarah Vaughan and Billy Eckstine. Nat "King" Cole sometimes sat in while he conducted.

After a three-year reunion with Armstrong, Hines formed a new sextet that played at San Francisco's Hangover Club in the mid-1950's. He led a band that toured with the Harlem Globetrotters in 1954. He was at the top of the jazz movement in the 1960s with such albums as *Spontaneous Explorations* and *Legendary Little Theatre Concert.* In 1965, he was inducted into the Jazz Hall of Fame. The next year, he was named to *Down Beat* magazine's Hall of Fame and named the world's No. 1 Jazz Pianist—he won the award six times. In 1979, he was inducted into the Black Filmmakers Hall of Fame.

Hines was influential in the development of jazz piano, releasing more than 100 albums on Columbia, RCA, Capitol, Verve, and other labels during his career. In 1974 alone, at age 71, he recorded 20 albums. Many of his performances went unrecorded, to the lament of his legions of fans. His were among the recordings destroyed in the 2008 Universal fire.

He toured the world, performing in Europe, South America, Asia, Australia, the Soviet Union, at the White House, for the Pope, and the President of France. Hines was married several times with his last performance a few days before he died at age 79 on April 22, 1983, in Oakland, California. Count Basie called him "The greatest piano player in the world." ◼

EDWARD MICKOLUS

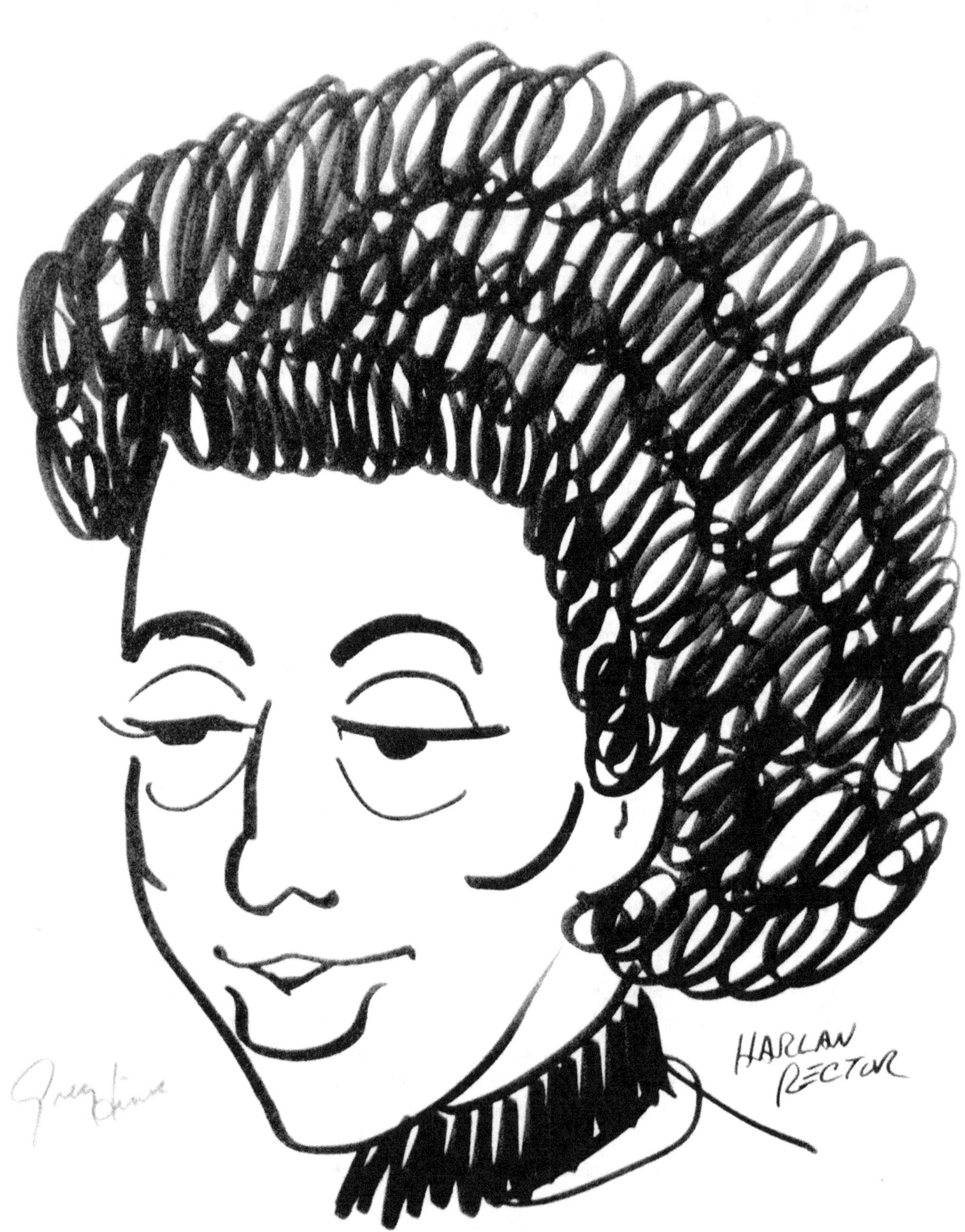

HARLAN
RECTOR

Gregory Hines

Gregory Hines began tap dancing at the tender age of two, made his Broadway debut with his older brother, Maurice, in *The Girl in Pink Tights* six years later, and at 26 years old he was interviewed by JP McCarthy on WJR. "He still had most of his entertainment future ahead of him when I sketched his caricature," Harlan Rector said, remembering that day in 1972.

Gregory Oliver Hines was born on February 14, 1946. Other notables born on Valentine's Day include Jack Benny, Jimmy Hoffa, Florence Henderson, Teller (from Penn & Teller) and Harlan Rector.

Hines was born in New York City to Alma Iola (Lawless) and Maurice Robert Hines, a dancer, musician and actor. Encouraged by his father, Gregory, and his brother Maurice, known as "The Hines Kids," made nightclub appearances at venues such as the *Cotton Club* in Miami with Cab Calloway. Later they grew up to become "The Hines Brothers" until their father joined the act as their drummer and they changed the name again to "Hines, Hines and Dad."

Hines broke out on his own and performed as the lead singer and musician in the rock band *Severance* from Venice, California in 1975 to 1976. The house band played at a music club called *Honky Hoagies Handy Hangout* otherwise known as the *4H Club* where they released their debut album with Largo Records. Now in his 30's, Hines's career took off in movies, on stage, and in television, at a speed almost as fast as his tapping feet.

Hines earned Tony Award nominations for *Eubie* in 1979, *Comin' Uptown* in 1980, *Sophisticated Ladies* in 1981, then won the Tony and Drama Desk Awards for *Jelly's Last Jam* in 1992. He created and hosted the PBS special called *Gregory Hines's Tap Dance in America* in 1989 then later co-hosted the Tony Awards in 1995 and 2002.

Despite Mel Brooks writing, producing, directing, and starring in *The History of the World, Part I*, in 1981, it was Hines's movie debut that critics noted for his comedic charm, setting him apart from such co-stars as Sid Caesar, Shecky Greene, Charlie Callas, Dom DeLuise (page 33 of this book), Madeline Kahn, Harvey Korman, Cloris Leachman, Bea Arthur, Hugh Hefner, Jackie Mason, Henny Youngman, and Orson Welles.

Hines starred in his own television series called *The Gregory Hines Show* on CBS in 1997 and had a recurring role on *Will & Grace*. Hines's 44 films and television appearances plus demanding schedules put strains on his marriage to Patricia Panell and then to Pamela Koslow—both ended in divorce. He had two children, a son, Zach, and a daughter, Daria, as well as a step daughter, Jessica Koslow.

Gregory Hines suffered from liver cancer for more than a year, but informed only his closest friends. He died on August 9, 2003, en route to the hospital from his home in Los Angeles. ■

HARLAN RECTOR

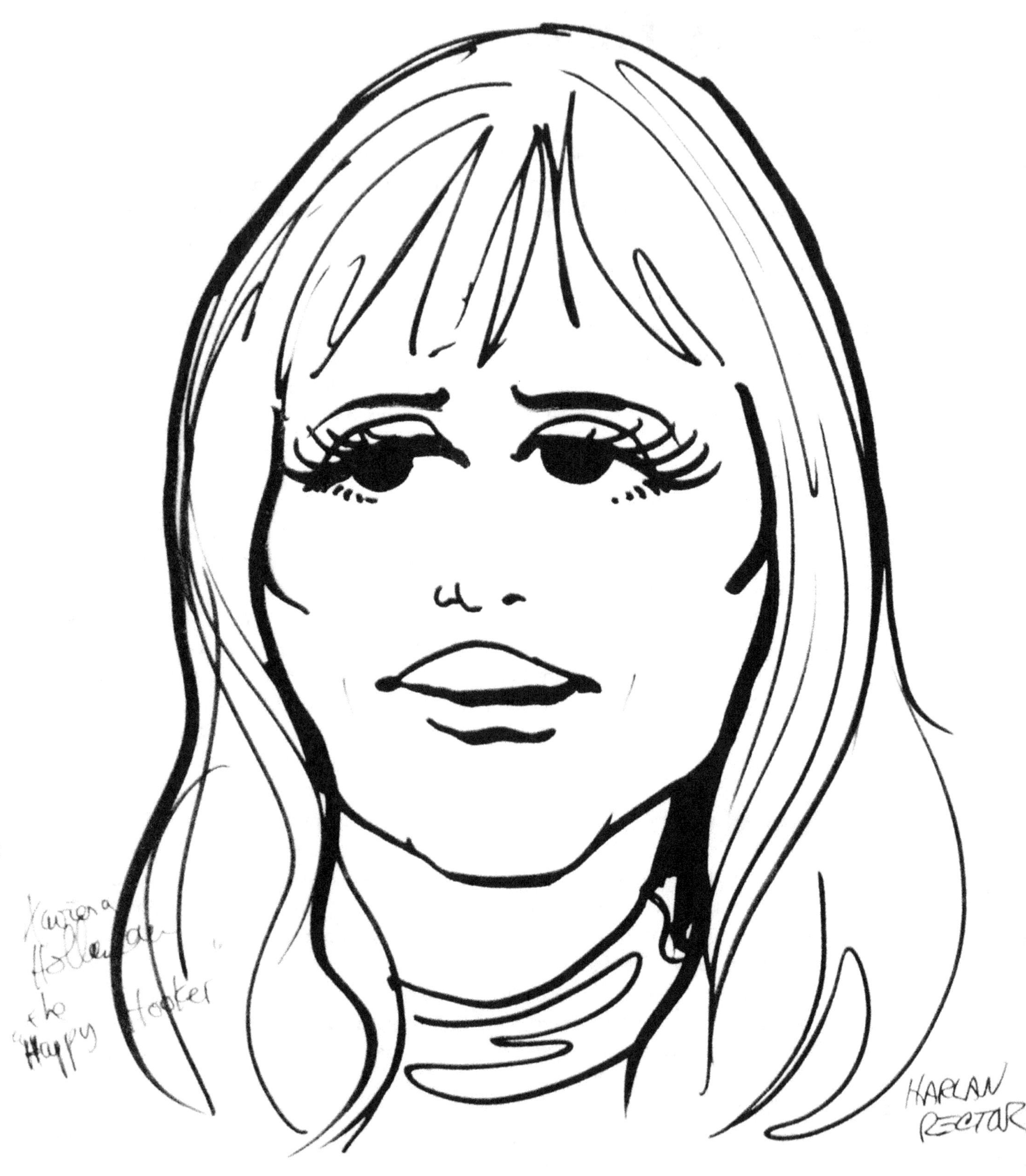

64

Xaviera Hollander

Do you remember when and how you first learned about sex? If you grew up in the late 1970s, as I did, particularly in Los Angeles, it may have come from a jubilantly lustful escort named Xaviera Hollander, better known as The Happy Hooker. Her personal stories were delightfully humorous, poignant and wild!

She was born Xaviera (Vera) de Vries in the Japanese-occupied Dutch East Indies, which later became part of present-day Indonesia. Her father was a Dutch Jewish physician, and her mother was French and German. She spent the first years of her life in a Japanese-run internment camp.

In her early 20s, she left Amsterdam for Johannesburg, South Africa where her stepsister lived. There she met and became engaged to John Weber, an American economist. When the engagement was broken off, she left South Africa for New York City.

In the era of sexual chaos in the late 1960s, when Playboy Clubs and love-ins were competing for national attention, a beautiful and intelligent young Dutch secretary named Xaviera de Vries arrived on the scene in New York City. She quickly became blasé about her desk job and resigned as secretary of the Dutch consulate in Manhattan to become a call girl. Even in the beginning, she was making $1,000 a night, today's equivalent of $7,400! She soon became the most prominent and glamorous madam the city had ever seen. A year later she opened the Vertical Whorehouse brothel and soon became New York City's leading madam. In 1971, she was arrested for prostitution by New York Police and was forced to leave the United States.

Later, in 1971, Hollander published a memoir, *The Happy Hooker: My Story.* Hollander also wrote a number of other books and produced plays in her beloved Amsterdam. In her book, *Child No More,* Xaviera tells the story of losing her mother. For 35 years she wrote an advice column for *Penthouse* magazine entitled *Call Me Madam.*

In 1975, she starred in the semi-autobiographical film *My Pleasure is My Business.* For several years in the 1970s, Hollander lived in Toronto where she married Frank Applebaum, a Canadian antique dealer who was a regular fixture in the downtown scene.

She mentions a lover named John Drummond, with whom she partnered and co-authored two books, including *Let's Get Moving* in 1988 about their amorous life together. "For years he had been the love of my life." She wrote, "He was a wild Scottish intellectual, however, sometimes he liked his whiskey, beer and wines too much and would become quite destructive towards me. He is the only one who managed to deprive me of my self-esteem or identity—temporarily."

Drummond is listed as one of Hollander's husbands despite claims she turned gay around 1997, establishing a long-term relationship with Dutch poet Dia. In 2005 she operated *Xaviera's Happy House,* a bed and breakfast within her Amsterdam home, and in January 2007, she married Philip de Haan, a Dutch man in Amsterdam. ■

JERRY RECTOR

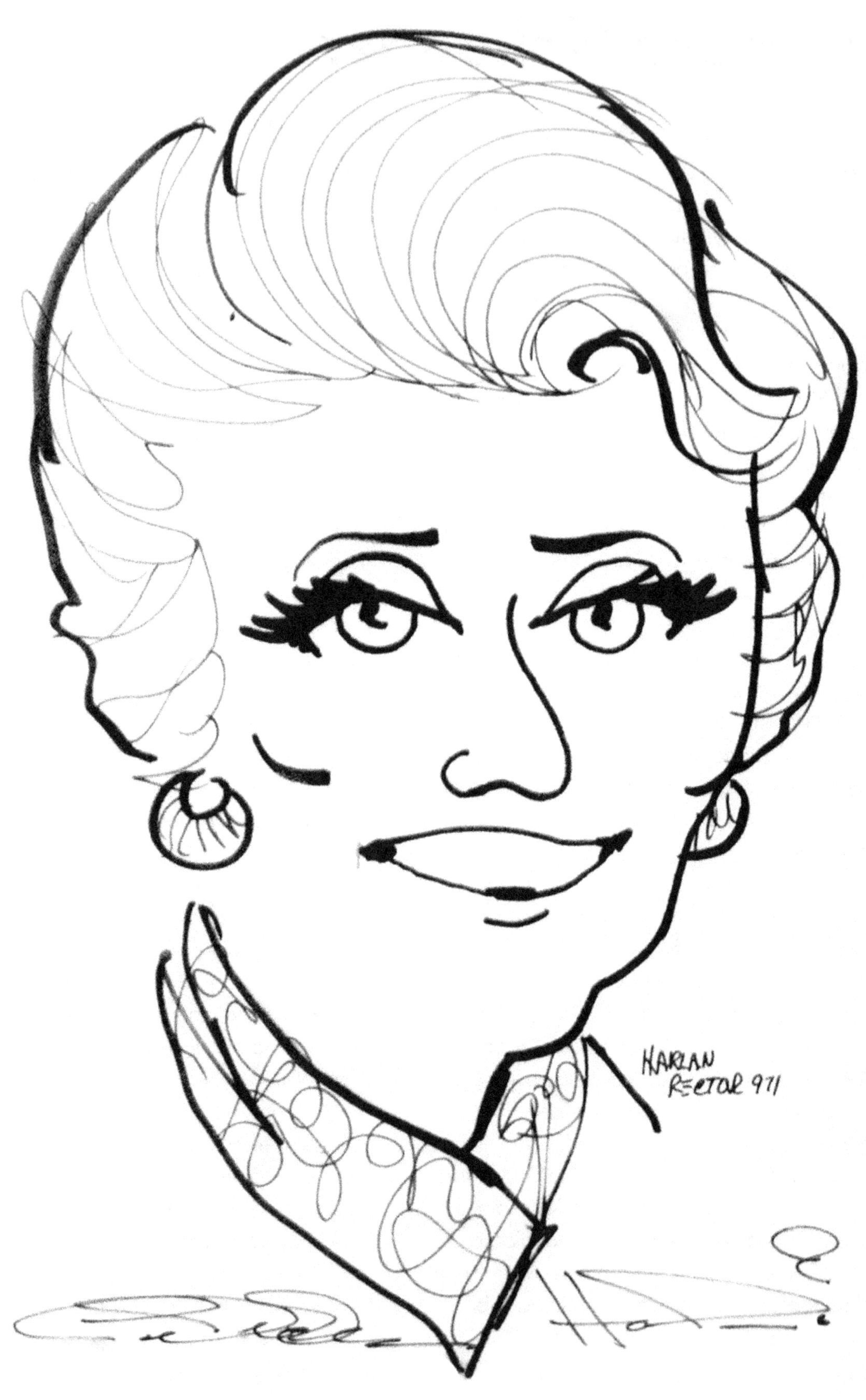

Celeste Holm

Celeste Holm was born on April 29, 1917, in *Brooklyn, New York*. Celeste's mother, Jean Parke, was an American portrait artist and author. Her father, Theodor Holm, was a Norwegian businessman. His company provided marine adjustment services for Lloyd's of London. Because of her parents' occupations, and being an only child, Celeste traveled often during her youth and attended various schools in the Netherlands, France and the United States.

She debuted at age 19 on Broadway in *The Time of Your Life*. That was just the beginning of many successful musicals like *The Women, Oklahoma*, and *Bloomer Girl*, but it was in her role as "Ado Annie" when she sang the show-stopper song *I Can't Say No* from *Oklahoma* that would be most memorable.

Then came her life as an actress. Her professional theatrical debut was in the production of *Hamlet*, co-staring Leslie Howard. This was followed by her first film, *Three Little Girls in Blue* in 1946. The following year, Celeste won the Supporting Actress Oscar and a Golden Globe award for her appearance in *Gentleman's Agreement*. In 1949 and 1950, Celeste won two more Academy Awards for *Come to the Stable* and *All About Eve*.

Celeste preferred the stage to the screen and briefly left Hollywood for the New York stage. It wasn't long before MGM had her return for the musicals—*The Tender Trap* (1955) and *High Society* (1956). Celeste also appeared in several shows on television including her own series, *Honestly, Celeste!* (1954). In 1992, she was inducted into the Theater Hall of Fame but many remember her best as playing the role of "Hattie Green" for *Promised Land* in 1996.

A lady of many talents, Celeste was appointed to the National Arts Council by President Ronald Reagan. She was also a spokeswoman for UNICEF. In 1957, King Olav V of Norway made her a Knight, First Class of the Order of St. Olav, for her help in saving the "Christian Radich" schooner, one of Norway's national treasures.

Celeste was married five times, with two husbands that died and the other three she divorced. She had two children, one was Ted Nelson, born in 1937 when Celeste was barely 20 so he was raised by his grandparents. He grew up to become the internet pioneer and sociologist known for inventing Hypertext.

At age 95, Celeste Holm was diagnosed with Alzheimer's and later died of a heart attack in New York City on July 15, 2012.

"Out of all the sketches I did, only two and a half people were displeased with their caricature. That one-half was Celeste Holm who simply added a question mark to her signature." Harlan recalled with a smile. "Her classy response was appreciated!" ∎

PATRICIA DALY-LIPE

Kindest regards to all
Sandy Novit

Gordie Howe

Gordon "Gordie" Howe was born in Saskatchewan, Canada on March 31, 1928, during the Great Depression. One of nine children in a poverty-stricken family, he was often sick because of poor nutrition. At age five, his mother bought him a pair of used hockey skates. He fell in love with the game immediately and began playing and practicing year-round.

At six feet tall by his mid-teens, Gordie felt shy and awkward around others his age. In 1943, fifteen-year-old Gordie attended the New York Rangers training camp. They offered him a contract, but he passed. A year later, Howe landed a tryout with the Detroit Red Wings. The coach and general manager of the team were impressed by the young player and signed him immediately.

After only three years in the NHL, Gordie Howe became a household name. From 1946 to 1980, he played twenty-five of his twenty-six National Hockey League seasons with the Detroit Red Wings, plus six seasons in the World Hockey Association. He could play left and right-handed, which worked well with the straight-bladed sticks of the time.

To sports fans he was "Mr. Hockey", but to opposing players, he was "Mr. Elbows", because if you went into the corner with Howe to battle for a puck, that's exactly what you got! He became known for the "Gordie Howe hat trick": a goal, an assist and a fight in the same game. Howe estimated that he had received over three hundred stitches in his face over his career. Howe was a 23-time NHL All-Star and surpassed Maurice "Rocket" Richard's scoring record in 1963.

In 1951 Howe met Colleen Joffa; two years later they were married. They had four children: Martin, Mark, Cathy, and Murray. The boys soon became involved in youth hockey, and years later, after Howe retired from the Red Wings, he went on to finish his career with the Hartford Whalers, playing side by side with two of his sons. Mr. Hockey passed away in 2016 at the age of 88. His record was surpassed decades later by Wayne, "The Great One", Gretsky.

Though I grew up in the Detroit suburbs, it wasn't until I was fourteen in 1973 that I finally got to watch the Red Wings play at the "Old Joe", (Joe Louis Arena). Unfortunately, Gordie had left the team a few years before. Still, it wasn't so bad to watch my first live NHL game with the likes of Marcel Dionne, Red Berenson, Alex Delvecchio, and Mickey Redmond, who is still a Red Wings commentator.

When the Red Wings organization got wind of my Dad's caricature of Gordie, they asked him to draw all of the players on the team. A "one-sheet" was created, and all the players signed their caricatures for the kids before one of the games. I was so proud of my Dad. I learned to play on a small lake nearby as a kid, and I am so grateful to still be playing today. I have the Red Wings' home and away uniforms, and I'm proud to honor the Wings' legacy every time I play. ■

JERRY RECTOR

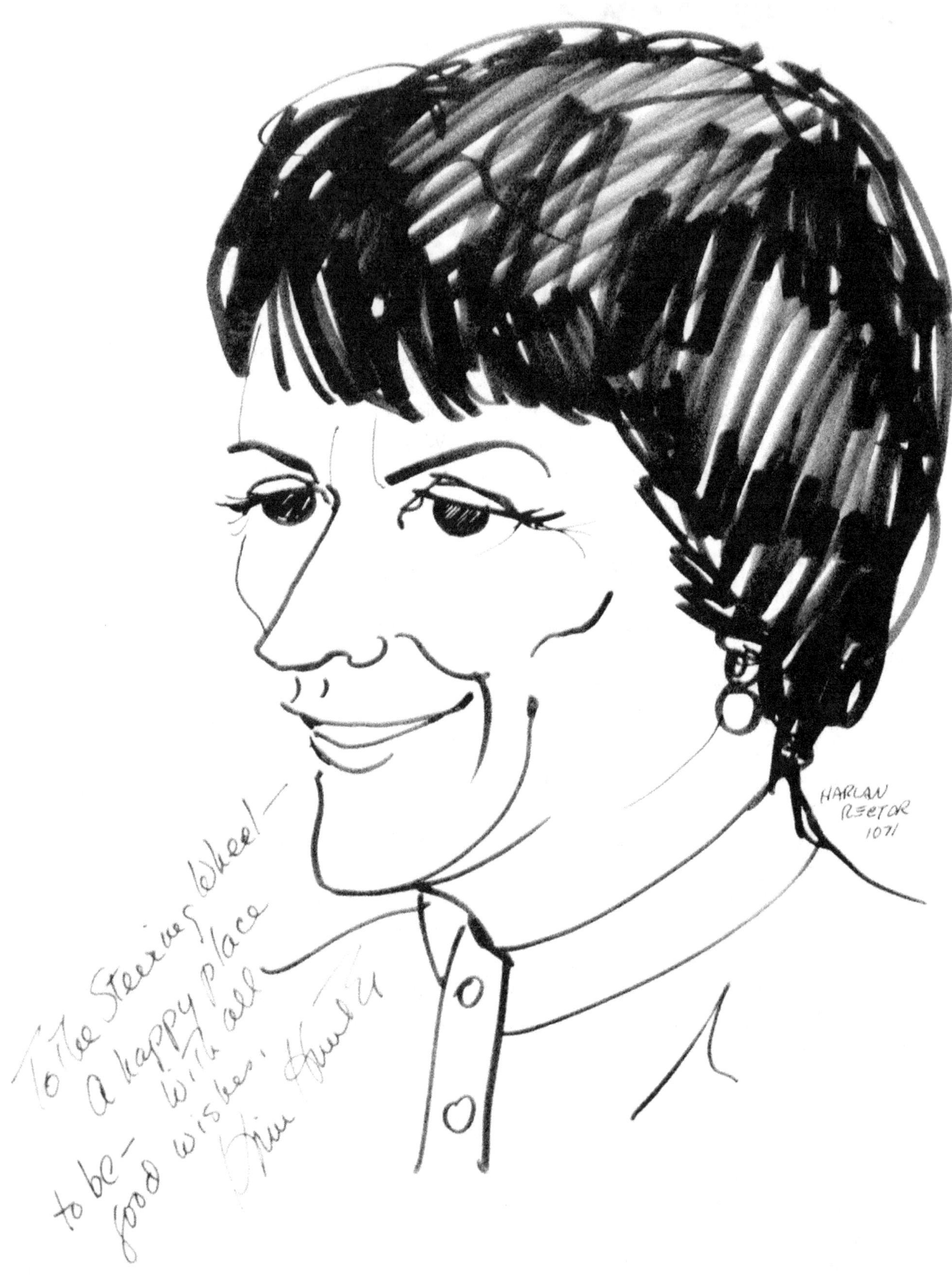

To the Steering Wheel —
a happy place
to be — with all
good wishes,
Jim Howell
HARLAN
RECTOR
1071

Kim Hunter

American film, theatre, and television actress Kim Hunter was born Janet Cole in Detroit, Michigan on November 12, 1922. The daughter of Grace Lind, a trained concert pianist, and Donald Cole, a refrigeration engineer, Kim was of English and Welsh descent and attended Miami Beach High School.

Hunter's first film role was in the 1943 film noir *The Seventh Victim*. Her first starring role was in the 1946 British fantasy film *A Matter of Life and Death*. In 1947, she was Stella Kowalski in the original Broadway production *A Streetcar Named Desire*. Hunter later recreated the role in the 1951 film version and won both the Academy and Golden Globe awards for Best Supporting Actress.

In the interim, she joined with the co-stars Marlon Brando, Karl Malden, and 47 others, to become one of the first members of the newly created, and now legendary, Actors Studio.

In 1952, Hunter became Humphrey Bogart's leading lady in *Deadline USA* but she was blacklisted from film and television amid suspicions of communism in Hollywood, during the era of the House Un-American Activities Committee (HUAC).

In 1956, with the HUAC's influence subsiding, she co-starred in Rod Serling's Peabody Award-winning teleplay on *Playhouse 90* and *Requiem for a Heavyweight*, winning multiple Emmy Awards. She appeared opposite Mickey Rooney in the 1957 live CBS-TV broadcast for *The Comedian*, written by *Twilight Zone* creator Rod Serling and directed by John Frankenheimer.

Other notable television roles she appeared included *Rawhide*, *Dr. Kildare*, *Ironside*, *Columbo*, *Cannon*, and the popular western series *Bonanza*. She also appeared in several soap operas, most notably ABC's *The Edge of Night*, for which she received a Daytime Emmy Award nomination. Hunter starred in the controversial TV movie *Born Innocent*, playing the mother of Linda Blair as well as David Niven's love interest in the film *A Matter of Life and Death*.

Hunter played Zira, the sympathetic chimpanzee scientist in the 1968 film *Planet of the Apes* (written by Rod Serling and starring Charlton Heston) and two sequels, *Beneath the Planet of the Apes* and *Escape from The Planet of the Apes*. *Planet of the Apes* remains one of the most iconic science fiction classics of all time, spawning a television series, a video game and eleven sequels. Hunter's last film role in a major motion picture was in Clint Eastwood's 1997 film, *Midnight in the Garden of Good and Evil*.

Hunter was married twice. Her first marriage in 1944 was to William Baldwin, a Marine Corps pilot. The couple had a daughter, Kathryn Deirdre. Her second marriage was in 1951 to actor Robert Emmett; they had a son, Sean Robert.

Hunter died in New York City on September 11, 2002, of a heart attack at age 79. She was survived by her children. ∎

JEFF RECTOR

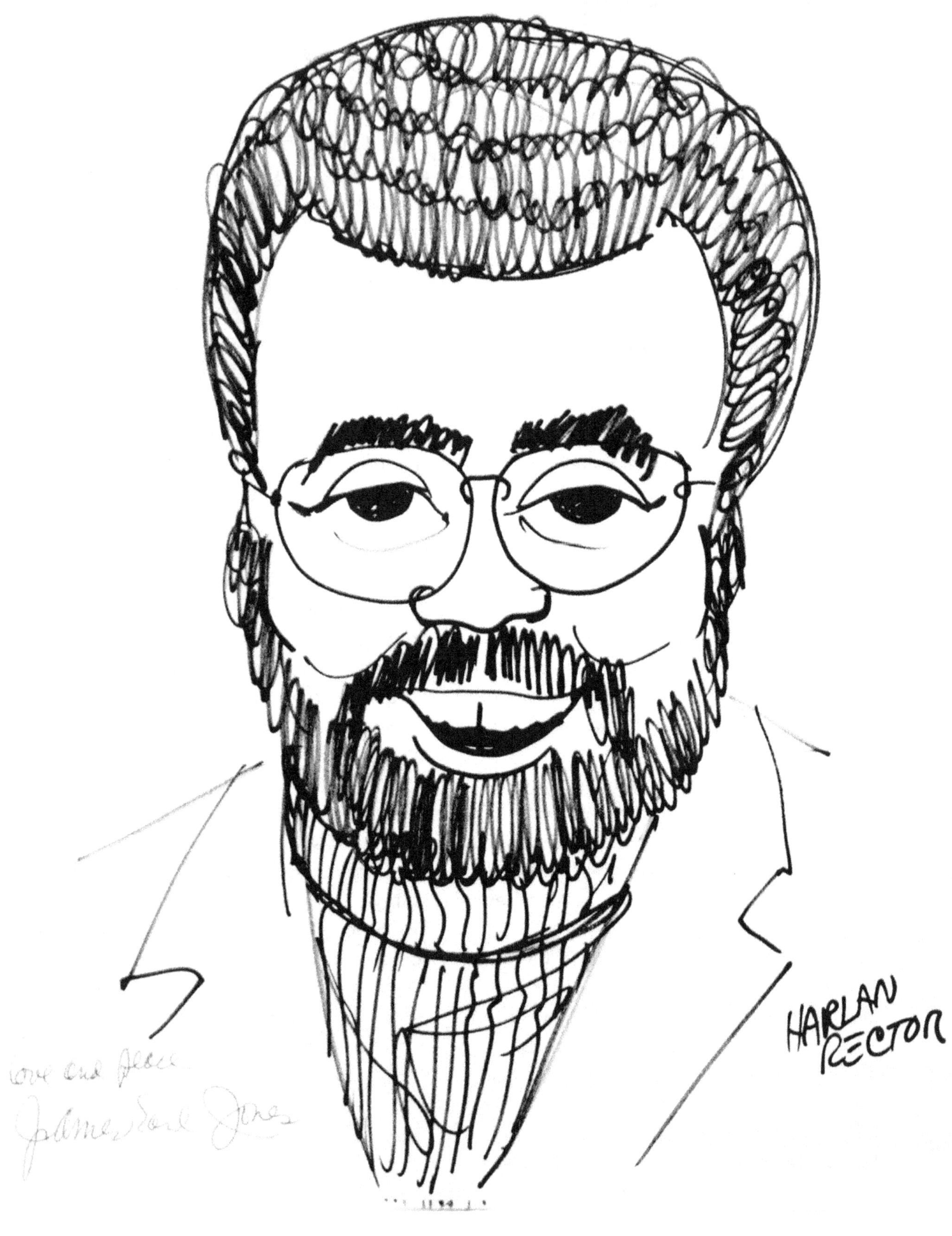

love and peace
James Earl Jones
HARLAN RECTOR

James Earl Jones

The voice that summons its sound from the deepest corner of a hollow cave was born in Arkabutla, Mississippi, on January 17, 1931. James Earl Jones was the son of Ruth (Williams) Jones, teacher and maid, and Robert Earl Jones, boxer, butler, and chauffeur. His father left shortly after James was born to pursue a career as a stage and screen actor in New York and Hollywood. That separation wasn't reconciled until the 1950s.

From age five, Jones was raised by his maternal grandparents, John and Maggie Williams, on their farm in Jackson, Michigan. The transition was so traumatic for James that he developed a stutter and refused to speak. When his family moved to rural Brethren, Michigan, a teacher helped him overcome his stutter but he remained functionally mute for eight years until he entered high school. An English teacher helped Jones end his silence.

After graduating as vice president of his class from Dickson Rural Agricultural School, Jones attended the University of Michigan. He entered as a pre-med major and joined the Reserve Officer Training Corps. Having dabbled in drama as a stage-hand, he was smitten by the allure of acting and changed his focus from pre-med to enroll at the University's School of Music, Theatre and Dance. He graduated in 1955 and was commissioned as a 2nd Lieutenant. The Korean War was ending, so Jones served his time in Ranger training in Georgia and later in a training unit in the rugged Rocky Mountains. He was promoted to 1st Lieutenant prior to his discharge.

Jones moved to New York and studied at the American Theatre Wing while working as a janitor to support himself. The name James Earl Jones appeared on marquees from Broadway to London's West End for major roles in five Shakespeare productions, many African-American adaptations of Pulitzer Prize-winning dramas including *Driving Miss Daisy* with Vanessa Redgrave and *On Golden Pond* with Leslie Uggams, who's caricature also appears in this book. Jones received two Tony Awards for *The Great White Hope* in 1969 and *Fences* in 1987.

Jones is the only actor to ever receive two Television Emmy Awards in the same year, for *Gabriel's Fire* and *Heat Wave* in 1991. Sometime between a stint on television's *Sesame Street* in 1969 and a revival of *The Iceman Cometh* on Broadway in 1973, Jones visited Detroit and I sketched his caricature when he was 40 years old.

Jones's filmography started with him playing a small part as a bombardier in *Dr. Strangelove*. His basso-profundo voice as Darth Vader has given him star status in the voiceover business, of which I am familiar as well. In 1995, as a voiceover announcer in New York, I was pitted against Jones to become the signature voice of A & E's new History Channel. A & E awarded the job to me and with a huge case of bloated ego, I went straight to my agent to tell them the good news. Their reaction, "That's great, but, before you think that you've reached star status, Jones's agent probably wanted too much money." Thud. ∎

HARLAN RECTOR

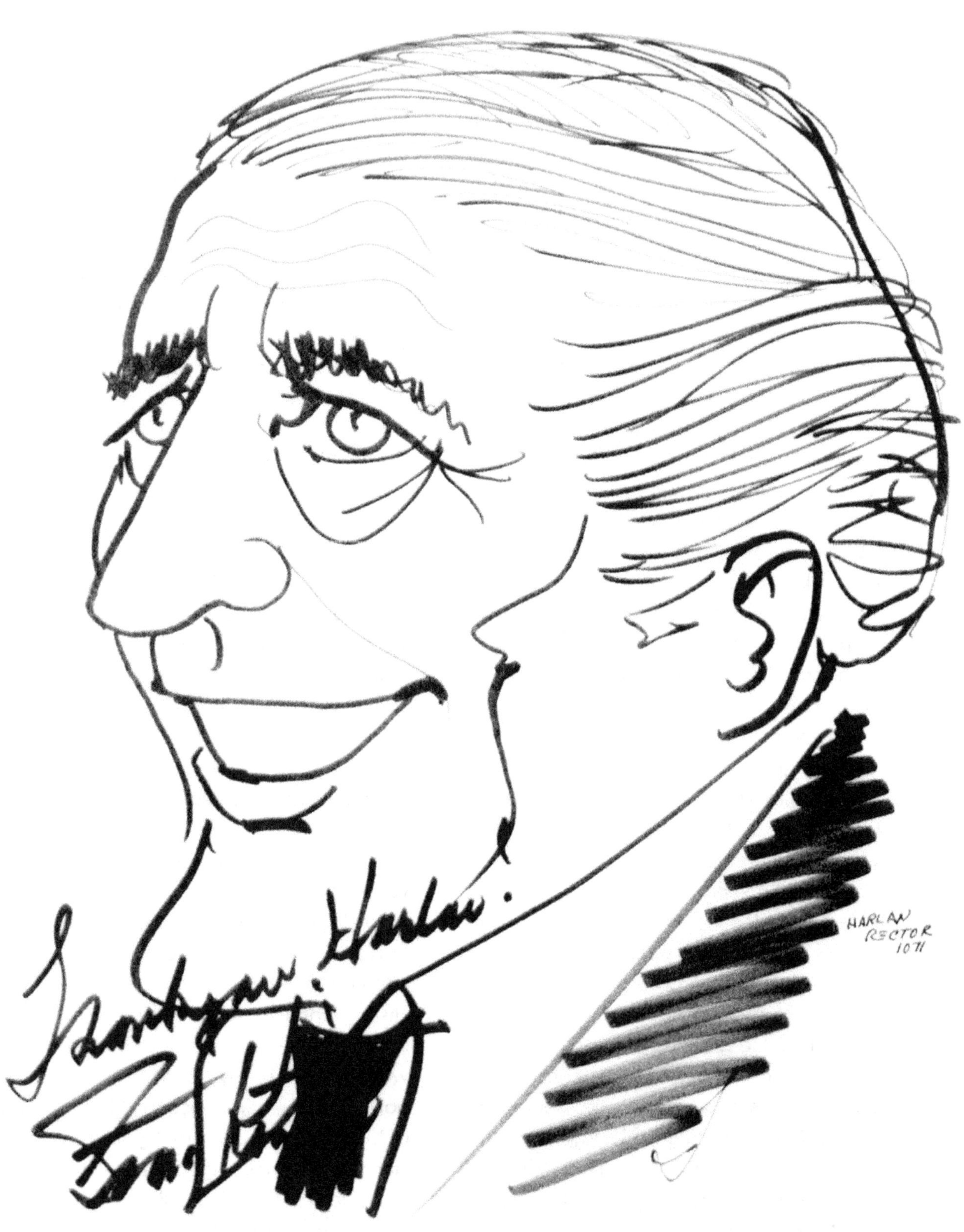

HARLAN
RECTOR
10 11

Stan Kenton

Stan Kenton was a highly accomplished bandleader, musician, composer, and arranger. In 1970-1971, Kenton traveled the country, visiting radio stations to promote his records. During that time, he was interviewed at WJR in Detroit.

Throughout his life, Kenton believed his birthdate was February 19, 1912. He was born out of wedlock, which at the time was considered controversial and immoral, putting his parents in a difficult position. His incorrect date of birth is carved onto his tombstone. A birth certificate from Wichita, Kansas, was discovered posthumously, citing his actual birthdate as December 15, 1911.

In 1924, his family moved from Wichita to Bell, California, located in the greater Los Angeles area. He attended Bell High School, where he was nicknamed "Old Man Jazz."

By age 16, he was playing the piano at a local hamburger stand for 50 cents per night.

By the 1930s, Kenton was playing in Gus Arnheim's orchestra, which was arranged in the style of Benny Goodman's band. He continued studying piano and composition with private instructors to help refine his natural musical ability.

Stan Kenton formed his first orchestra in 1940, which included bassist Howard Rumsey and trumpeter Chico Alvarez. In 1943, he signed a contract with newly formed Capitol Records and produced the popular record *Eager Beaver.*

The Stan Kenton Orchestra developed into one of the most recognized musical ensembles on the entire West Coast. They played at the best theaters and produced a string of successful recordings including *Artistry in Rhythm*, *Machito*, and *Interlude.*

Looking to expand his musical horizons, Stan ventured into a relatively new art form, progressive jazz. His music introduced Cuban rhythms into complex jazz compositions. Stan worked to enhance his existing orchestra by recruiting some of the finest jazz players in the country. They tirelessly toured the nation, playing at Carnegie Hall, Boston's Symphony Hall, The Hollywood Bowl, and dozens of similar venues from coast to coast. They became the first jazz orchestra to gross $1,000,000 in a year.

In the mid-1950s, Kenton changed his musical direction by composing bebop and standard dance recordings, including *Contemporary Concepts* and *Kenton in Hi-Fi*, a greatest hits record combining his past and current sounds.

In the early 1960s, Stan tried his hand at developing a more "pop" sound. He wrote some Country/Western songs, including the 1962 hit *Mama Sang a Song*. He also teamed up with Tex Ritter and released the album *Stan Kenton! Tex Ritter!*

Stan Kenton was instrumental in moving big band orchestras from the dance hall to the concert hall. Among jazz legends, the four longest running touring bands were helmed by Stan Kenton, Woody Herman, Count Basie, and Duke Ellington.

Kenton was married three times, fathering two children from his first two marriages.

After suffering a stroke, Stan Kenton died on August 25, 1979. ■

GREG BARRY

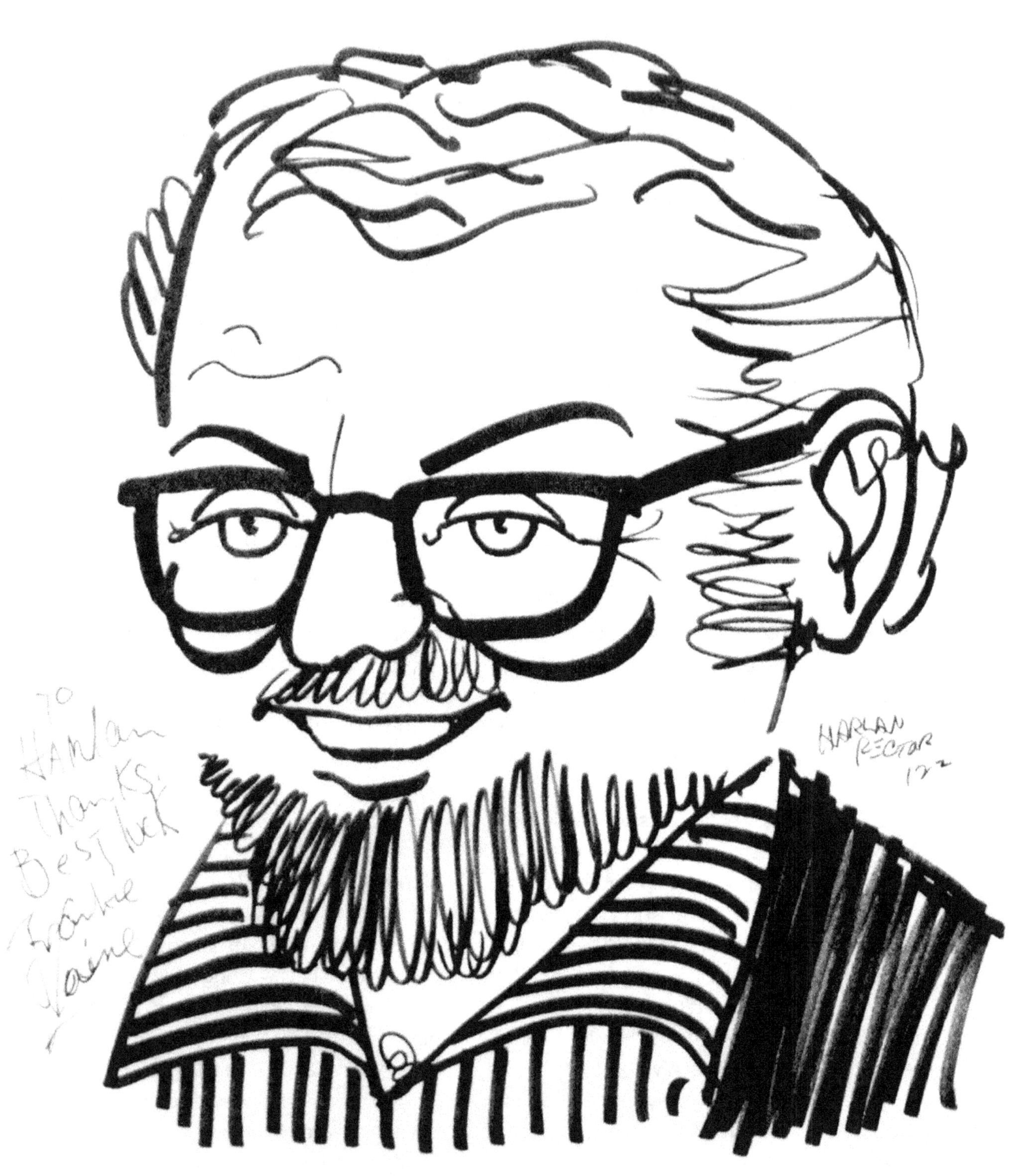
To
Harlan
Thanks!
Best luck
Frankie
Paine
HARLAN
RECTOR
'22

Frankie Laine

Frankie Laine was known to almost everyone in the seventies after recording more than 60 Top Forty hits during the previous four decades.

Francesco Paolo LoVecchio was born in Chicago on March 30, 1913. He got his first taste of performing as a member of his elementary school's choir. He joined a dance company shortly after graduating high school. Billed as Frank LoVecchio, he would sing for the spectators when the dancers took breaks.

Francesco chose his professional name, Frankie Laine, in 1938 upon getting a job singing for New York City radio station WINS.

Frankie moved to California in 1943 and became a house singer at a Los Angeles club soon after. When he began performing an old song that few people remembered, called *That's My Desire*, Laine quickly became the star attraction at the club. He was soon recording for Mercury Records, and *Desire* was one of the songs cut in his first recording session. It quickly became a Top 10 hit and listeners initially thought Laine was black.

Desire became Laine's first Gold Record and established him as a force in the music world. A series of hit singles quickly followed but he really reached the big time in 1948 after teaming up with Mercury Records A&R man, Mitch Miller.

Their first collaboration, *That Lucky Old Sun*, became the number one song in the country three weeks after its release in 1949. *Sun* was a folk spiritual that became both an affirmation of faith and a working man's yearning to bring his earthly sufferings to an end.

Laine and Miller released their second collaboration, *Mule Train*, a few weeks later. *Mule* knocked *Sun* into second place, making Frankie the first artist to hold the Number One and Two positions simultaneously. *Cry of the Wild Goose* in 1950 would be his last number-one hit on the American charts.

Frankie signed with Capitol Records in 1963, but his two years there produced only one album and a few singles of an inspirational nature. However, he performed regularly during that time, including a South African tour. On television, he hosted *The Frankie Laine Hour* in 1950, *The Frankie Laine Show* in 1954, and *Frankie Laine Time* in 1955.

Frankie played a significant role in the civil rights movement in the mid-twentieth century. When *Nat King Cole's* television show was unable to get a sponsor, Frankie became the first white artist to appear as a guest. During that time period, Laine joined several African American artists in performing a free concert for Martin Luther King's supporters.

Frankie donated his time and talent to many charities and homeless shelters. He was an emeritus member of the Mercy Hospital Foundation board of directors. He died of heart failure in San Diego on February 6, 2007. He was inducted into the Hit Parade Hall of Fame a year later. Two stars on the Hollywood Walk of Fame are dedicated to him. ∎

RICHARD WILLITS

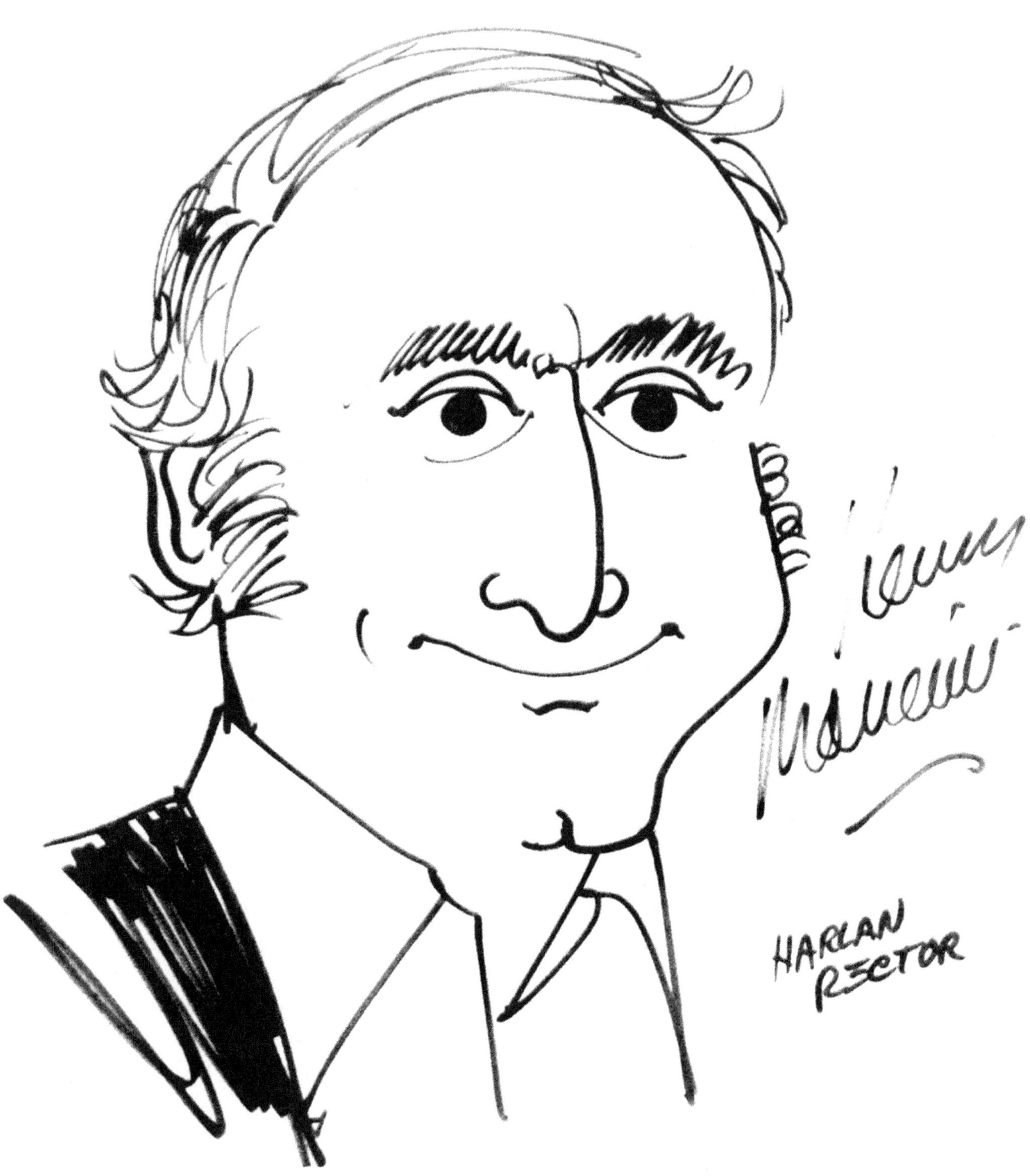
HARLAN RECTOR

Henry Mancini

Henry Nicola Mancini was born on April 16, 1924 and was named Enrico Nicola Mancini. His parents emigrated from Italy to the United States when they were young. Henry's father brought music into the home. He worked long days in the steel industry but was a natural talent as an amateur musician.

Although music was in his blood, Henry's father hoped that his son would become a teacher. That was not in the cards, because when Henry attended the cinema to watch *The Crusaders* in 1935, he was entranced by the score created by Rudolph Kopp—he had found his focus.

His path to stardom had some zigzags. Upon completing high school in 1942, he attended the Carnegie Institute of Technology for one year then enrolled at the Juilliard School of Music in New York but by 1943 things weren't working out so well, the United States were heavily involved in conflicts abroad.

Henry enlisted and connected with Glenn Miller while in boot camp. Mancini joined the 28th Air Force Band, which actually saved his life because the unit to which he was originally assigned was wiped out to a man in the Battle of the Bulge. Later, he was assigned to the 1306th Engineering Brigade, who were involved in the liberation of the *Mauthausen-Gusen concentration camp* in Austria.

The year 1946 brought Mancini into the spotlight as the pianist for the world-renowned Glenn Miller Orchestra. Although he was a skilled musician, Henry's interests were less as a performer and more as a composer so in 1952 he switched gears and joined Universal Pictures Music department where he settled for the next six years. He was involved in musical scores for more than 100 films, including *The Creature from the Black Lagoon, Tarantula, Touched by Evil* (Orson Welles), and he received an Academy Award Nomination for his work for the *Glenn Miller Story.*

In 1958, Mancini went on to do independent work as a composer for film and television. As a prolific recording artist his many albums, mostly for RCA, sold in the millions and included *"Music from Peter Gunn", "Music from Mr.Lucky"* and *"The Mancini Touch".*

In recognition of his work, he earned over a half dozen Grammys, Golden Globes, and Academy Awards for the musical scores of films such as *Breakfast at Tiffany's, The Pink Panther, Days of Wine and Roses,* and *Victor/Victoria.*

When asked "What's your favorite piece of all of them you've written?", Mancini said, "I'd have to say my favorite out of all the pieces of music I've ever written is "The Pink Panther". When asked why, Mancini replied, "Because I own half of it!"

Henry Mancini died of pancreatic cancer in 1994. His legacy continues not only through his recordings, but in the Henry Mancini Institute for young musical talent, which was created in 1996 in his honor, as well as the Henry Mancini Arts Academy, which opened its doors in 2005. ◼

JOHNNY DALY

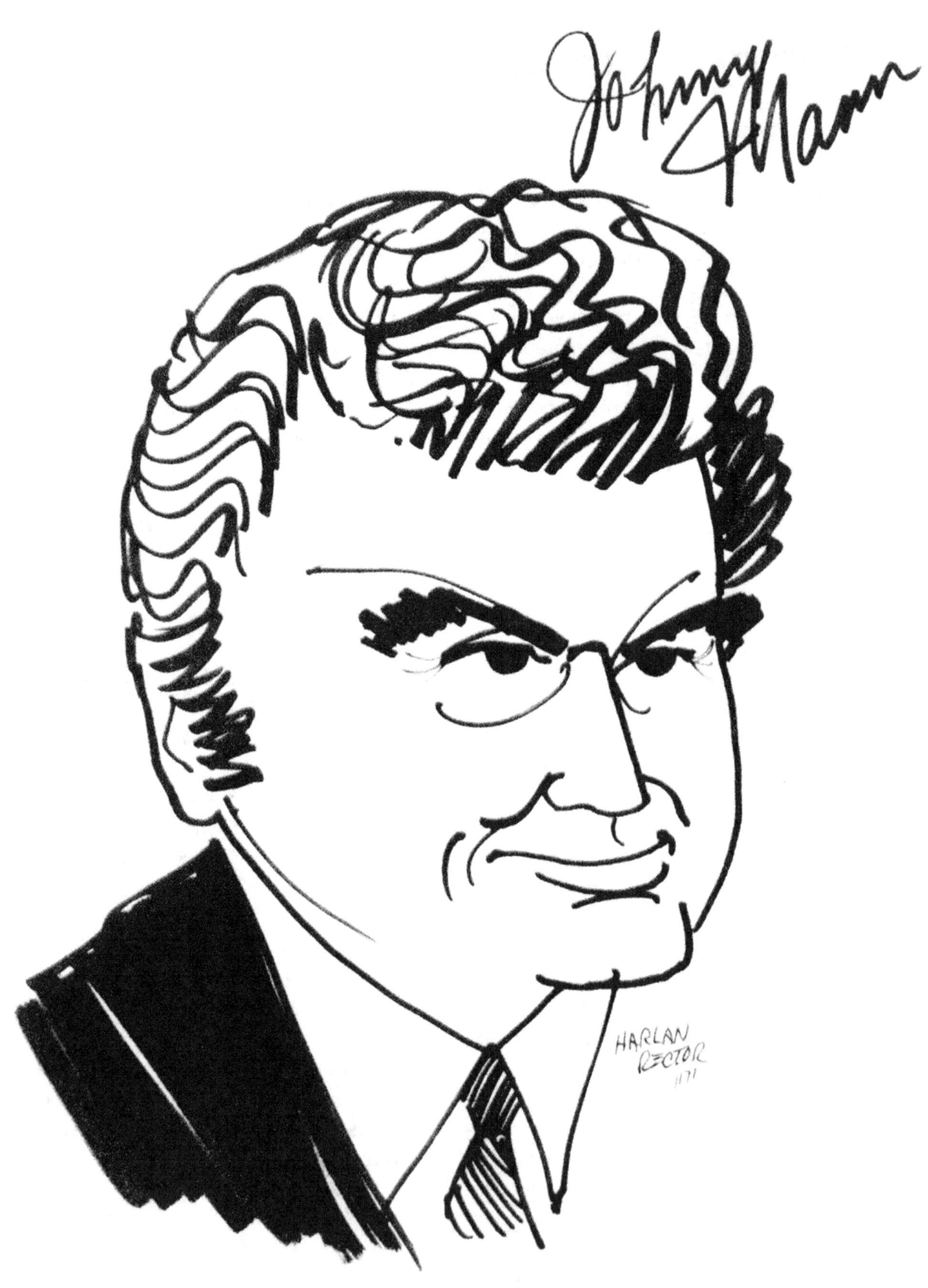

HARLAN
RECTOR
1971

Johnny Mann

John Russell Mann was an American arranger, composer, conductor, and recording artist. Along with Norman Luboff and Ray Conniff, he was one of the premier chorus directors of the "golden age of mood music."

Born on August 30, 1928, in Baltimore, Mann got his start in Hollywood by penning musical scores for major motion pictures before becoming the choral director of the *NBC Comedy Hour*.

He eventually formed the Johnny Mann Singers and signed with Liberty records. During the 1960s, that group released several albums, including *Invisible Tears, Up-Up and Away*, and *We Wish You a Merry Christmas*. The Johnny Mann Singers were also involved in several classic rock 'n' roll and rockabilly recording sessions with Johnny Burnette, The Crickets, and Liberty recording artist Eddie Cochran.

The group's instrumental *Cinnamint Shuffle* (*Mexican Shuffle*) hit the US Pop chart in 1966 and can still be found on YouTube today. Their next single was a cover version of *Up, Up and Away*, which became a hit on the UK Singles chart, overtaking the US hit version by The 5th Dimension. It also won a Grammy Award in 1968 for "Best Performance by a Choir of Seven or More Persons."

The group had numerous best-selling albums on Liberty Records from 1958-1969, including *Ballads of the King: The Songs of Sinatra, Golden Folk Song Hits*, and *Great Band with Great Voices*.

He and his singers also recorded radio jingles for many different radio stations, most notably KHJ and KRTH-FM in Los Angeles, all RKO Top 40 radio stations, and many oldies stations in the US.

In addition to his work with the Johnny Mann Singers, he served as musical director for the original *Alvin & the Chipmunks* TV series, even supplying the voice of the character Theodore. From 1971-1974, Mann also hosted the TV series *Stand Up and Cheer* and was the musical director for the 1967-69 ABC-TV late-night *Joey Bishop Show*.

During his career, Johnny worked with all the greats, including George Gobel, Johnny Mathis, Nat "King" Cole, Dean Martin, Frank Sinatra, Julie London, and Steve Allen, in addition to serving as Danny Kaye's conductor on an extended tour.

Strongly patriotic, Johnny received a host of awards from Veterans groups and performed at the White House twice. The Johnny Mann Singers performed a patriotic musical presentation at the 1972 Emmy Awards telecast that was hosted by Johnny Carson. Mann also hosted celebrity golf tournaments in his adopted hometown of Palm Springs and often served as a speaker for local charity fundraisers.

Mann was nominated for five Grammys, winning two. In 1998, a Golden Palm Star on the Palm Springs Walk of Stars was dedicated to him. In April 2014, he was a guest conductor at Anderson University's spring gala and he led the university choir in performing the Johnny Mann Singers arrangement of *Up, Up and Away*.

Johnny died on June 18, 2014, of heart failure at age 85 at his home in Anderson, South Carolina. ∎

RICHARD WILLITS

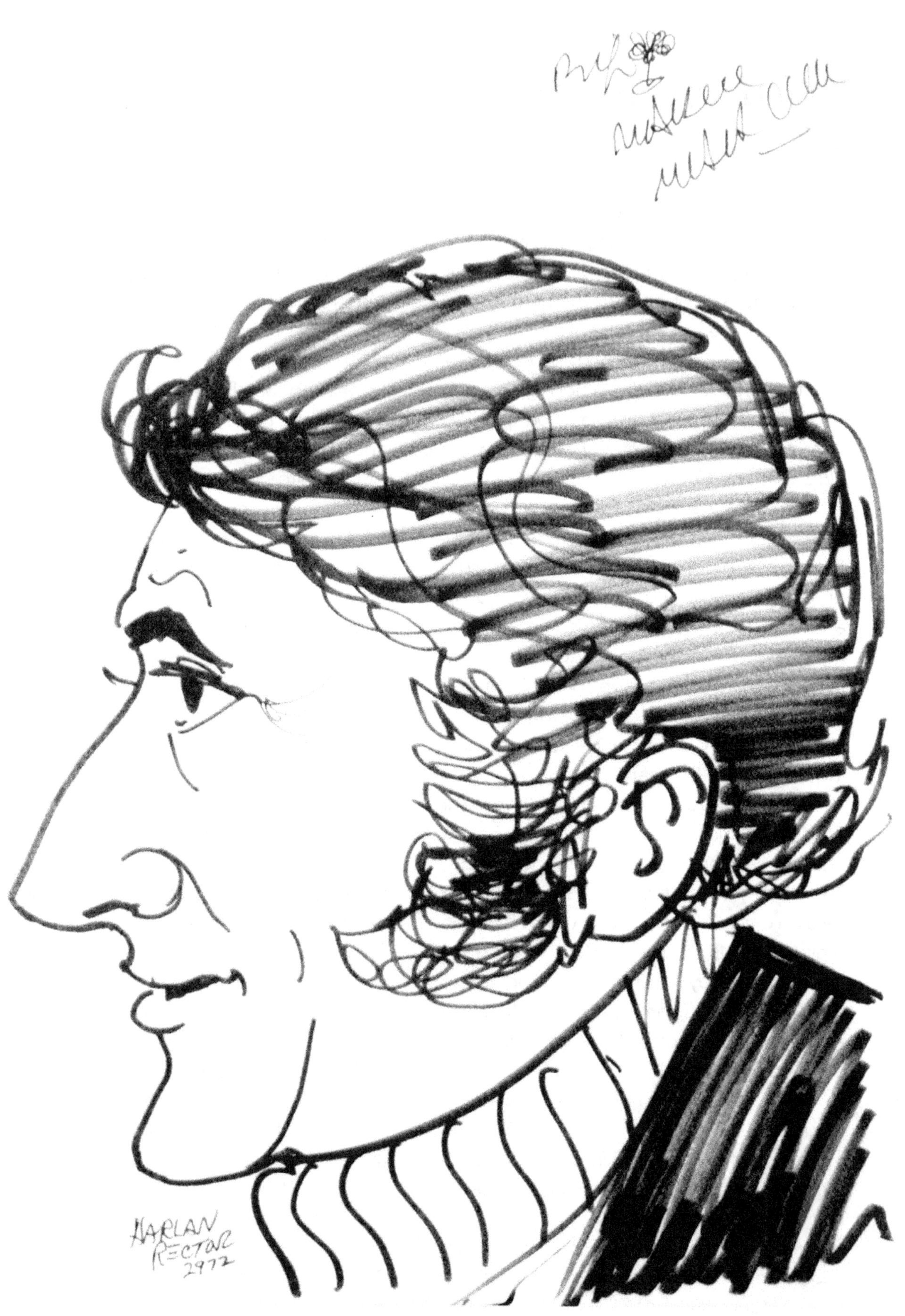

Marcel Marceau

How many of us have had a chance to hear the world's most famous mime speak? WJR listeners did when Marcel Marceau sat down for his interview. Despite his public silent persona, he was talkative off-stage, giving numerous interviews with Studs Terkel, NPR's Scott Simon, and several French and German interlocutors.

He also talked a lot at his pantomime school in Paris when training numerous performers, including original *Saturday Night Live* cast member Laraine Newman. Longtime friend Michael Jackson even credited him with the moonwalk dance steps.

Marcel Mangel was born in Strasbourg, France, to a Jewish family on March 22, 1923. At the start of World War II, the Gestapo deported his Polish father to Auschwitz, where he was killed.

Marcel took the name of Marceau in honor of a general in the French Revolution. As part of the French underground, he used mime to keep Jewish children quiet while helping them escape to Switzerland. He also worked with the French Resistance against the Nazi occupation and was a trilingual liaison officer between DeGaulle's forces and General Patton's Third Army.

In 1944, Marceau gave his first major performance to 3,000 troops celebrating the liberation of Paris. His exploits earned him the Grand Officier de la Legion d'Honneur and National Order of Merit.

He went on to study dramatic art and mime in Paris, inspired by the work of Charlie Chaplin, Buster Keaton, and the Marx Brothers.

He performed "the art of silence" professionally in "mimodramas" for more than 60 years. He created his iconic character, Bip the Clown, in 1947. Bip sported a white face and was clad in a striped pullover, red flower, and a battered silk opera hat.

He performed his most famous routines such as *The Cage, Walking Against the Wind, The Mask Maker, In the Park* and *Youth, Maturity, Old Age and Death* on five continents to standing room only crowds. He also performed in numerous stage plays and movies such as *Barbarella, First Class* (in which he played 17 roles), and Mel Brooks's *Silent Movie* (where he famously said the film's only word, "Non!").

He wrote two children's books, an art book, and a memoir. He won an Emmy for his television work and earned honorary doctorates from Ohio State, Linfield College, Princeton, and the University of Michigan.

He married three times, had two sons and two daughters.

He died in a retirement home in Cahors, France, on September 22, 2007, at the age of 84, and is buried in Paris. ■

EDWARD MICKOLUS

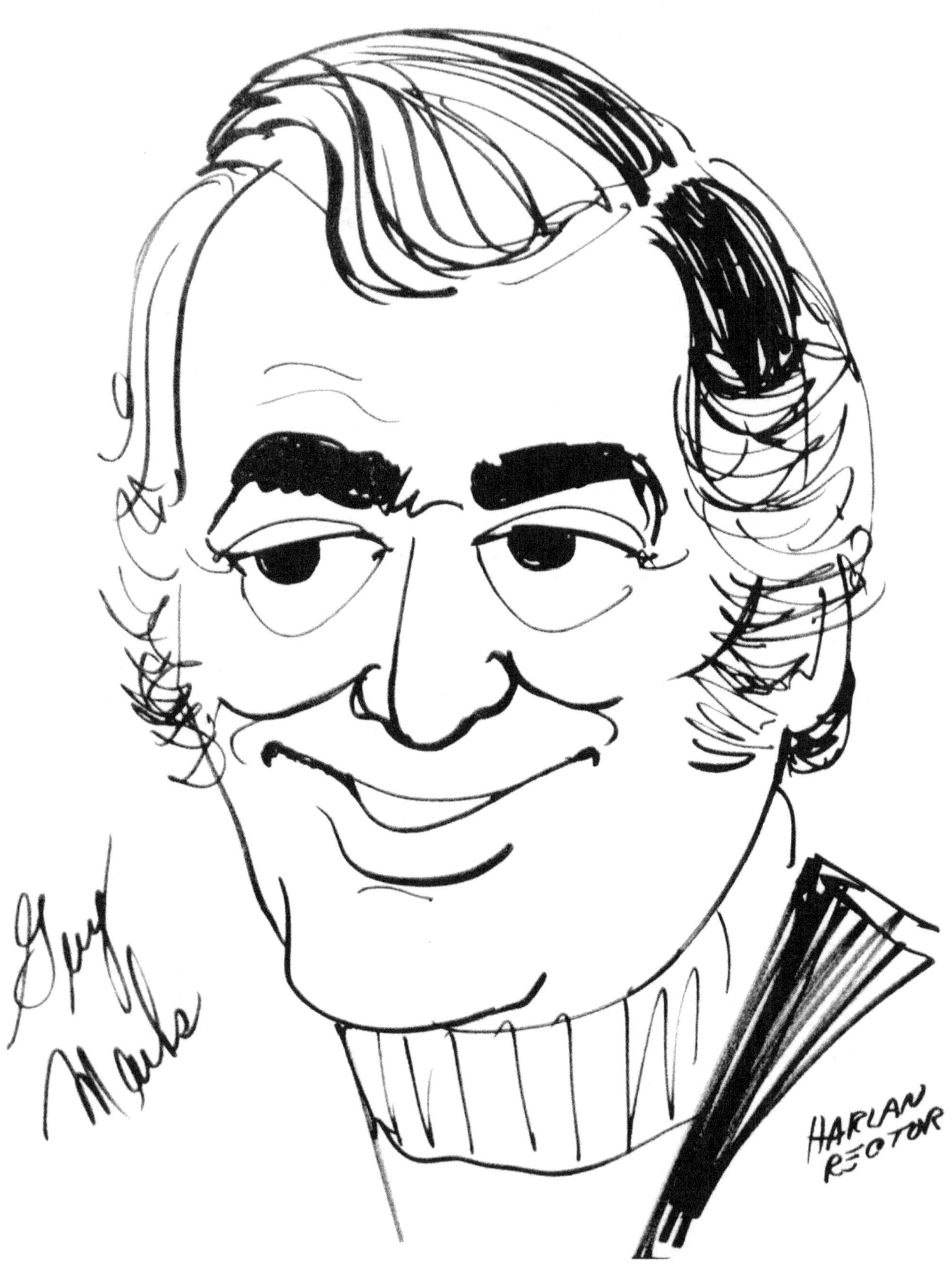
HARLAN
RECTOR

Guy Marks

Guy Marks was a familiar face and voice when he arrived for his WJR interview. He was a popular impressionist, known for mimicking Humphrey Bogart, Gary Cooper, Boris Karloff, Tony Bennett, and even Margaret Truman. You could find Guy on TV sitcoms and variety shows, regularly appearing on *The Ed Sullivan Show*, *The Merv Griffin Show*, *The Dean Martin Show*, *The Mike Douglas Show*, and *The Joey Bishop Show*.

Mario Scarpa was the last of 11 children, born on October 31, 1923, in South Philadelphia. His parents, Ermelindo and Adelina, emigrated to America from Italy. His father, a clarinetist with the RCA recording orchestra, named all of his children after opera characters. Mario was named after the hero in *La Tosca*, a favorite opera his mother watched while she was pregnant with him. The family included Victoria, Yolanda, Gioconda, Mafalda, Alba, Melba, Thenistocles (Domisticles) and Aristides. All sang opera for their suppers; the family took requests from their neighbors.

Following only three years of high school, running away from home several times, he eventually served in the Army for two years. After December 12, 1940, he switched to a six-year stint, sailing around the world with the Merchant Marines.

Upon his return, he tried a series of odd jobs until he stumbled into show business. Friends pushed him to try the stage in South Philadelphia where he did impressions of Wendell Willkie, W.C. Fields, and the Ink Spots. He moved to New York City and rented a room with five others included Eddie Fisher and Al Martino. By the end of the 1950s, the three of them all won on *Arthur Godfrey's Talent Scouts*.

Marks expanded his impressions to others sounds including a housefly on a slippery oil cloth, neon signs, alligators, driftwood furniture, rubber bands, frozen chickens, frogs, a flamingo, a praying mantis, and an ostrich.

He appeared on dozens of popular variety shows, was cast as a regular in the 1962-1963 season of the *Joey Bishop Show*, portraying Freddy, Bishop's manager and eventually America's favorite second banana. He was often cast as the funny sidekick, acting on the *Dick Van Dyke Show, Hollywood Palace, My Living Doll, My Favorite Martian, Western Rango, American Bandstand, The Odd Couple, The Ghost and Mrs. Muir, Police Woman*, and *Here's Lucy*. He frequently headlined nationwide in night clubs, including Las Vegas and Atlantic City. His lone movie was the long-forgotten *Train Ride to Hollywood*.

His notoriety wasn't limited to acting and impressions. As a singer, he became internationally famous for the novelty hit *Loving You Has Made Me Bananas*. In 1968 the song made it to #19 on the Hot Adult Contemporary, #51 on the Hot 100 charts, and in 1978, the re-released hit #25 on the UK singles chart. He released two albums, including *Hollywood Sings* as impersonated by Guy Marks.

Thrice-married, Marks died on November 28, 1987, in Pomona, New Jersey at age 64. ■

EDWARD MICKOLUS

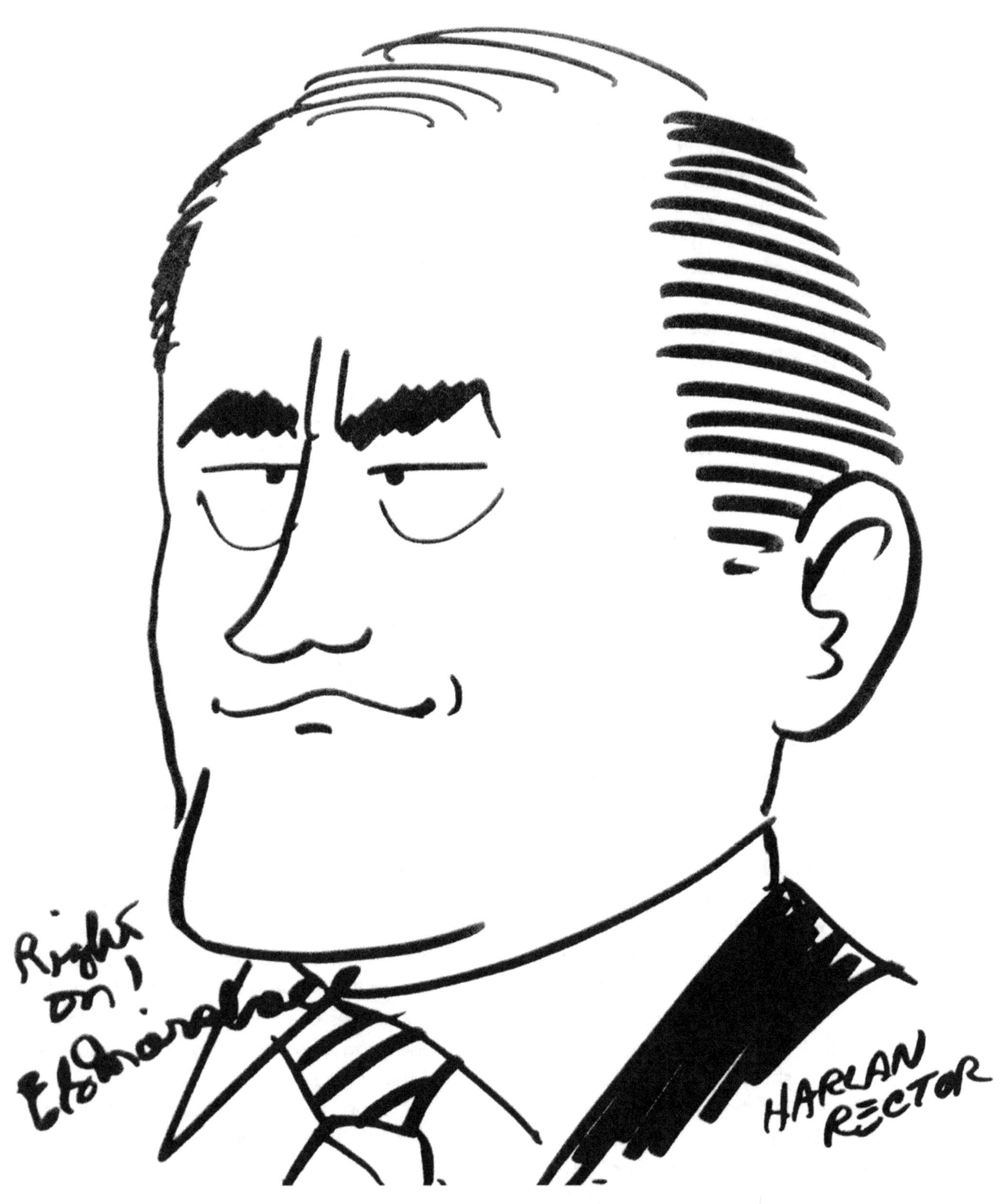

Right on!
Ed Shanahan
HARLAN RECTOR

E.G. Marshall

Everett Eugene Grunz was born in Owatonna, Minnesota on June 18, 1914, the son of Hazel Irene and Charles Grunz. No one was sure when he changed his name to E.G. Marshall, but obviously, "Everett Grunz" no doubt accounts for the E.G. One can only speculate on how he took the name Marshall. During his life he chose not to reveal what E.G. stood for, telling most people it was for "Everybody's Guess."

E.G. was married three times with five children in all. His third wife, Judith, combined a long E with the G to create the "Eeej" sound.

E.G.'s filmography of 57 movies spans 52 years from 1945 to 1997. He also had distinguished careers in theater, television and a host of nightly radio drama series with *The CBS Radio Mystery Theater*. His various bios established him as one of the greatest actors of stage, screen, and television.

Here's my ad agency experience with him:

In 1973, we chose E.G. to be the spokesman for Rockwell International's corporate television commercials. Working with him, as the creative team, was pure pleasure. His on-camera performance was outstanding and confident, which complemented Rockwell's corporate personality. Off-camera, we welcomed his easy, modest personality and witty humor to our team.

I drew his caricature on location during a break in filming at one of Rockwell's aerospace facilities. We produced five commercials, highlighting five different areas of Rockwell's corporate interests. One of the five was shot in Kitty Hawk, North Carolina.

My creative partner, Joe Paonessa, brilliantly wrote the commercial later chosen as one of the best 100 commercials produced that year—one out of thousands from ad agencies entries all over the US. As art director, part of my job was color coordinating the "look" of each commercial. I was given a Saks Fifth Avenue credit card and sent to New York to take E.G. wardrobe shopping. We had fun buying five different suits, shirts, ties, shoes and socks—everything except underwear.

Once, when I was at the New York Boat Show with our client Hatteras Yacht, I phoned E.G. just to say, "Hi." He said he was doing a Henrik Ibsen play in Connecticut. Thinking he said, "Henry Gibson," I invited the ad director of Hatteras on a drive up to the Long Wharf Theater in New Haven to see E.G. in the play written by that comedian on *Laugh In*. I had no idea who Henrik Ibsen was. My idea of "theater" was seeing *Hair* on Broadway. Ibsen, a Norwegian playwright, writes heavy, dark dramas. I managed to stay awake, and, graciously, E.G. met us afterward in his dressing room, where we were entertained by this humble actor. It was the last time I saw "Eeej."

E.G. Marshall died of lung cancer at his home in Bedford, New York on August 24, 1998, at age 84. ∎

HARLAN RECTOR

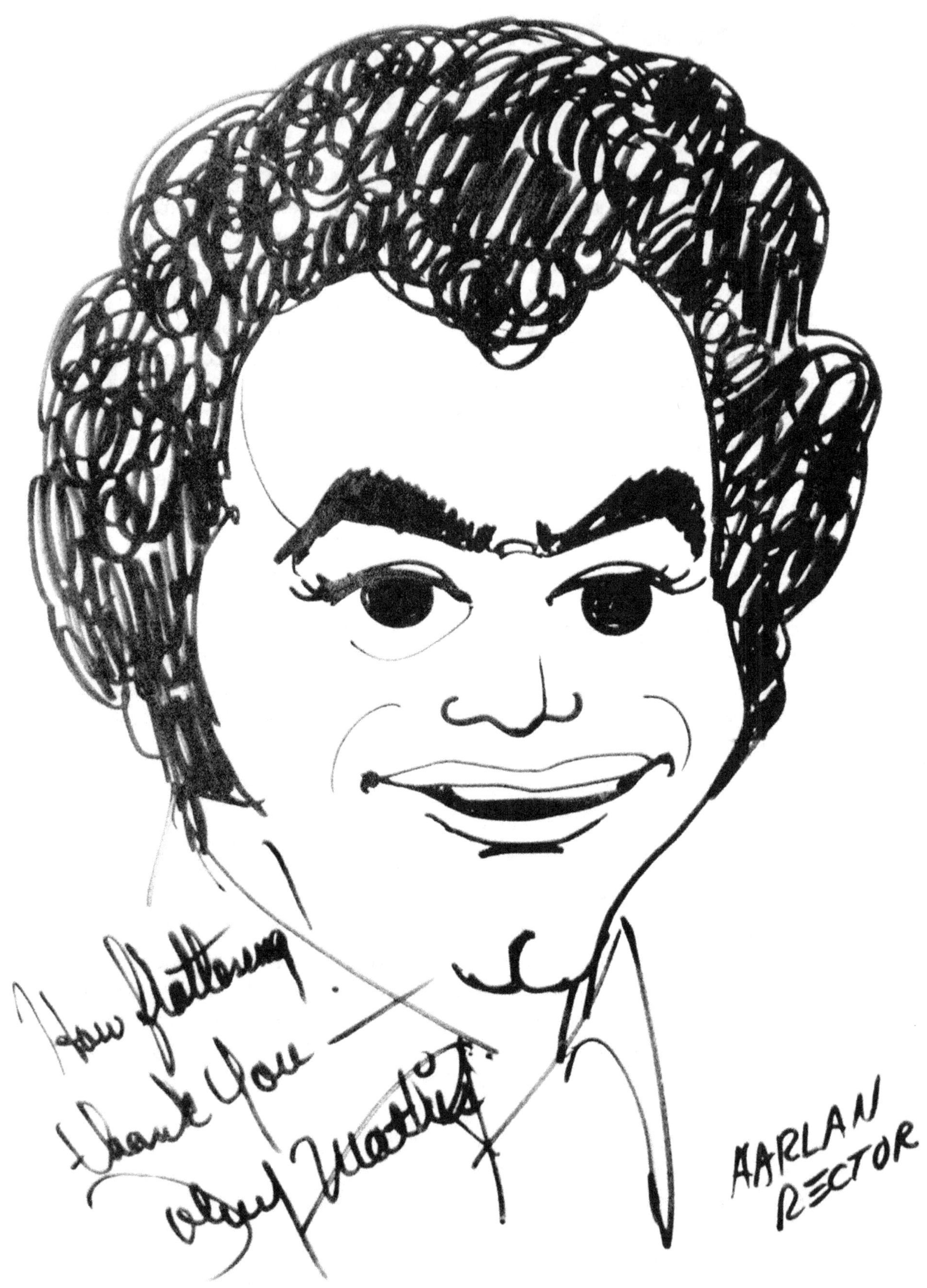
AARLAN
RECTOR

Johnny Mathis

John Royce Mathis was born in Gilmer, Texas, on September 30, 1935, the fourth of seven children of Clem Mathis and Mildred Boyd. The family moved to San Francisco early in Johnny's life. His ethnic origin is African American and Native American. When his father heard Johnny's voice, he invested $25 in a piano and encouraged Johnny with songs and routines from his vaudeville days.

At age 13, voice teacher Connie Cox accepted Johnny as her student in exchange for doing work around her house. For six years, Mathis learned vocal scales, voice production and classical as well as operatic singing. In high school, Johnny was a star athlete high jumper, hurdler, and basketball player on the team.

In 1954, Johnny entered San Francisco State College on an athletic scholarship with an eye on becoming an English teacher. He set a high jump record of 77.5 inches while in college, only two inches short of the Olympic record at the time.

He was singing with a friend's jazz sextet at a club in San Francisco and attracted the attention of the club's co-founder, Helen Noga. She became Mathis's music manager and in 1955 she booked him to sing on weekends at Ann Dee's 440 Club.

Noga persuaded George Avakian, head of Music A & R at Columbia Records, to come hear Mathis. He wasn't disappointed. Avakian sent a telegram to his record company saying, "Have found phenomenal 19 year old boy who could go all the way. Send blank contracts."

Back at school, Mathis was asked to try out as a high jumper for the US Olympic Team going to Melbourne, Australia. However, Mathis had an appointment in New York City to make his first recordings. On his father's advice, Johnny opted to embark on a professional singing career. His first LP record album, *Johnny Mathis: A New Sound In Popular Song*, was released late 1956.

In 1957, my wife and I saw Johnny Mathis at the Starlight Roof of the famous Chase Hotel in St. Louis. She was pregnant with our twin boys. The MC announced that Johnny was ill and couldn't promise a good show, but he was still sensational. As of this writing, those twin boys are 61 years old and Johnny Mathis is still going strong, as always, an incredible entertainer.

Johnny Mathis's biography would fill pages, but one has to see him perform or actually meet him to appreciate his humility. When his interview was over, he just walked out of the studio to the elevator. I jumped off my stool and ran after him to give him his caricature and get him to sign the other one. He stopped the elevator door and graciously wrote, "How flattering." A class act in every way. ∎

HARLAN RECTOR

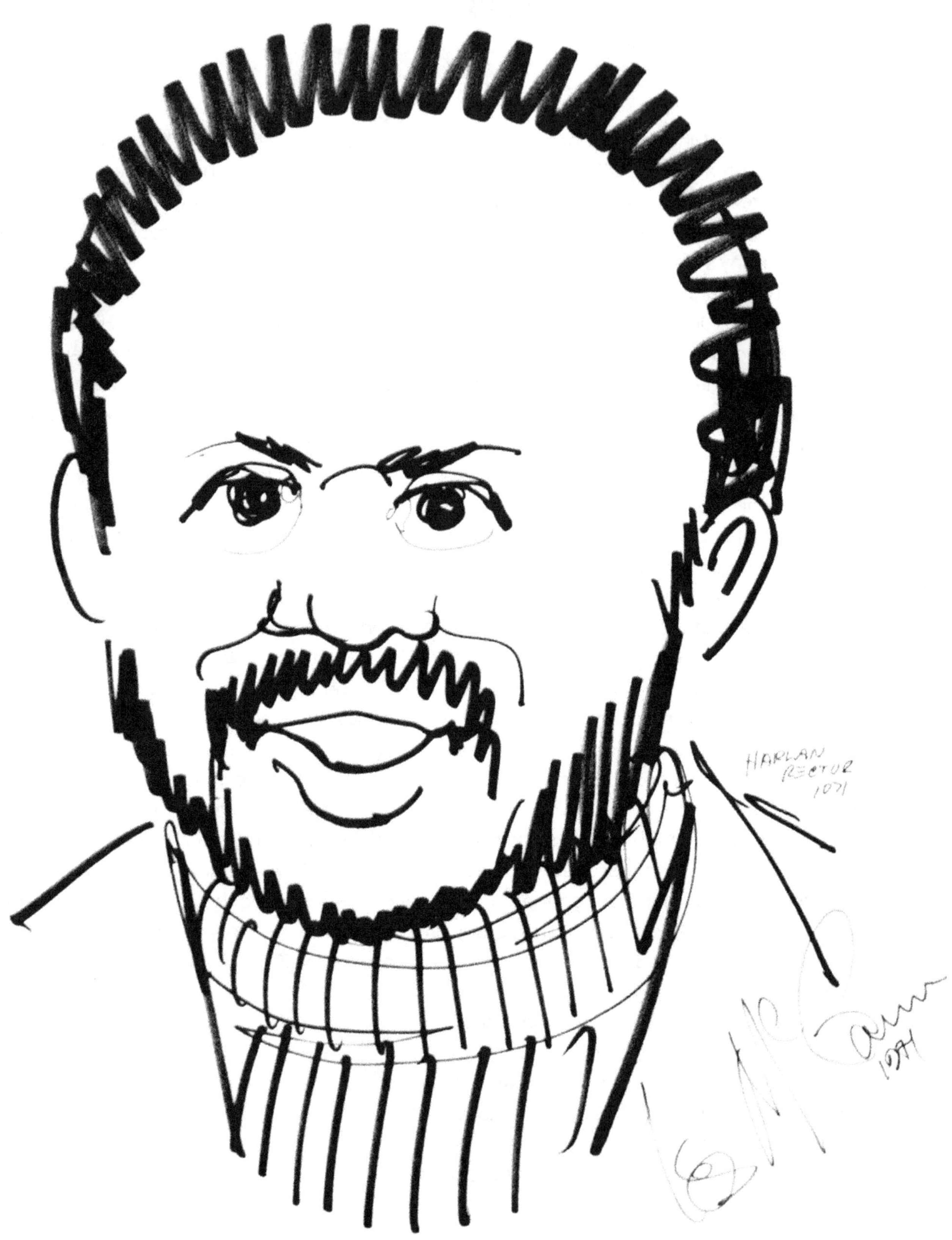

HARLAN
RECTOR
1971

Les McCann

American jazz and soul pianist, the gravelly-voiced singer Les McCann, certainly had a lot to talk about when he visited WJR. In 1970-1972 alone he released six albums: *Les McCann Ltd. Plays the Shout, New from the Big City*, and Atlantic Records hits *Comment, Second Movement, Talk to the People*, and *Invitation to Openness*.

Leslie Coleman McCann was born on September 23, 1935, in Lexington, Kentucky. He was a self-taught musician whose musical family got him started with church music. He played in his high school's marching band before joining the armed forces.

He won a Navy singing contest that got him on *The Ed Sullivan Show* in 1956. In the early 1960s, he played the piano on recordings with his trio for Pacific Jazz. He played at the Montreux Jazz Festival in 1969, generating his album containing *Compared to What*—a critique of the Vietnam War. Both the album and the single made it to the *Billboard* pop charts.

He was a cross-over artist, moving from jazz into rhythm and blues and soul. He kitchen-sinked a bit of everything into his soul jazz, mixing in dance-based funk, bop, soul, gospel, and world rhythms. He was a pioneer in adding electric piano, clavinet (electrically amplified clavichord), and synthesizer to soul jazz.

He played with all the jazz greats, performing in the 1960 and 1962 Antibes Jazz Festival with Ray Charles and Count Basie (included in this book), and touring Europe the next year with Charlie Byrd. He mentored Roberta Flack, Mahalia Jackson, and Nancy Wilson.

In 1971, McCann, Wilson Pickett, the Staple Singers, Santana, Ike and Tina Turner, plus many others performed a 14-hour concert for more than 100,000 fans in Accra, Ghana. The concert was used in the documentary film *Soul to Soul*. The movie and soundtrack album were released in 2004.

Overcoming a stroke and carpal tunnel syndrome in the mid-1990s, he returned to music in 2002, releasing *Pump it Up*, featuring Billy Preston and Bonnie Raitt. Musing on his career he said, "It was evidently meant to be. Thanks to the people who have helped me, including the musicians, hospitals, and the incredible amount of angels in my life."

The 2008 Universal Fire destroyed the works of hundreds of artists, including McCann's. He had exhibited watercolor paintings and over 8,000 photos of friends such as Miles Davis and Duke Ellington. In his lifetime he released 53 albums, 47 singles and EPs, and played as a sideman on nine other albums, including those headlined by Herbie Mann and Lou Rawls. A 2009 NPR interview celebrated the 40th anniversary of his *Swiss Movement*.

As of 2019, he was still active in the music business, playing "Volkswagen Blues" with lifelong friend Eddie Harris. ∎

EDWARD MICKOLUS

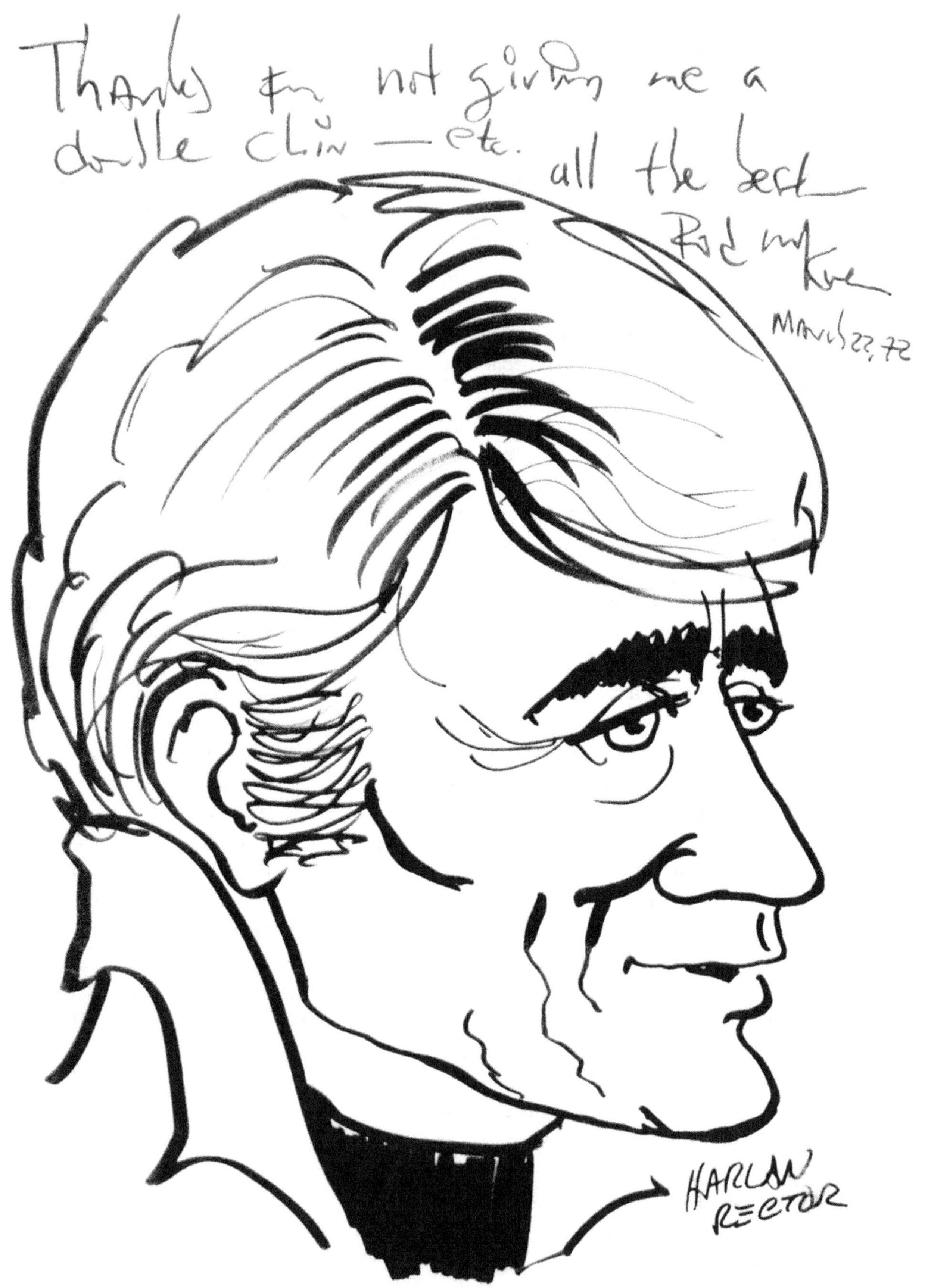
Thanks for not giving me a
double chin — etc.
all the best
March 22, 72
HARLAN
RECTOR

Rod McKuen

By the time I drew Rod McKuen's caricature in early 1972, he had garnered two Academy Award nominations, won a Grammy Award, saw his poems translated into eleven languages, and sold over one million copies of his books.

Rodney Marvin McKuen was born on April 29, 1933, in a Salvation Army hostel in Oakland, California. He never knew his biological father, who took off when Rod was still an infant. Physically and sexually abused by relatives, raised by his mother and stepfather—a violent alcoholic, McKuen ran away from home at age 11. During the late 1940s, he worked as a ranch hand, surveyor, railroad worker, lumberjack, rodeo cowboy, stuntman and radio disc jockey, always sending money home to his mother.

In 1951, McKuen dropped out of Oakland Technical High School. Compensating for his lack of formal education, he began keeping a journal which he later drew on for his first poetry and song lyrics. He continued writing and settled in San Francisco, where he would read his poetry in clubs alongside other Beat poets like Jack Kerouac and Allen Ginsberg. He was a folk singer at the famed *Purple Onion* and started to incorporate his own songs into his act.

The 1950s were a golden time for Rod McKuen. Decca Records signed him, he released several pop albums, appeared as an actor in three feature movies, and he sang with the Lionel Hampton band. All the while, he kept writing. He wrote 1,500 songs during his career, which accounted for the sale of over 100 million records worldwide.

In the early 1960s, McKuen moved to France where he met and befriended Belgian singer-songwriter Jacques Brel. McKuen began to translate the work of Brel into English, which led to the song *If You Go Away*—an international pop standard. Another Brel song, *Le Moribond*, translated loosely into *Seasons of the Sun*, was recorded later by Terry Jacks. In 1978, upon hearing of Jacques Brel's death, McKuen locked himself in his room and drank for a week, ruminating over their unfinished life together.

Rod McKuen's songs have been performed by Robert Goulet, Glenn Yarbrough, Barbra Streisand, Perry Como, Petula Clark, Waylon Jennings, The Boston Pops, Chet Baker, Jimmy Rogers, Johnny Cash, Andy Williams, the Kingston Trio, Percy Faith, the London Philharmonic, Nana Mouskouri, Dusty Springfield, Al Hirt, Greta Keller, Aaron Freeman, Frank Sinatra, Pete Fountain, and Johnnie Mathis (the last two celebrities are included in this book). McKuen's collaboration with composers include Henry Mancini (also in this book), John Williams, and Anita Kerr. His symphonies, concertos, and other orchestral works are performed by orchestras around the globe.

Despite Rod McKuen's achievements, awards and popularity, he was never taken seriously by critics or academics. Rod McKuen lived out his life in Beverly Hills, California with his partner, Edward, in a rambling Spanish house which held one of the world's largest private record collections. He died of respiratory pneumonia at age 82 on January 29, 2015. ■

HARLAN RECTOR

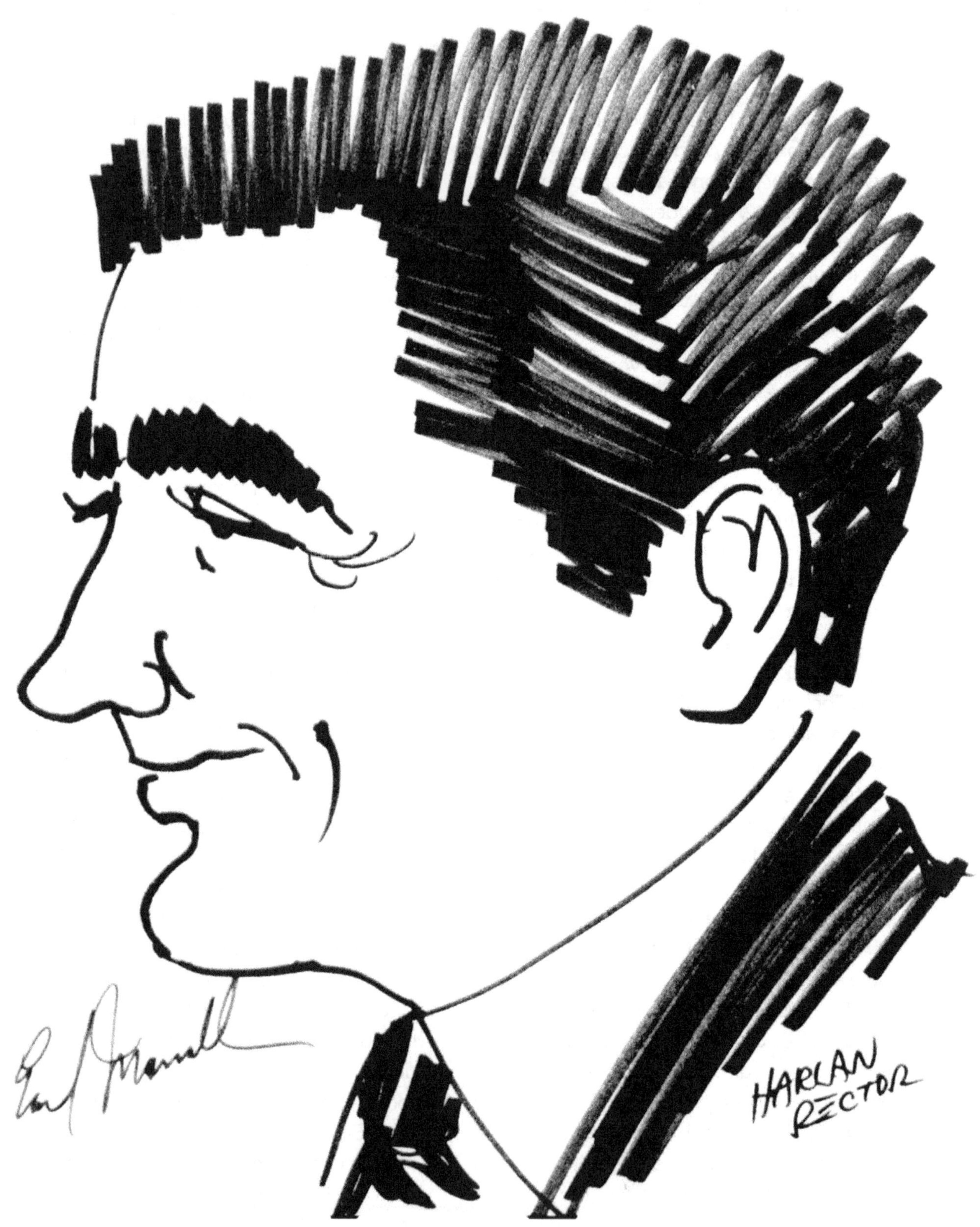

HARLAN
RECTOR

Earl Morrall

Earl Morrall was a quarterback in the National Football League (NFL) for 21 seasons. Though he was a successful starter, he was considered by many, including Hall of Fame coach Don Shula, to be one of the greatest reserve quarterbacks in the history of the league. He was a member of three Super Bowl championship teams.

Morrall was born on May 17, 1934 in Muskegon, Michigan. He achieved success early, leading the Muskegon High School football team to the Michigan state championship in 1951. Morrall then attended Michigan State University in East Lansing, Michigan, where he led his team to a 9-1 season in his senior year and defeated the UCLA Bruins in the Rose Bowl.

Morrall was heavily scouted by NFL teams during his time at Michigan State. In 1956, he was drafted second overall by the San Francisco 49ers. Throughout his career he played for six NFL teams. After his rookie season, he was traded to the Pittsburgh Steelers for Marv Matuszak and two future number one draft picks.

In 1956, Morrall was traded to the Detroit Lions for future Hall of Famer Bobby Layne. He played for the Lions for the next seven seasons, where he had his best statistical year in 1963, throwing for more than 2,600 yards and 24 touchdown passes.

Morrall played the next several seasons for the rebuilding New York Giants. Eventually, he was traded in 1968 to the Baltimore Colts as a backup for starter Johnny Unitas. During the first exhibition game of the 1968 season, Unitas suffered a season-ending injury, thrusting Morrall into the starting role.

Morrall led the Colts to a 13-1 record, winning two playoff games and the Most Valuable Player Award that season. The heavily favored Colts lost in the Super Bowl to Joe Namath and the upstart New York Jets, with a score of 16-7. It was one of the greatest upsets in Super Bowl history.

During the 1970 season, Morrall again replaced an injured Johnny Unitas in the second-to-last game of the regular season, leading the Colts to a Super Bowl victory over the Dallas Cowboys, 16-13.

In 1972, Morrall replaced injured quarterback Bob Griese during the fifth game that year after being traded to the Miami Dolphins. The team was 5-0 at that point in the season, until Morrall led the Dolphins to victory in the next 11 games. Though Griese eventually returned during the playoffs, Morrall was largely responsible for the Miami Dolphins achieving the only perfect record in NFL history at 17-0.

Morrall continued as backup quarterback for the Dolphins for the next four seasons, finally retiring in 1977.

Throughout the 1980s Morrall served as quarterbacks' coach for the University of Miami. He helped developed future NFL players Jim Kelly, Vinny Testaverde, and Bernie Kosar. In 1989, Morrall won a seat on the Davie, Florida, city council and eventually became mayor of Davie.

Earl Morrall died on April 25, 2014, in Fort Lauderdale, Florida. He was survived by his wife, Jane. ■

GREG BARRY

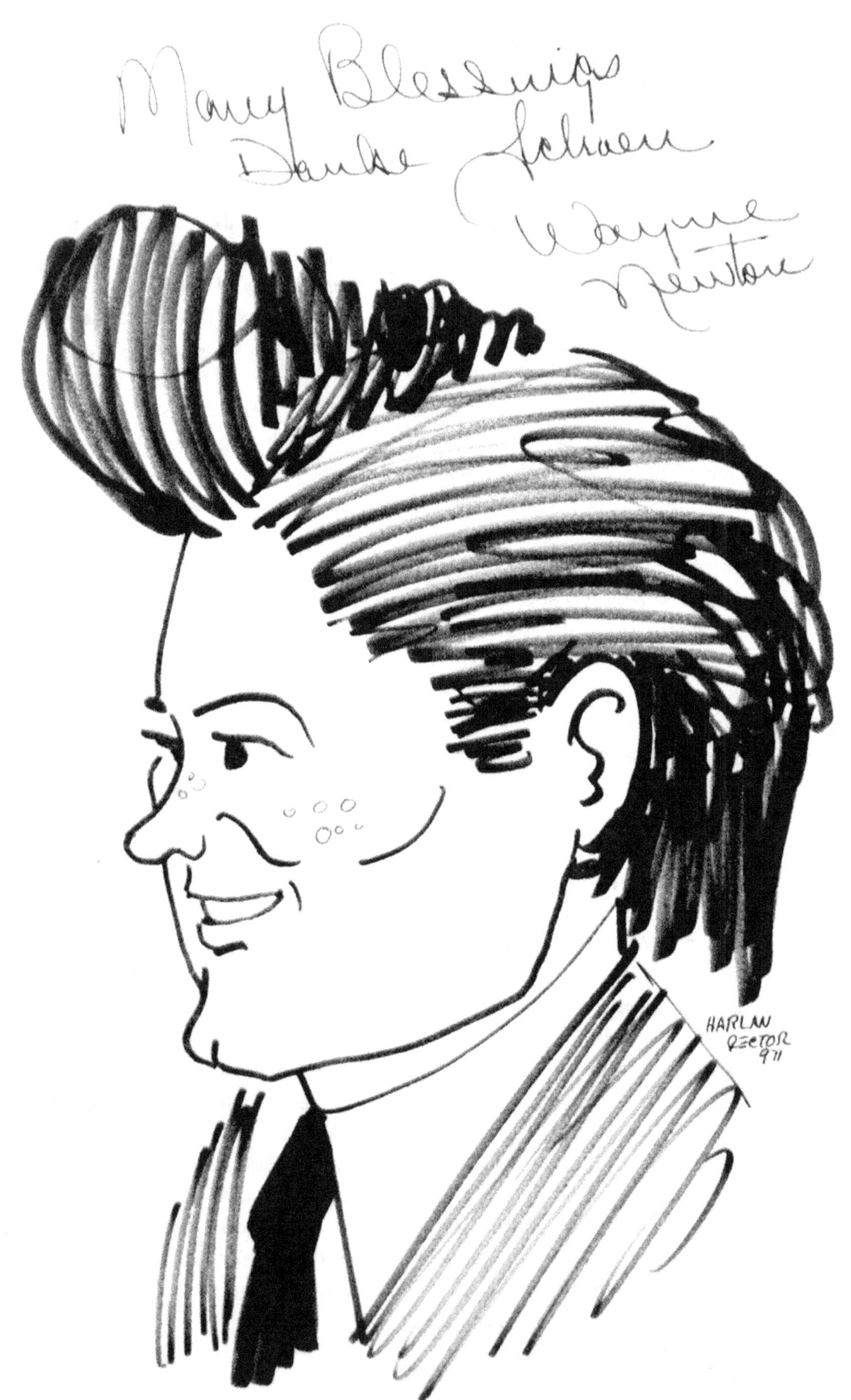

Many Blessings
Danke Schoen
Wayne
Newton

HARLAN
RECTOR
9 71

Wayne Newton

Danke Schoen is a song that has transcended time and generations. The level of familiarity varies, but few have never heard the lyrics belted out in movies, such as the trailer for *Wolfenstein II: The New Colossus*, *The Grudge Match*, and the most well-known, *Ferris Bueller's Day Off.*

Carson Wayne Newton was born on April 3, 1942, in Norfolk, Virginia, later moving to Newark, Ohio, with his parents and brother, Jerry. His parents, both of Native American descent (his mother was half Cherokee and his father half Powhatan), moved their family to Arizona due to Wayne's severe asthma. His love of music began early, and he found his inspiration for singing from watching Kitty Wells and Hank Williams. Newton also learned to play the banjo, piano, and guitar at a very young age.

Newton began singing for pay at age six, known for his soprano voice and chubby features. Wayne and his brother traveled to The Grand Ole Opry, where they were known as the "Rascals in Rhythm." They also performed on a local television show, *Lew King Rangers Show.* Soon they caught the eye of a booking scout in Las Vegas.

In 1958, still a boy at age 16, Wayne and Jerry traveled to Vegas, where they performed six days and nights a week for five years at the Fremont Hotel. While performing in a Vegas lounge act Jackie Gleason spotted him, and on September 29, 1962, Wayne made his first of four appearances on *The Jackie Gleason Show.*

In a town known for its big-name performers such as Frank Sinatra, Sammy Davis, Jr, Elvis Presley, and Bobby Darin, Newton learned to stand out and become one of Vegas's most successful stars. How did he do it? He worked the crowd with lively charisma and talent. He built them up, egged them on, and encouraged them to give just a little bit more as he did the same.

Newton enjoyed the years with his fellow stars. According to him, there was camaraderie at that time that does exist among performers today. In fact, the song that made him famous was given to him by Bobby Darin, who had originally been intended to sing the song.

Of course, to the Wayniacs, there are many titles that will forever be synonymous with his name: *Daddy Don't Walk So Fast*, *Red Roses for a Blue Lady*, *I'll Be With You in Apple Blossom Time*, *Summer Wind*, *Remember When* (*We Made These Memories*), and *Hello, Dolly*, to name just a few. Another celebrity that helped Newton make it to the top was Jack Benny. He hired Newton as an opening act for his show. When this job ended in 1972, Newton was given a headline show of his own at the Flamingo Hotel in Vegas.

Wayne Newton recently said goodbye to his 52-acre estate, Casa de Shenandoah, due to a bankruptcy reorganization. The property, once thought to be worth $70 million, recently sold for only $5.56 million. He had once hoped to open his property to the public, but this plan failed. His new $3 million mansion sits on 20 acres about a mile away from the estate and will have plenty of room for the Arabian horses Newton breeds, his peacock, and Charlie the penguin. ■

TRACY TRIPP

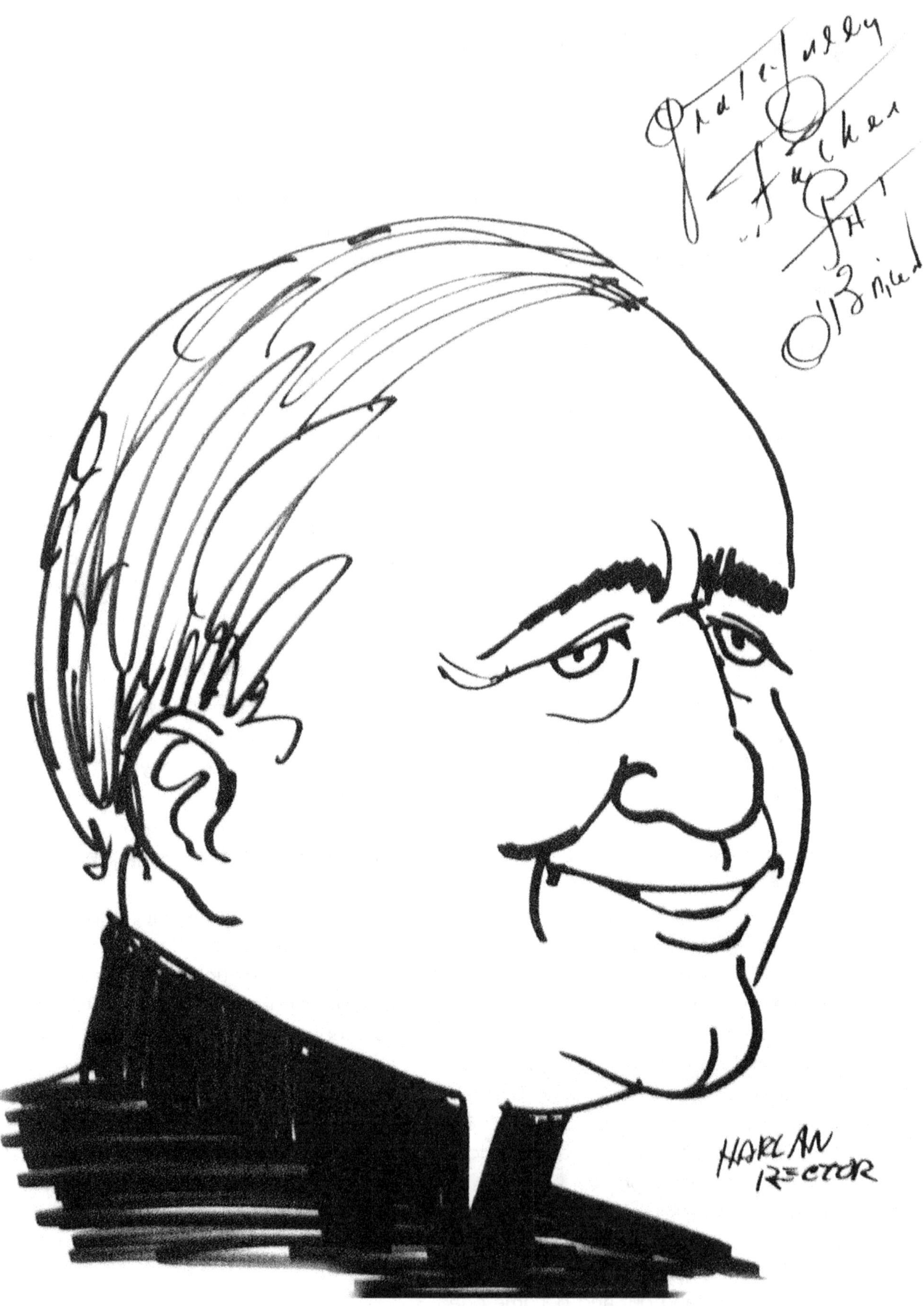

Pat O'Brien

Veteran movie star Patrick O'Brien was doing quite well as a television actor when he was interviewed at WJR in the early 1970s. O'Brien wore a regular shirt for his interview however, the drawing shows a 'clerical' collar. I was told when O'Brien saw the drawing he laughed and signed it "Father" Pat O'Brien.

William Joseph Patrick O'Brien was born in Milwaukee, Wisconsin, on November 11, 1899, as the grandchild of Irish immigrants. After he graduated from Marquette University, he and Spencer Tracy moved to New York to attend the American Academy of Dramatic Arts.

In 1930, Patrick made his film debut in *The Nightingale*. His first starring role was in the original 1931 version of *The Front Page* with Adolphe Menjou. The 1934 release *Here Comes the Navy* was O'Brien's first film with James Cagney, while the two were under contract with Warner Brothers. The two remained close friends for decades.

Cagney and O'Brien reunited in 1935 with *Devil Dogs of the Air*, *The Irish in Us*, and *Ceiling Zero*. They co-starred in the 1938 movie *Angels with Dirty Faces* and the 1940 picture *The Fighting 69th*.

O'Brien got his best-known role in 1940, portraying the famous University of Notre Dame football coach in *Knute Rockne, All American*.

In the late 1930s, Patrick and a small group of his actor friends would meet to converse and exchange opinions and stories. A Hollywood columnist dubbed them the "Irish Mafia," but they preferred the sobriquet, "The Boys Club." In addition to O'Brien, the original members of the club were James Cagney, Spencer Tracy, Allen Jenkins, and Frank McHugh, all of whom were Irish Americans.

Shortly after he left Warner Brothers in 1940, O'Brien signed a contract with RKO and appeared in several movies for that studio in authority or military roles, including *The Navy Comes Through* in 1942, and *Bombardier* in 1943.

Patrick's movie career slowed considerably by the early 1950s, but he appeared in another one of his best-known movies in 1959 as a police detective in *Some Like It Hot*.

O'Brien often worked in television. He performed in two episodes of *The Virginian* in the mid-1960s. In the 1960-1961 television season, Patrick joined Roger Perry in the 34-episode ABC sitcom *Harrigan and Son*, in which he played the lead role. From the 1960s through the early 1980s, O'Brien traveled the country in road shows as a one-man act.

Patrick and his wife, Eloise, had four children: Mavourneen, Sean, Terry, and Brigid, three of whom were adopted. The youngest, Brigid O'Brien, born in 1946, was his biological child. Eloise O'Brien occasionally appeared on stage with her husband.

Friends said O'Brien was known for his love of storytelling, jokes, and late-night parties. Bob Hope remembered him as a raconteur, while another friend recalled that he was always, "The life, and I mean the lively life, of the party."

Patrick died at age 83 on October 15, 1983, in Santa Monica from a heart attack.

O'Brien was a movie star at a time when Hollywood ruled the culture. He was also an emblem of Irish America and the American Catholic church, when ties to either were still considered controversial. ∎

RICHARD WILLITS

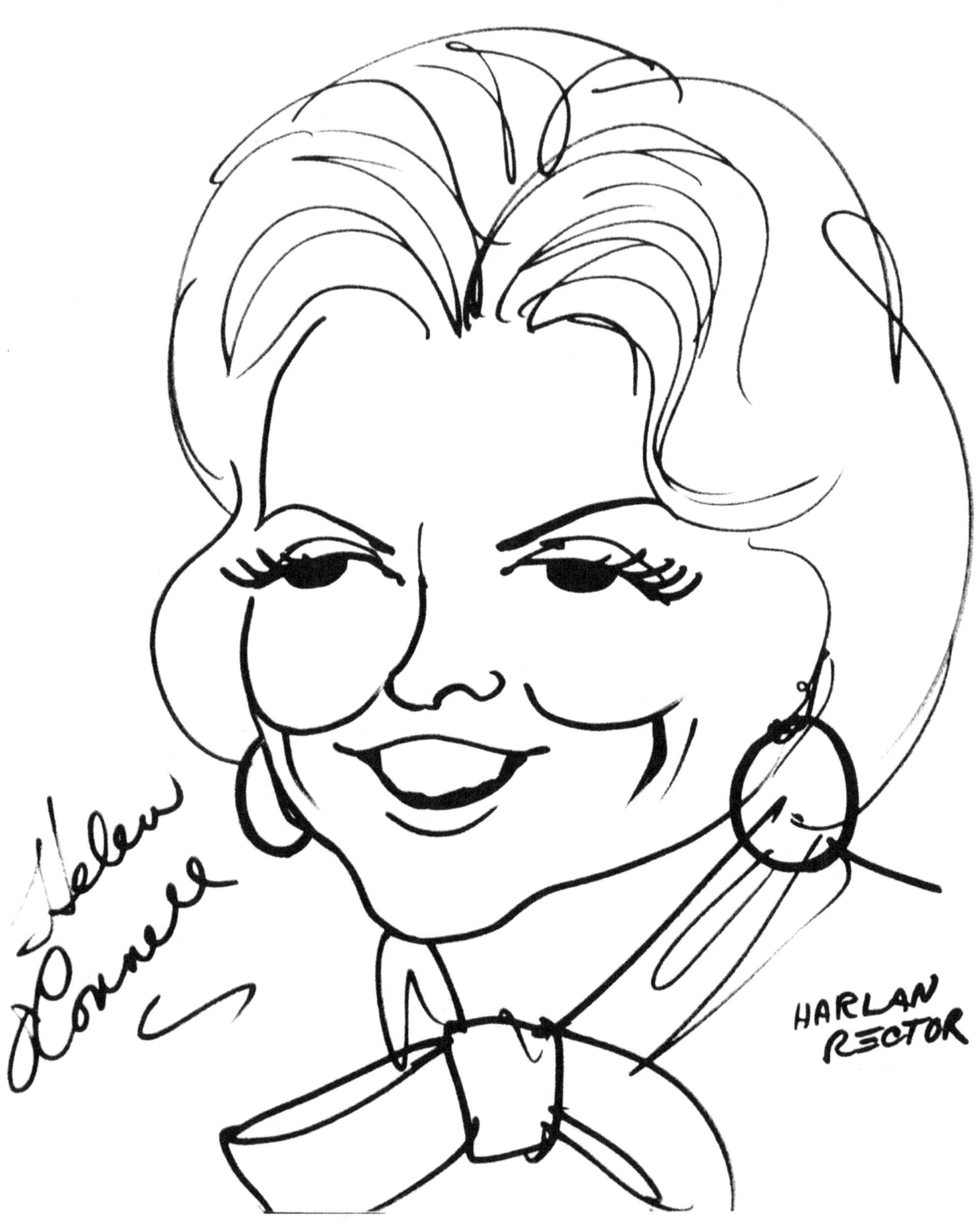
HARLAN
RECTOR

Helen O'Connell

Helen O'Connell, the petite girl next door with the sunny disposition, achieved fame as a big band singer. When WJR Detroit interviewed her, she was co-hosting the Miss USA and Miss Universe pageants with Bob Barker of *The Price is Right*.

Helen was born on May 23, 1920, in Lima, Ohio. By the age of 15, she and her older sister, Alice, were singing in clubs, hotels, and could be heard on radio stations around Toledo. One night, while singing with Larry Funk and his Band of a Thousand Melodies, Jimmy Dorsey's manager discovered Helen and hired her the next day.

Her collaboration with the Dorsey band and Bob Eberly earned her best-selling records in the early 40s. They produced such hits as *Green Eyes*, *Amapola*, *Tangerine*, and *Yours*. She and Bob Eberly became the most popular male-female singing duo on the big band circuit. At the height of her fame, Helen appeared in two movies: *The Fleet's In* (1942) and *I Dood It* (1943).

Helen married Navy aviator Clifford Smith, Jr in 1941, and then took a break from show business to raise her four daughters. Although she was grateful for what music and singing did for her, she acknowledged it was not a healthy lifestyle for young children. Except for an appearance in the movie *The Fabulous Dorseys* (1947), she pretty much stayed out of the limelight. Helen used this time to finish her high school diploma at Hollywood High School.

When the marriage ended in 1951, she resumed her career, achieving chart success and making regular appearances on television. Helen starred with Bob Eberly on *TV's Top Tunes* in 1953. In March 1955, Helen went with singer Johnnie Ray on his landmark tour in Australia. It set a box office record that stood until the Beatles went Down Under in 1964.

In 1957, Helen landed a job as a host on NBC's *The Today Show*, where she joined Dave Garroway. She covered the weather and features but sang very little. During one of these telecasts she met the author Thomas T. Chamales, who she married just two weeks later. Unfortunately, he died in a house fire in 1960, leaving her single once again. In 1961, she co-hosted the Desilu-NBC program *Here's Hollywood*, where she interviewed celebrities, often from their homes.

Helen had a short marriage to musician Bob Paris, which she annulled after only ten months. Soon after, her career had another resurgence when she became co-host of the Miss USA and Miss Universe pageants with Bob Barker, continuing until 1980. She was nominated for an Emmy Award in 1976 for her coverage of the Miss Universe pageant.

In the late 1970s and 1980s, O'Connell toured with the show *4Girls4* for several years with singers Rosemary Clooney, Margaret Whiting, Rose Marie, and, on occasion, Kay Starr. She also sang the National Anthem for Super Bowl XV in 1981.

In 1991, she married composer-conductor Frank DeVol and was married to him at the time of her death from cancer in 1993, in the midst of a big band show tour in Pennsylvania. ∎

DORRI HALL

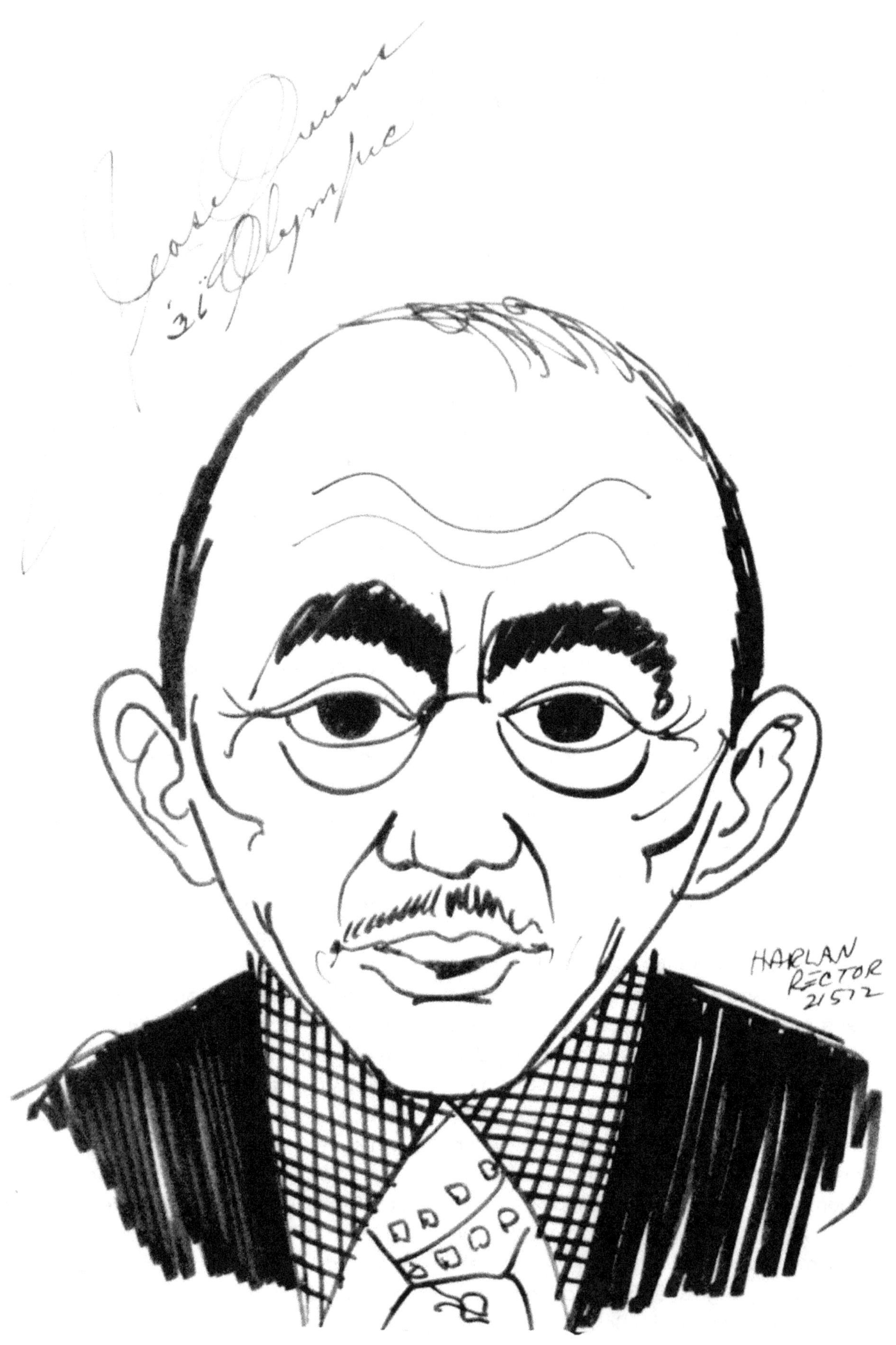

HARLAN
RECTOR
2/5/72

Jessie Owens

It is always fun to discover that you share a birthday with a celebrity. Such is the case with this honoree, born on September 12 in Oakville, Alabama, but a few years earlier, in 1913.

Affectionately known as the "Buckeye Bullet," James Cleveland Owens, better known as Jesse Owens, a world-renowned American track-and-field athlete, eventually set a world record in the running broad jump (also known as the long jump), which stood for 25 years.

Jesse Owens, originally known as JC, was the youngest of ten children, three girls and seven boys, born to a sharecropper. At the age of nine, he and his family moved to Cleveland, Ohio, for better opportunities. They were part of the Great Migration, when 1.5 million African-Americans left the segregated south for the urban and industrial north. When his new teacher asked his name to enter in her roll book, he said, "JC." Because of his strong southern accent, she thought he said, "Jesse." The name stuck, and he was known as Jesse Owens for the rest of his life.

His greatest acclaim came when he won four gold medals at the 1936 Summer Olympic Games in Berlin, Germany. He was the most successful athlete at the Games and, as a black man, was credited with single-handedly crushing Hitler's myth of Aryan supremacy.

In the months prior to the Games, there was much discussion of boycotting the Olympics due to the world's political climate. Owens was persuaded by the NAACP to declare, "If there are minorities in Germany who are being discriminated against, the United States should withdraw from the 1936 Olympics." Despite this statement, he and others eventually took part even after Avery Brundage, president of the American Olympic Committee, branded them "Un-American agitators."

Owens specialized in sprints and the long jump. He was recognized in his lifetime as perhaps "the greatest and most famous athlete in track and field history." He set three world records and tied another, all in less than an hour at the 1935 Big Ten track meet in Ann Arbor, Michigan. This was a feat that has never been equaled and has since been called "the greatest 45 minutes ever in sport."

The Jesse Owens Award is the USA Track and Field's highest accolades given to the year's best track and field athlete. Owens was ranked by ESPN as the sixth greatest North American athlete of the 20th century and the highest-ranked in his sport. In 1999, he was on the six-man short-list for the BBC's Sports Personality of the Century.

Throughout his life, Owens attributed the success of his athletic career to the encouragement of Charles Riley, his junior high school track coach at Fairmount Junior High School in Cleveland. Owens also met his wife Minnie Ruth Solomon at Fairmont Junior High School when he was just 15 and she was 13. They dated steadily and were eventually married. They had three daughters together and remained married until his death in 1980. ∎

JERRY RECTOR

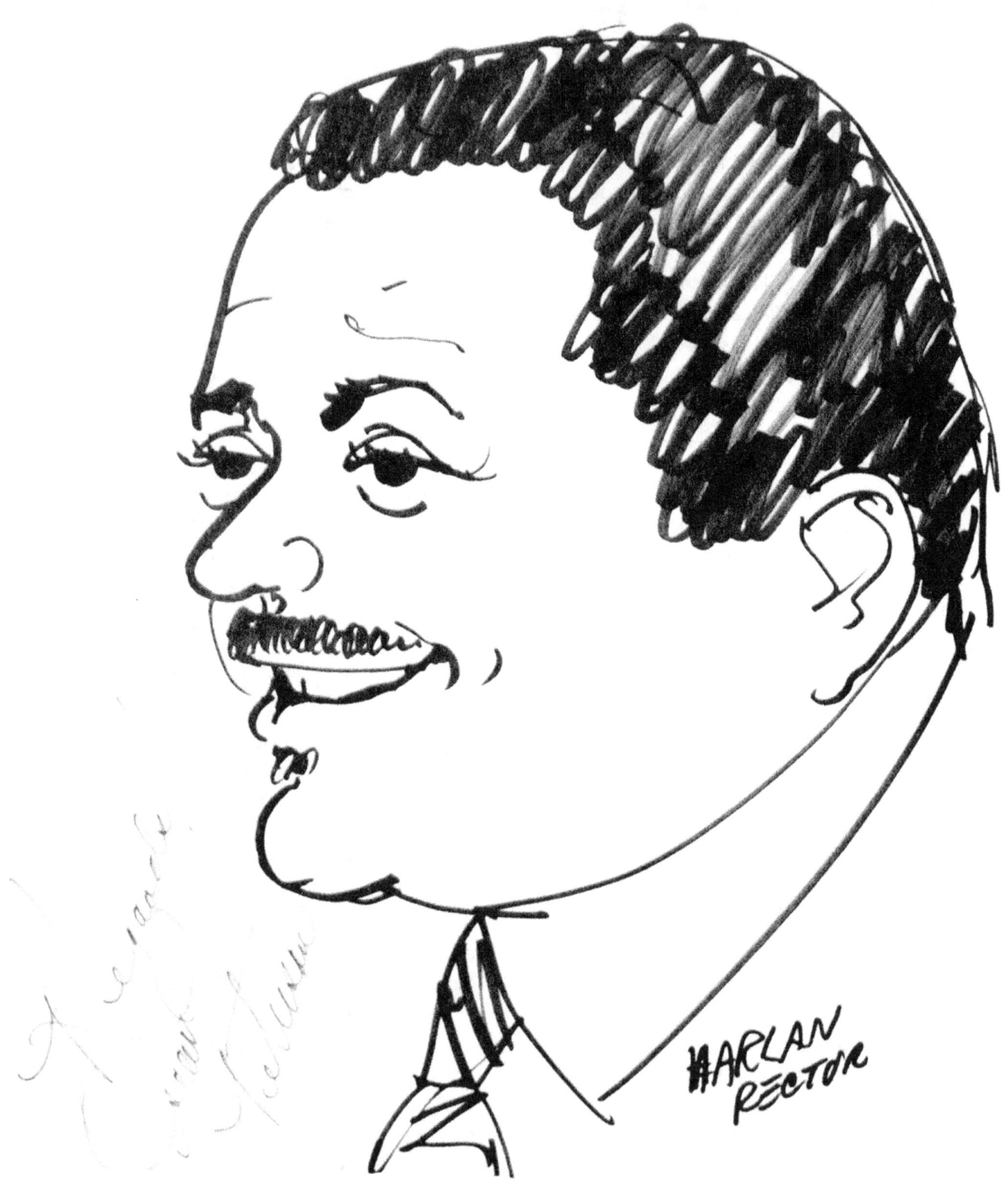
HARLAN
RECTOR

Oscar Peterson

Oscar Emmanuel Peterson—dubbed the "Maharajah of the Keyboard" by Duke Ellington—was interviewed at WJR to promote his newest albums including *Tristeza on Piano*, *Tracks*, and *Reunion Blues*.

He was born in Montreal, Quebec, Canada on August 15, 1925, to West Indian immigrants, where he began playing classical piano at age five.

In 1940, he won a national music competition organized by the Canadian Broadcasting Corporation. After the victory, he dropped out of school to play in hotels and music halls, and to star in a weekly radio show. This experience led him to join the Johnny Holmes Orchestra while still in his teens.

In the early 1950s, he joined bassist Ray Brown and drummer Charlie Smith to perform as the Oscar Peterson Trio.

He founded the Advanced School of Contemporary Music in Toronto during the 1960s, but it closed because touring called him and his associates away, and it had no government funding.

In addition to playing the piano, Oscar sometimes sang. One of his vocal recordings can be found on a 1965 tribute album to Nat King Cole. In the 1970s, Peterson formed a trio with guitarist Joe Pass and bassist Niels-Henning Ørsted Pedersen. Their album *The Trio*, won the 1974 Grammy Award for Best Jazz Performance by a Group. He later played in a duo with Herbie Hancock in the 1980s.

Peterson had trouble with arthritis from early on in his youth, which gave him difficulty with everything, including buttoning his shirts in his later years. Never slender, his mobility was further hindered when his weight increased to 276 pounds.

In 1993, he suffered a stroke which weakened his left side and knocked him out of performing for two years. Although he recovered some dexterity in his left hand, his piano playing was diminished forever. Still, Oscar returned to occasional public performances in 1995. Two years later he received the Grammy Lifetime Achievement Award and the International Jazz Hall of Fame Award. He toured the US and Europe for a month in 2003, with considerable rest between concerts.

Throughout his esteemed career, Oscar also taught the piano. He published jazz piano etudes for practice, and usually asked his students to study the music of Johann Sebastian Bach, especially *The Well-Tempered Clavier*, the *Goldberg Variations*, and *The Art of Fugue*. He considered those piano pieces essential for every serious pianist.

According to pianist and educator Mark Eisenman, some of Peterson's best playing was as an understated accompanist to singer Ella Fitzgerald.

Peterson died on December 23, 2007, of kidney failure at his home in Mississauga, Ontario. ■

RICHARD WILLITS

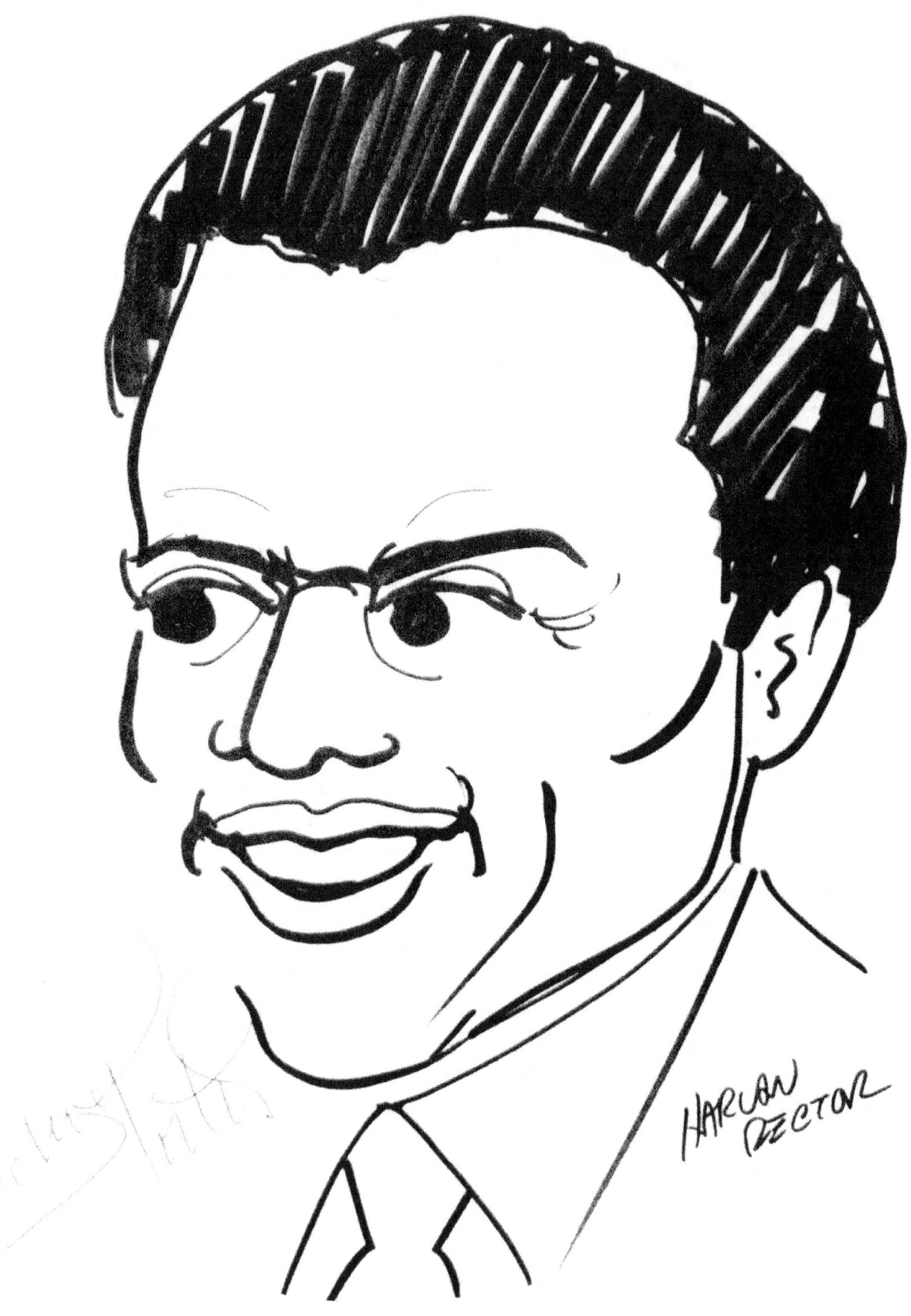
HARLAN
RECTOR

Sidney Poitier

When the debonair American actor, Sidney Poitier, spoke to WJR in Detroit, he was embarking on the next chapter of his career —directing.

Sidney Poitier was born on February 20, 1927, in Miami, Florida. His parents were visiting Miami when Sidney, surprising everyone when he was born two-and-a-half months premature. They remained in Miami until Sidney was strong enough to return to their farm on Cat Island in The Bahamas.

At the age of 10, his family moved to Nassau. Sidney was exposed to modern conveniences like electricity, plumbing, and automobiles for the first time. He moved to Miami when he was 15 to live with his brother's family, before eventually moving to New York City. There he worked various menial jobs and learned to read by skimming newspaper stories.

He served in the Army's medical unit during World War II. After his discharge, Sidney earned a spot with the American Negro Theater. Initially, he wasn't accepted by audiences due to his inability to sing but his determination to improve his acting skills and get rid of his strong Bahamian accent proved successful, leading to numerous other roles.

In 1950, Sidney's film debut in *No Way Out* was critically acclaimed, and he earned more complex roles, leading to his breakout role in *Blackboard Jungle* in 1955. He married Juanita Hardy on April 29, 1950, with whom he had four daughters.

In 1958, Stanley Kramer's *The Defiant Ones* achieved both commercial and critical acclaim, earning Poitier an Academy Award nomination for Best Actor. He was the first African American male to be nominated.

Sidney won an Academy Award in 1963 for Best Actor performance in the movie *Lilies of the Field* but he had mixed feelings about it, because he felt it might have been more about the industry celebrating itself for having him as a token rather than an award truly recognizing his talent. Subsequent roles offered to him were mostly type-cast as the soft-spoken appeaser.

He starred in *A Raisin in the Sun* on Broadway in 1959, as well as the film version, which was released in 1961. Sidney was the most successful draw at the box office in 1967, with films such as *Guess Who's Coming to Dinner, To Sir, with Love*, and *In the Heat of the Night*. Many of the movies Sidney starred in during the 1960s were social thrillers dealing with race and race relations.

Some criticized the roles he played as being over-idealized and without flaws. Still, Sidney felt it was essential to set an example with his characters, challenging racial stereotypes of the time.

A Western, *Buck and the Preacher*, was his directorial debut. But his most successful film was the comedy *Stir Crazy*, the highest-grossing movie directed by an African American.

Among Sidney's various honors was a knighthood from Queen Elizabeth in 1974. From 1997-2007, he served as ambassador of the Bahamas to Japan. Sidney was awarded an Honorary Academy Award in 2001 for his outstanding achievements as an artist and humanitarian. He is also a recipient of the Presidential Medal of Freedom, America's highest civilian honor. ∎

DORRI HALL

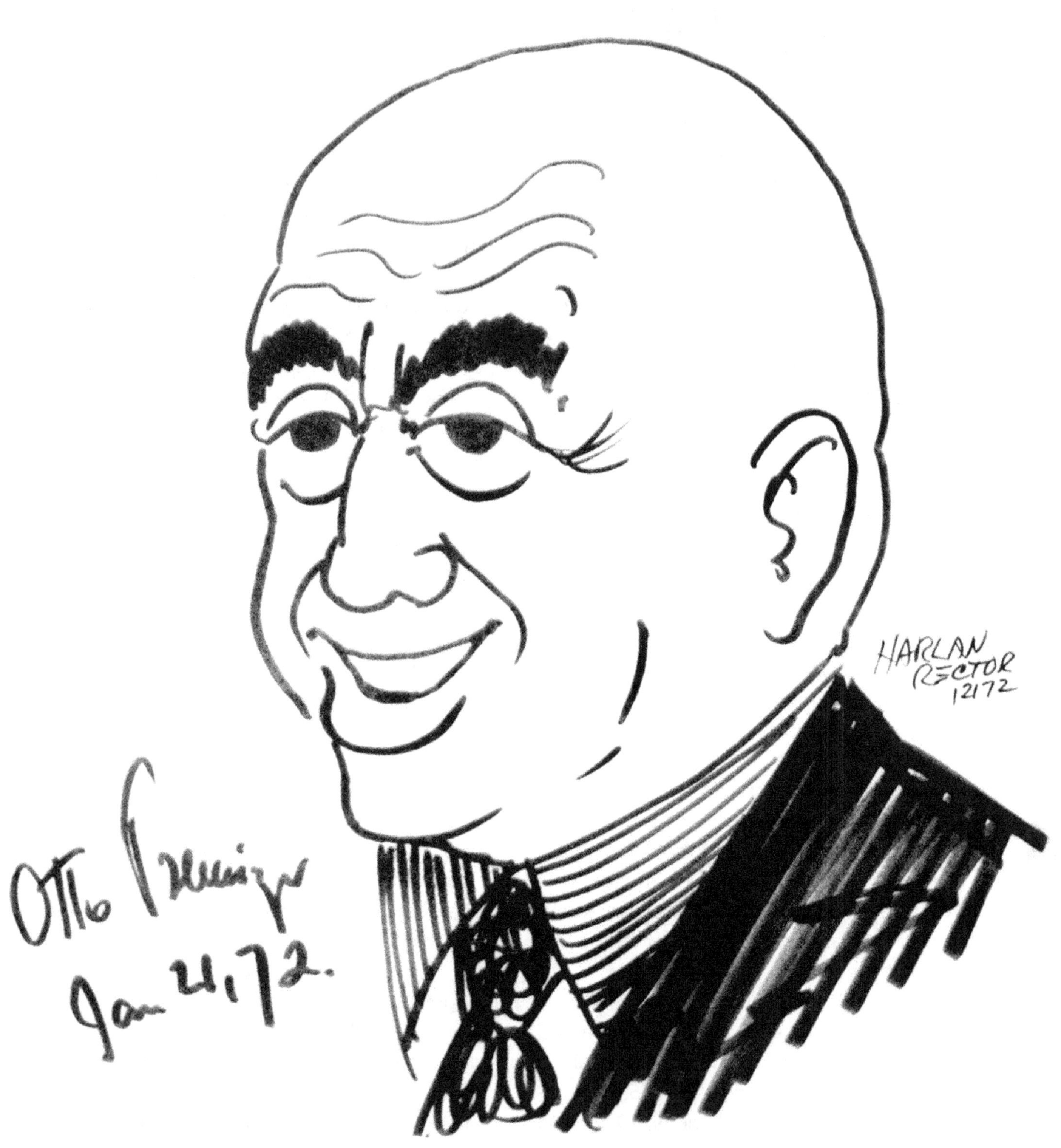

Otto Preminger

Otto Ludwig Preminger was born on December 5, 1905 in present day Ukraine. As World War I was ramping up, the Preminger family moved to Graz, Austria. His father, an attorney, instilled in young Otto the importance of fairness and to respect alternative viewpoints. These early life lessons served Preminger throughout his lifetime.

Otto Preminger became a prolific film director who wasn't afraid to take chances with provocative subject matter including rape in *"Anatomy of a Murder"*, homosexuality in *"Advise and Consent"* and drug addiction in *"The Man with the Golden Arm."* During his career he directed more than 35 films and was nominated for two Academy Awards for Best Director for "Laura" and "The Cardinal."

Preminger had hoped to become a stage actor. While living in Austria he acted in several plays including *"The Servant of Two Masters"* and *"The Merchant of Venice."*

When Preminger was 25 he was offered to direct the movie *"The Great Love"*, which became a critical and commercial success. He continued to direct stage plays and movies in Europe until 1935 when he was offered a contract to direct movies in Hollywood for Darryl F. Zanuck at Twentieth Century Fox studios.

Preminger's first two assignments were low budget screwball comedies which were both met with a tepid response from film critics. Despite Preminger's early struggles, Zanuck had enough confidence in him assigning him to direct the big budget movie *"Kidnapped,"* based on a Robert Lewis Stevenson novel which Zanuck himself had adapted for the screen. Preminger made changes to the script on location, infuriating Zanuck. After a heated argument, Preminger stormed out of Zanuck's office effectively ending their short working relationship.

Two years after arriving in Hollywood and lacking job prospects, Preminger relocated to New York City to pursue a career in stage. Success came quickly. Preminger directed a string of hits including *"Outward Bound," "My Dear Children,"* and *"Margin for Error."* He even resurrected his acting career casting himself as a Nazi in "Margin for Error."

Preminger's success was noticed by Hollywood. Ironically, while William Goetz was running Twentieth Century Fox in Darryl Zanuck's extended absence, he rehired Preminger. Goetz assigned the filming of *"Laura"* to Otto Preminger to direct which became one of Preminger's greatest cinematic achievements.

Other successes followed including *"Daisy Kenyon," "Anatomy of a Murder," Exodus"* and *"Carmen Jones"* which had an all-Black cast. He even acted in several films including *"Stalag 17,"* directed by Billy Wilder.

Preminger regularly pushed the boundaries of the decency standards of the time. In 1953 he released the comedy, *"The Moon is Blue"* which included the words virgin and pregnant. He brazenly released the film without obtaining The Production Code Seal of Approval.

While he continued to direct and act in films from the mid-1960s through the 1970s, Preminger struggled to produce material as well-received as his earlier works. Films such as *"Hurry Sundown," "Rosebud"* and *"The Human Factor"* had difficulty finding an audience and were critically panned.

Preminger was married three times. He also had a relationship with burlesque performer Gypsy Rose Lee which produced a son. While filming *"Carmen Jones"* in 1954 he entered into a four-year relationship with actress / singer Dorothy Dandridge.

Otto Preminger died at his home in Manhattan of lung cancer on April 23, 1986. ■

GREG BARRY

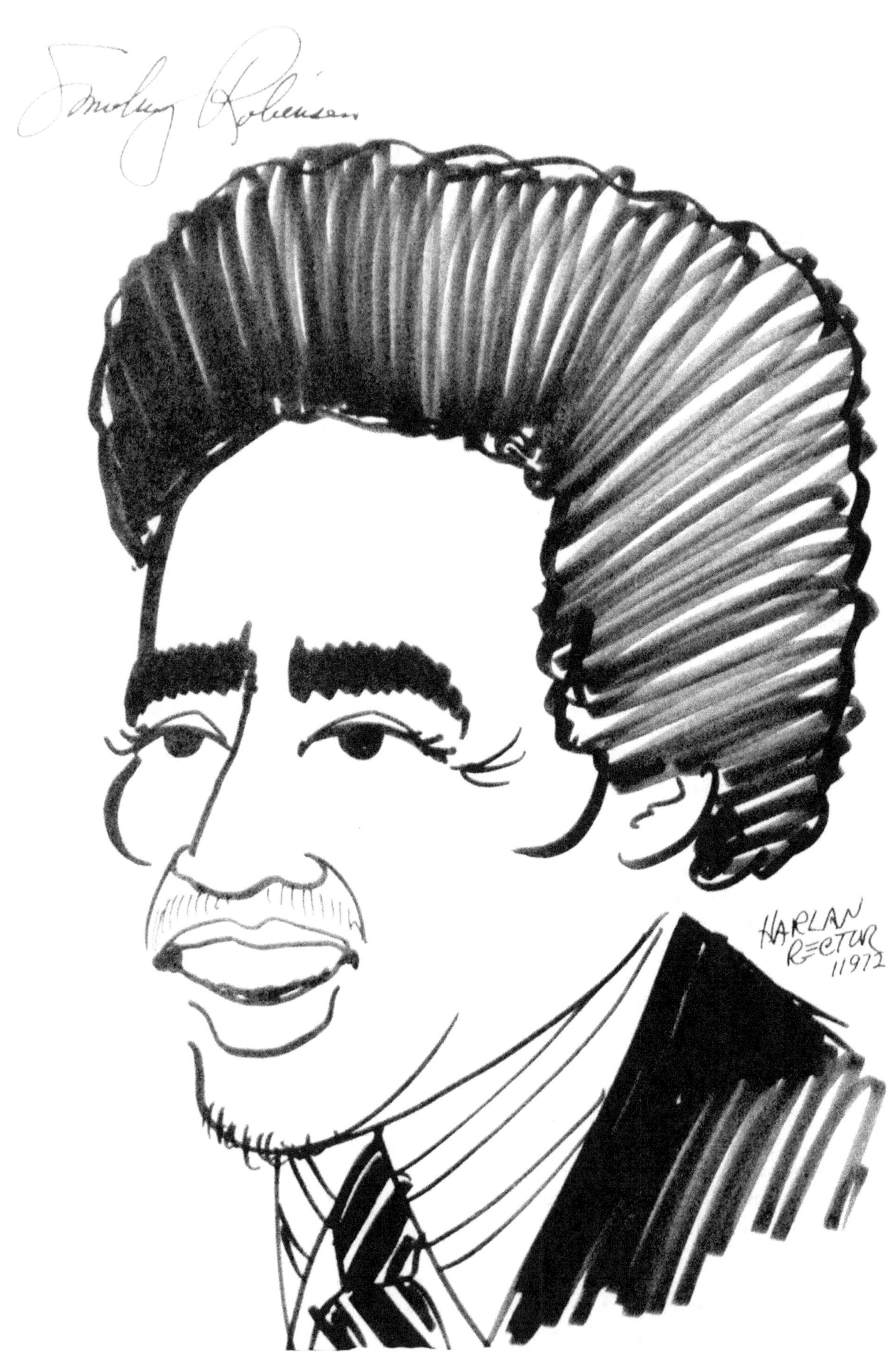

HARLAN
RECTOR
11972

Smokey Robinson

American singer, songwriter, record producer, and former record executive William "Smokey" Robinson Jr was born on February 19, 1940, to an African-American father and a mother of African-American-French ancestry—a poor family in Detroit, Michigan. His uncle Claude gave him the nickname "Smokey Joe" when he was a child and Robinson eventually became known as "Smokey."

He attended Northern High School, where he was above average academically and a keen athlete, though his main interest was music. He formed the doo-wop group the *Five Chimes*. Two years later, they were renamed the *Matadors* and began touring Detroit venues. Later they changed their name to *The Miracles*.

The Miracles released their first single *Got a Job* as an answer song to the *Silhouettes'* hit single *Get a Job*. During this time, Robinson attended college, studying electrical engineering. Robinson dropped out after only two months following the release of their first record.

The Miracles were one of the first groups ever to be signed by Motown Records, owned by now-legendary record producer Berry Gordy. Their first hit, *Shop Around* became Motown's first million-selling hit record. Other hits included *Tears of a Clown*, *You've Really Got a Hold on Me* and *Baby, Baby Don't Cry*. In 1965, they were the first Motown Group to change their name, to *Smokey Robinson & The Miracles*. Smokey would go on to write, produce and sing 26 more top forty hits with *The Miracles*.

By 1969, Robinson wanted to retire from touring to focus on raising his kids with his wife Claudette Robinson. The couple had two children, Berry Robinson named after Berry Gordy, and Tamla Robinson named after the original Tamla label set up by Gordy that would eventually become Motown. At the time Robinson also served as Motown's vice president and he wanted to focus more on that as well.

However, the success of *Tears of a Clown* made Robinson stay with the group until 1972. Robinson's last performance with the group was in July 1972 in Washington DC, former Beatle George Harrison featured the track *Pure Smokey* on his 1976 album *Thirty Three & 1/3* as a tribute to Robinson. On November 9, 1972, Smokey dropped by WJR to chat about his last performance and what was in store for the future and to get his caricature drawn by my father.

In 1981, Robinson topped the charts once again with the ballad *Being with You* peaking at number two on the Billboard Hot 100. In 1987, Robinson made a comeback with the album *One Heartbeat* and the singles *Just to See Her* and *One Heartbeat*.

On February 22, 1983, Smokey was awarded an individual star on the Hollywood Walk of Fame. He was inducted into the Rock and Roll Hall of Fame in 1987. In 2016, he received the Library of Congress Gershwin Prize for his lifetime contributions to popular music and that year, he was inducted into the Rhythm & Blues Hall of Fame in his hometown of Detroit, Michigan. ∎

JEFF RECTOR

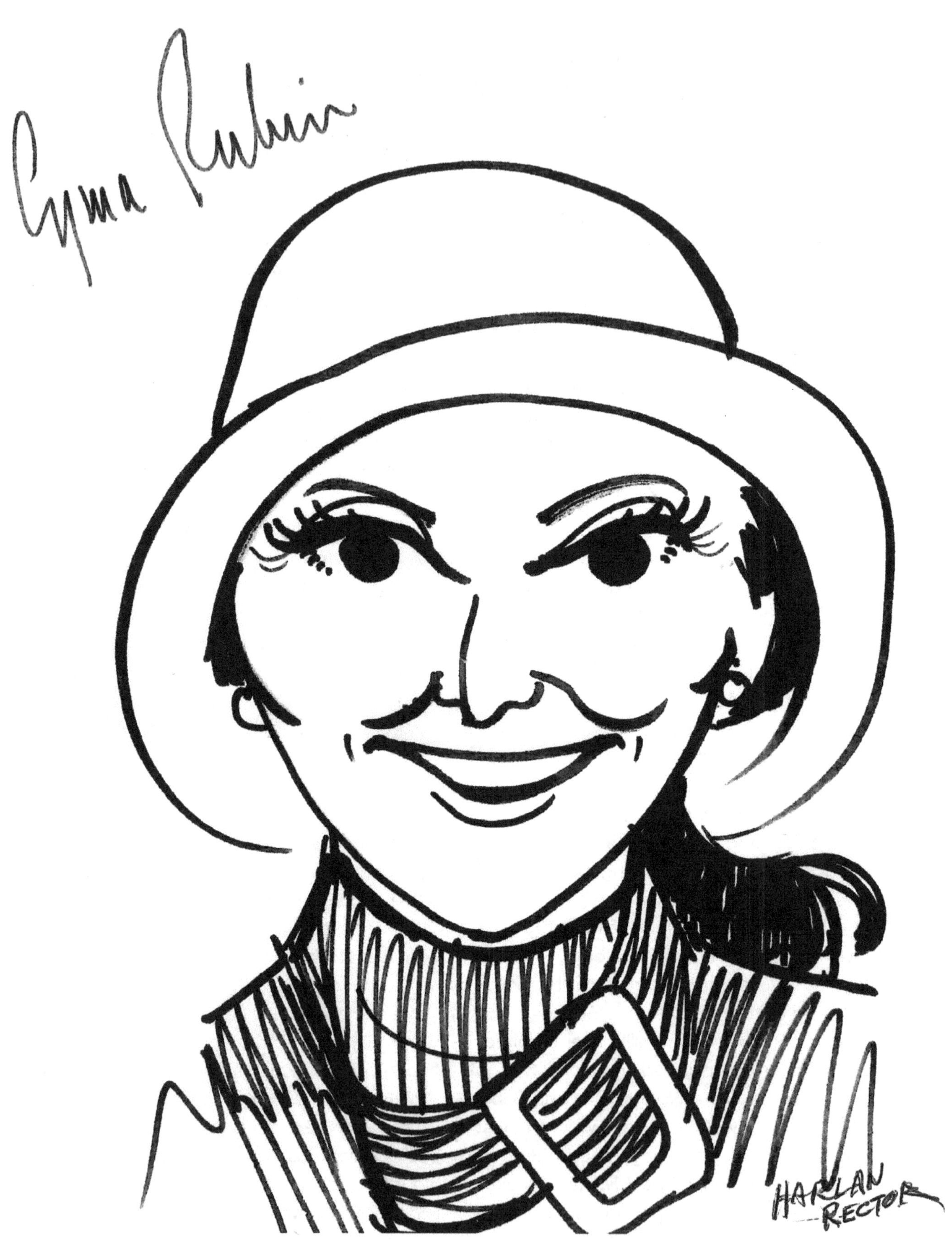

Gena Rubin
HARLAN
RECTOR

Cyma Rubin

Cyma Rubin, Tony and Emmy Award-winning producer, director, writer and president of Business of Entertainment, Inc. in New York, was at the top of her game when she was interviewed on WJR. Her feature film *Greaser's Palace*, released in 1972, was named Outstanding Film of the Year at the London Film Festival.

Cyma Saltzman was born in 1926 and grew up in Brooklyn. She earned a degree in textile engineering from North Carolina State University and graduated from the New York School of Interior Design. North Carolina State awarded her an Honorary Doctorate in Fine Arts and the Distinguished Alumni Award in 2003. Upon graduation, she founded the Pyxidium, Ltd. production company. She has produced a variety of media, including stage, television, movies, ads, ballet, and education, picking up numerous awards.

For her opening act, she produced the smash-hit revival of *No, No, Nanette*, which was nominated for six Tony awards and won four of them. Other theater credits include *Doctor Jazz* (which closed after five performances), *Mike, Porgy and Bess, I Love a Piano, Guys and Dolls,* and *Oh, Kay!*

She produced educational programs for Pepsi Cola, Movies-of-the-Week for CBS, and documentaries for Japanese television. In 2000, she curated, designed, and produced the first American exhibition of "Capture the Moment: The Pulitzer Prize Photographs," which 3 million people saw during its 13-year tour. She produced and directed a documentary on the collection entitled "Moment of Impact," which won a 2000 Emmy for Outstanding Historical Programming with Limited Dramatization-Programs. "Capture" is also available in book form.

Another million people have seen "The American Soldier: A Photographic Tribute from the Civil War to the War in Iraq," which she curated and produced. She was inspired to create the exhibit and subsequent book from her older brother's WWII experiences.

For Turner Network Television, she produced and directed "Moment of Impact: Stories of the Pulitzer Prize Photographs." It won the 1999 Emmy and Telly Awards for Best Documentary. Her feature film *Greaser's Palace* was named Outstanding Film of the Year at the London Film Festival. TV movies included *A Few Days in Weasel Creek*.

She appeared as herself in the 2006 movie *Jack Mitchell: My Life is Black and White*. She was the American producer for the American Ballet Theatre's tours to Japan. She married but divorced Dr. Martin Ackerman; they were the parents of Loni Ackerman, a tv, stage actress and cabaret singer. She later married Sam Rubin, president of Fabergé Perfume.

She is a member of the National Academy of Television Arts and Sciences, the Writers Guild of America East, the Overseas Press Club, National Press Photographers Association, the executive committee of the Weill Cornell Medical Council, and a trustee of the North Carolina Society of New York. Exhibits at the North Carolina Art Museum benefit from the Cyma Rubin Photography Fund. ∎

EDWARD MICKOLUS

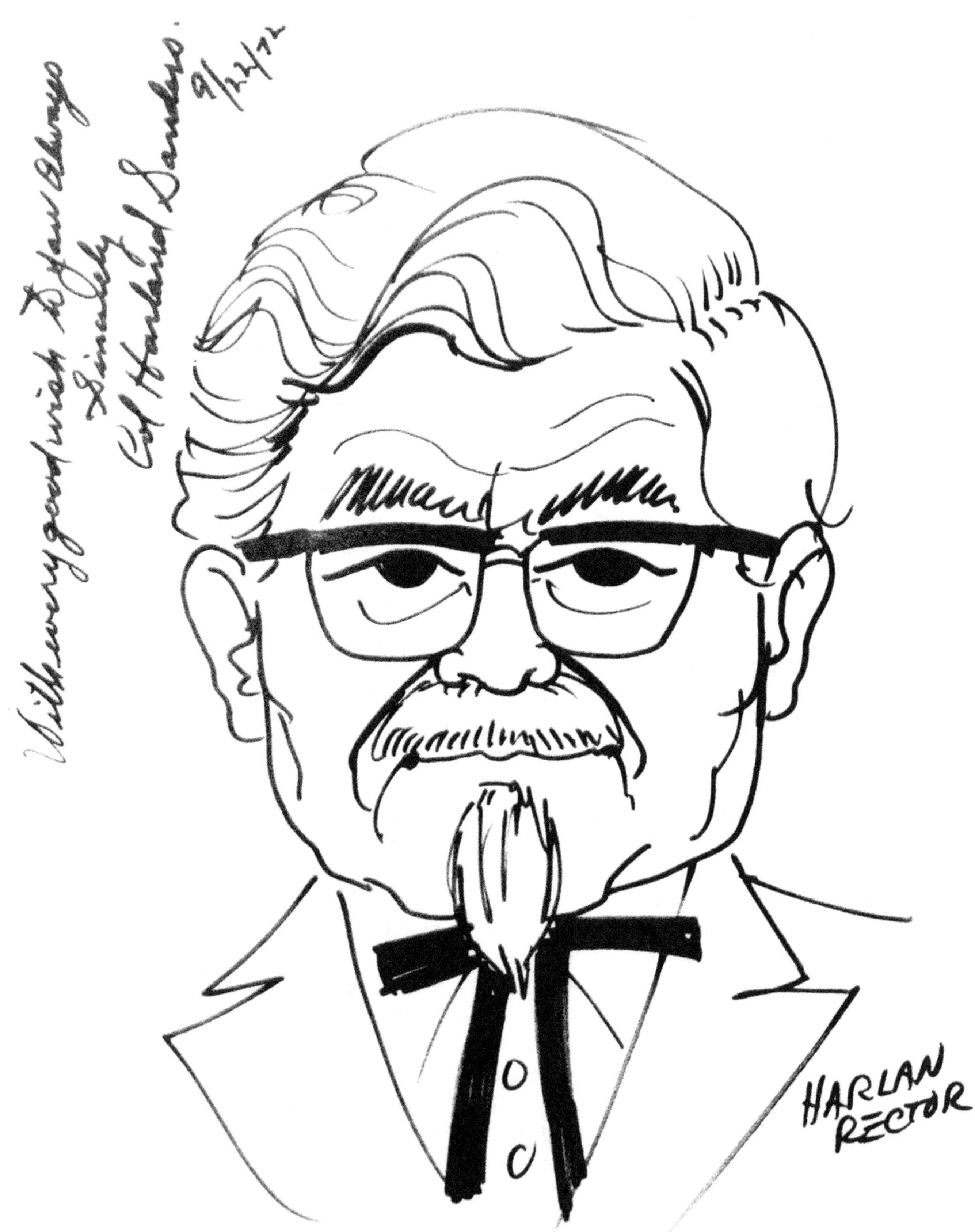

With every good wish to you always
Sincerely
Col Harland Sanders. 9/22/72
HARLAN
RECTOR

114

Col. Harland Sanders

Colonel Sanders achieved pop icon status with his Kentucky Fried Chicken empire in his mid-60's. His life story became an inspiration to millions.

Harland David Sanders was born into poverty on September 9, 1890, near Henryville, Indiana. His father died when Harland was five years old so his mother was often absent—working. "Algebra's what drove me off," Harland quit the seventh grade and left home only 13 years old. He drifted through many trades—farmer, blacksmith, buggy painter, janitor, streetcar conductor, railroad fireman, lawyer, insurance salesman, steamboat operator, secretary, and lighting manufacturer. He married, joined the Army with a falsified birth date, served in Cuba as a wagoner, was later honorably discharged before his wife left him, taking their baby and all before he turned twenty.

In 1929, North Corbin, Kentucky, Sanders opened a Shell service station that served food at one dining table set for six. Duncan Hines included the Café in his 1935 road-food guide. Sanders's popularity as a chef grew as he developed the pressure-cooker method of frying chicken. In 1937 he opened the Sanders Café, which seated 142. Fire destroyed the facility in 1939, the year he perfected the "finger-lickin' good" chicken recipe featuring his secret blend of 11 herbs and spices. He opened a restaurant/motel complex in 1940 along route US 25 and sold it sixteen years later to sell his KFC franchises—five sold the first two years with the first one in Salt Lake City, Utah.

Feeling like a failure, he contemplated suicide but while writing his will, a *Christmas Carol* moment changed him. "What might happen if he continued to live?" His wondering motivated him to find out. He borrowed $87 dollars and sold his chicken door to door. By 1964, more than 600 franchises dotted the US and Canada.

At 73 years old, Sanders signed most of KFC over to a group of investors for $2 million with a lifetime salary of $40,000 a year and a seat on the board of directors. He also made $1 million in a settlement lawsuit against his successors serving allegedly inferior fare. KFC was listed on the New York Stock Exchange in 1969. Heublein Corporation acquired the company in 1971 for $285 million—it had grown to 3,500 franchises and $700 million in annual sales. PepsiCo purchased KFC for $840 million in 1986.

Sanders continues to be KFC's public face. He donated hundreds of thousands of dollars to Canadian hospitals until he died of leukemia at age 90 in Shelbyville, Kentucky on December 16, 1980. By then, 6,000 KFC restaurants peppered 48 countries.

Check out his autobiographies: *Life as I Have Known It Has Been Finger Lickin' Good* and *The Autobiography of the Original Celebrity Chef*. He also released three Christmas albums. His image as a southern gentleman, sporting white hair and goatee, white double-breasted suits and black string ties, lives on in KFC television commercials. The restaurant he ran from 1940-1956, where he invented his secret recipe, is now the Harland Sanders Café and Museum in North Corbin. ■

EDWARD MICKOLUS

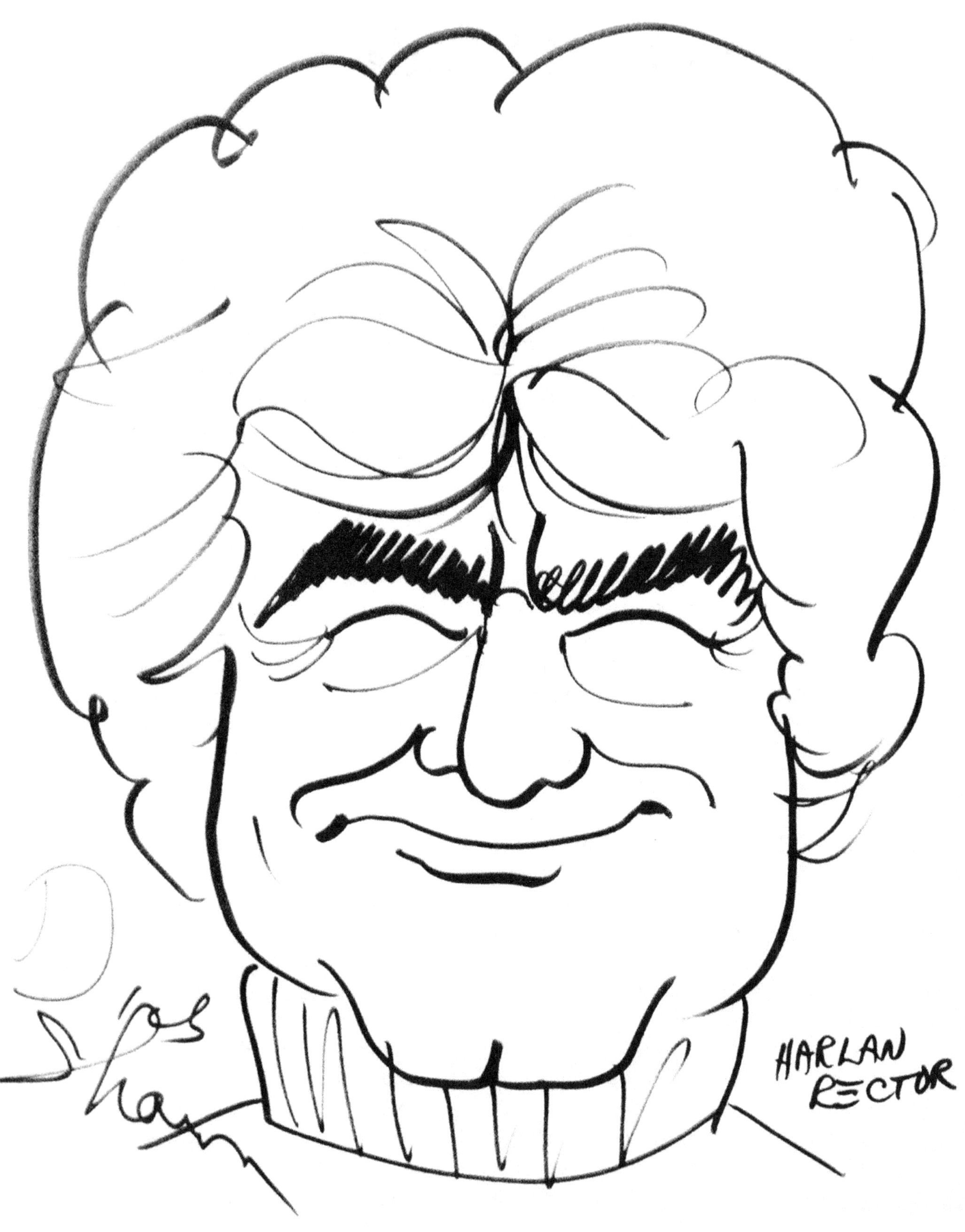

HARLAN
RECTOR

Dick Shawn

Dick Shawn was one of the greatest comedians ever. You can see his whacky style in the later work of Andy Kaufman, Steve Martin and Robin Williams. When he interviewed with WJR, his credits included the 1971 TV adaptation of *Dames at Sea* and the 1972, *Evil Roy Slade.*

Richard Schulefand was born in Buffalo, New York on December 1, 1923. His parents raised him and his brother in the back room of his father's clothing store in Lackawanna.

His baseball playing career ended days after signing with the Chicago White Sox when he was drafted into the Army. The USO featured him as a comedian. Upon discharge, he studied at the University of Miami, but left early for a successful audition as a comic for Arthur Godfrey's Talent Scouts, shortening his name to Shawn.

Shawn worked as a stand-up comedian for 35 years in nightclubs around the world. His signature one-man show, "The Second Greatest Entertainer in the Whole Wide World," started with him emerging from a pile of bricks in the center of the stage.

Shawn appeared in more than 30 movies, seven Broadway productions, released an album and four singles. His most remembered performances were as a counterculture character in such madcap classics as *The Producers*, where he portrayed a singing Adolf Hitler, and *It's a Mad, Mad, Mad, Mad World.*

He succeeded on stage in *A Funny Thing Happened on the Way to the Forum.* His voiceover work included *The Year Without a Santa Claus.* He was a frequent guest on various incarnations of *The Tonight Show* hosted by Steve Allen and Johnny Carson. He filled in as guest host for a vacationing Carson on January 1, 1971, on *The Tonight Show* which ran its last televised cigarette ad for Virginia Slims before such ads were banned.

He played on *Password*, performed on the *Ed Sullivan Show*, the *I Love Lucy Show*, the *Judy Garland Show*, and *Celebrity Cabaret*. He also played in television dramas and comedies including such titles as *Three's Company*, *St. Elsewhere*, *Magnum PI*, *Amazing Stories*, and *Faerie Tale Theater*. Shawn was even in a music video for the raucous rock band Ratt. Some credit Shawn with inventing the High Five during the Springtime for Hitler scene in which David Patch as Joseph Goebbels slapped his outstretched raised hand.

Shawn and his wife had four children. One of his daughters married John Travolta's older brother Joey.

Shawn died at age 63 on stage at the University of California, San Diego's Mandeville Hall of a heart attack on April 17, 1987. Ironically, his last line was, "If elected, I will not lay down on the job," after which he collapsed face-down on the stage. The audience assumed it was part of the shtick. The stage crew knew Shawn could do anything, anytime, on stage, so they didn't react because they too thought it was all part of his bit. This time they were all wrong, but even in death, he still got the laughs. ■

EDWARD MICKOLUS

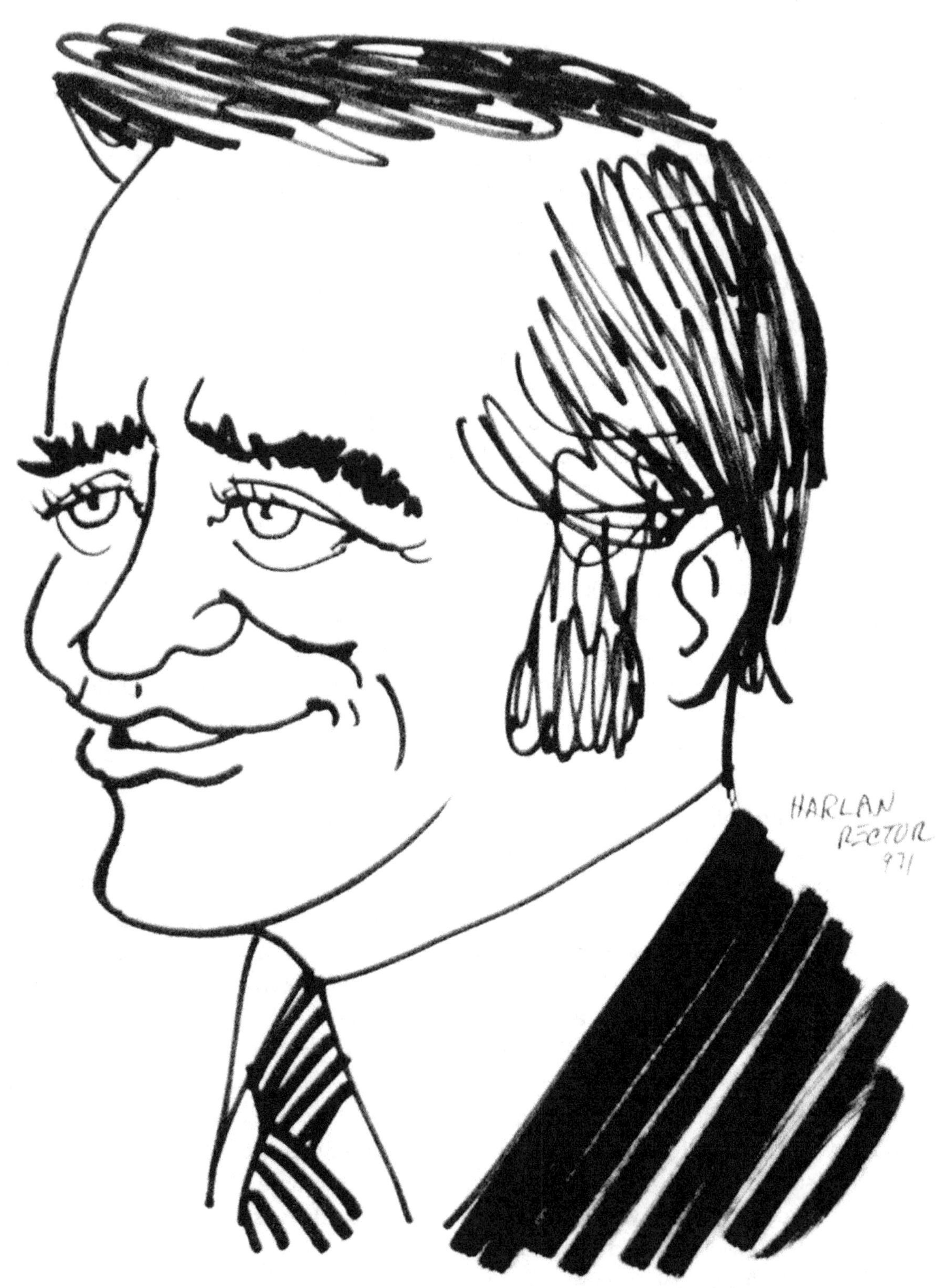

Max Showalter
HARLAN
RECTOR
971

Max Showalter

By the time Max Showalter visited WJR radio for his interview in 1972, he had performed multiple roles on stage, appeared in 41 movies, and 28 television shows. Showalter was 55 years old when I sketched his caricature.

Max Showalter was born on June 2, 1917, in Caldwell, Kansas, the son of Elma Roxana, a music teacher, and Ira Edward Showalter, a banker, farmer, and oil man. As a toddler, Max accompanied his mother to local theaters where she played piano as a soundtrack to silent movies. Elma taught and encouraged Max's musical interest, and even though his career was sustained by acting, he was also a composer, singer, and pianist.

Showalter's most memorable stage role was as Horace Vendergelder in the Broadway hit show *Hello, Dolly!* opposite Carol Channing, whose caricature and bio are included in this book.

20th Century Fox signed Showalter as a featured contract player in the late 1940s. Darryl F. Zanuck, Fox's founder, changed Showalter's name to Casey Adams because he thought it sounded more "bankable." As Casey, his feature film debut was in *Always Leave Them Laughing* in 1949, and his second feature film, *With a Song in my Heart*, had him singing along with David Wayne. Showalter wrote the film's song, "Hoe That Corn." Adams appeared alongside Marilyn Monroe in *Niagara* in 1953 and in the movie *Bus Stop* in 1956.

Of the 41 movies in which Showalter appeared, one of the most memorable roles was that of a deaf man being "spiritually touched" by a female evangelist, played by Jean Simmons, in 1960s *Elmer Gantry*. Showalter's breathtaking, sobbing portrayal stole the show. Showalter had impressive roles in two other big budget movies, *The Music Man* in 1962, and *How to Murder Your Wife* in 1965.

Showalter appeared in television shows like *The Loretta Young Show*, *The Doris Day Show*, and *The Lucy Show* and series such as *The Twilight Zone, Gunsmoke, Bewitched, Dr. Kildare, Surfside 6*, and *Kojak*. As Casey Adams, he portrayed Ward Cleaver in the original pilot for the 1950s sitcom *Leave It to Beaver*. By the time the sitcom premiered, however, Adams was replaced by Hugh Beaumont.

Max Showalter worked constantly, although his roles were mostly supporting actor types. He was a very good visual actor and most of his roles were lighthearted, so film and stage goers felt that he enjoyed talking and playing to an audience. Showalter's distinctive voice and exuberance left an indelible mark on audiences, as his fun was contagious.

In 1984, Max Showalter retired to Chester, Connecticut near his good friend Katharine Hepburn who lived in Old Saybrook, Connecticut. He died of cancer at age 83 on July 30, 2000. ∎

HARLAN RECTOR

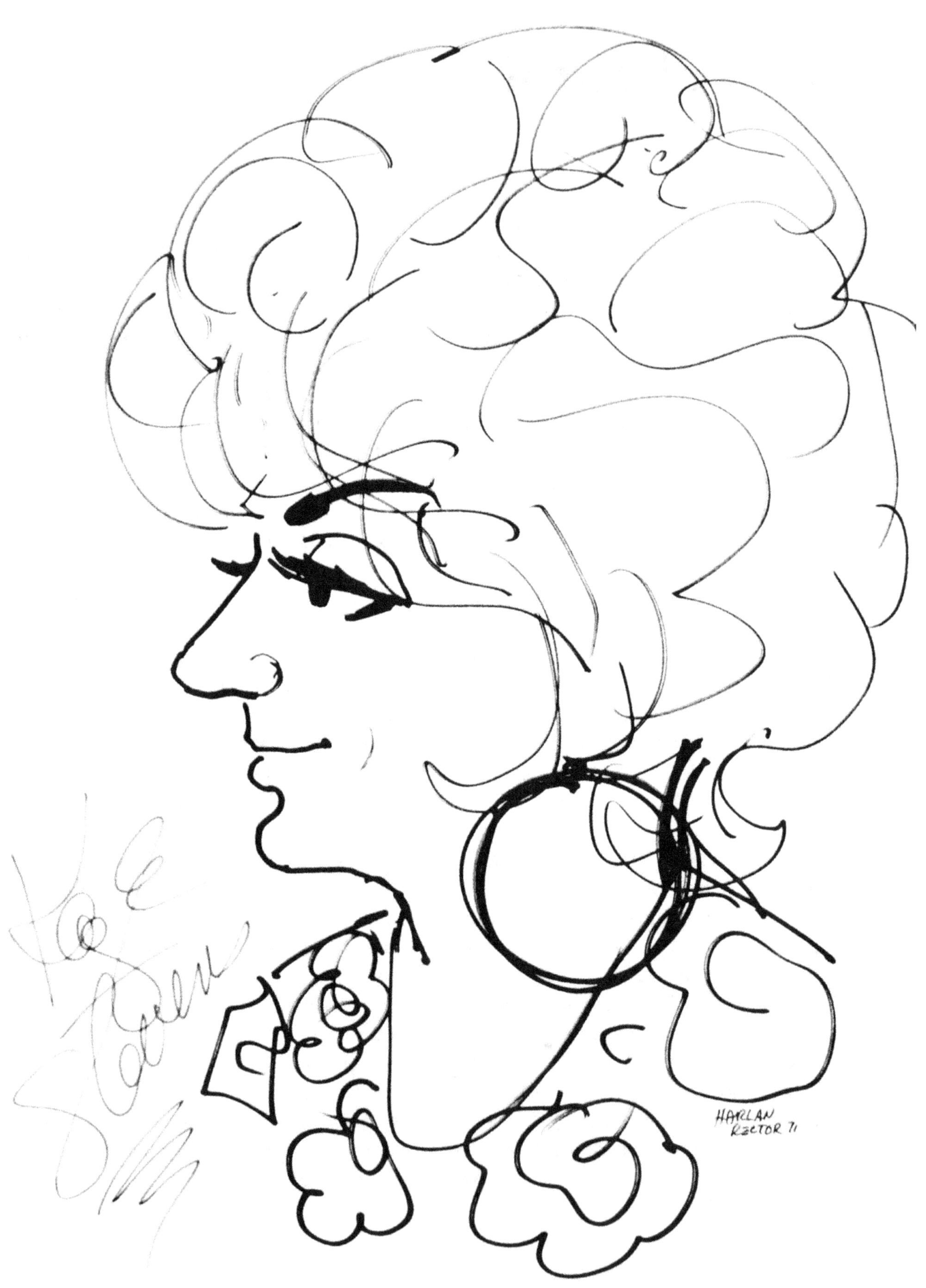

HARLAN
RECTOR 71

Kaye Stevens

The always striking Kaye Stevens was a popular singer, soap opera and movie actress, and game show contestant when she visited WJR.

Catherine Louise Stephens was born in Pittsburgh on July 21, 1932. An only child, in her teenage years in Cleveland she became a drummer and singer.

She got her big break as a lounge singer at the Riviera Hotel in Las Vegas when headliner Debbie Reynolds took ill and Stevens filled in. She went on to perform shows in New York City's Waldorf Astoria and Caesar's Palace on the Strip. She soon was singing to SRO audiences in New York City, Miami, and Los Angeles, and eventually touring with The Rat Pack, Johnny Carson, and Bob Hope's USO tour to Vietnam.

During the USO tour, she gave each soldier a pair of her iconic elbow-length gloves, vowing that if they brought them to any performance, she'd give them free admission. Over the next 40 years, nearly 2/3 of the gloves were returned by former servicemen.

She sang on the *Dean Martin Show*, *The Tonight Show, Hollywood Palace, Toast of the Town, Playboy After Dark*, and *The Ed Sullivan Show*. Her four singles and six albums included *Not So Great Songs That Were Left Out of Great Movies for Obvious Reasons*.

At the height of the television celebrity game show fad, her sunny disposition landed her on *Match Game, Hollywood Squares, Celebrity Sweepstakes, $25,000 Pyramid, The Price is Right, Password*, and *Tattletales*. She placed a sign next to her nameplate that read "Hello Margate," a reference to her home town for 50 years, landing her the nickname "The First Lady of Margate." The town would eventually name a city park for her.

Her movie career began in 1962 with *The Interns*, followed two years later by *The New Interns*, for which she received a Golden Globe nomination for Best Supporting Actress. She also acted in *The Man from the Diners' Club*, the TV movie *Let's Switch!*, and *Jaws 3-D*. She was in consideration for the leading role in *Funny Girl*, a role that eventually went to a then newcomer named Barbra Streisand.

During her longtime role on the soap opera *Days of Our Lives*, she premiered her song "You Light Up My Life." Inspired by its success, she created an album of inspirational, motivational, and spiritual pop music. Her growing fame led to guest starring appearances on *CHiPs, Police Woman, Superboy, BL Stryker*, and *Hour of Power*.

Kaye Stevens died at age 79 on December 28, 2011. Scores of people left remembrances on her digital memorial page detailing how their lives were touched by her kindness and grace. Bob Hope included her in his book *Five Women I Love*. ∎

EDWARD MICKOLUS

To J.P.
Very Best
Wishes +
congratulations
Larry
Storch
HARLAN
RECTOR

Larry Storch

The effervescent Larry Storch was always a good interview. Quick on his feet, refined comedic skills, he always had a comeback for anything thrown his way. For that reason, he was often invited back to variety and talk shows, including Johnny Carson's *The Tonight Show*.

Larry Storch was born in New York City on January 8, 1923. He attended De-Witt-Clinton High School in The Bronx with fellow actor Don Adams of *Get Smart*. They remained close friends all of their lives.

Storch hit the stage early. He began working as a stand-up comic for $12 per week in local theaters at the young age of twelve.

When World War II broke out, Storch enlisted in the Navy and served on the *USS Proteus* submarine alongside fellow crew member Tony Curtis.

After his stint in the Navy, Storch hitchhiked his way from Los Angeles to New York City and was picked up by bandleader Phil Harris. Storch told Harris he was a comedian and proceeded to regale Harris with a stream of impressions. Arriving in Los Angeles, Harris pulled into Ciro's Nightclub on Sunset Boulevard, where Lucille Ball was watching Desi Arnaz rehearsing with his band. After hearing some of Storch's impressions, Ball told him to show up the next night, because he would serve as the opening act for her husband.

Storch leveraged his impressions and comedic stage act as a springboard, being cast on many TV programs including *Car 54, Where are You?, Get Smart, I Dream of Jeannie, Gilligan's Island,* and many others.

He was a regular on numerous variety shows including *Sonny and Cher, Laugh-In, The Ed Sullivan Show, The Tonight Show,* and *The Jackie Gleason Show*, where he was a favorite of Gleason's. Storch kept his hosts and TV audiences entertained with his quick-witted comebacks, hundreds of impressions and dialects, including spot-on imitations of Muhammad Ali, Frank Morgan, and Claude Rains.

Because of his versatility, Storch was in high demand as an actor, comedian, impressionist, and voiceover actor. He notably performed as Mr. Whoopee on *Tennessee Tuxedo and his Friends*. Some of his other TV and film voiceover work included *The Batman/Superman Hour, The Brady Kids, Koko the Clown,* and *Treasure Island*.

Storch is best remembered for his portrayal of the bumbling Corporal Agarn in *F-Troop*. The show ran from 1965–1967, but the Corporal Agarn character is indelibly imprinted in the memories of millions of baby boomers. With his cavalry hat brim sticking straight-up, viewers immediately knew this zany character was destined to be consistently used in memorable ways. Many years after *F-Troop* had been cancelled, Storch continued to be approached by fans both on the street and in his appearances, wanting to talk about Corporal Agarn. Storch always said, "It tickles me every time Agarn is mentioned."

Larry Storch was married to Norma Catherine Greve for 43 years, until her death in 2003. In 2019, Larry was named Honorary Friary at a ceremony with Dick Cavett at the New York Friars Club and on his 97th birthday, Storch was presented with a Proclamation from New York. ∎

GREG BARRY

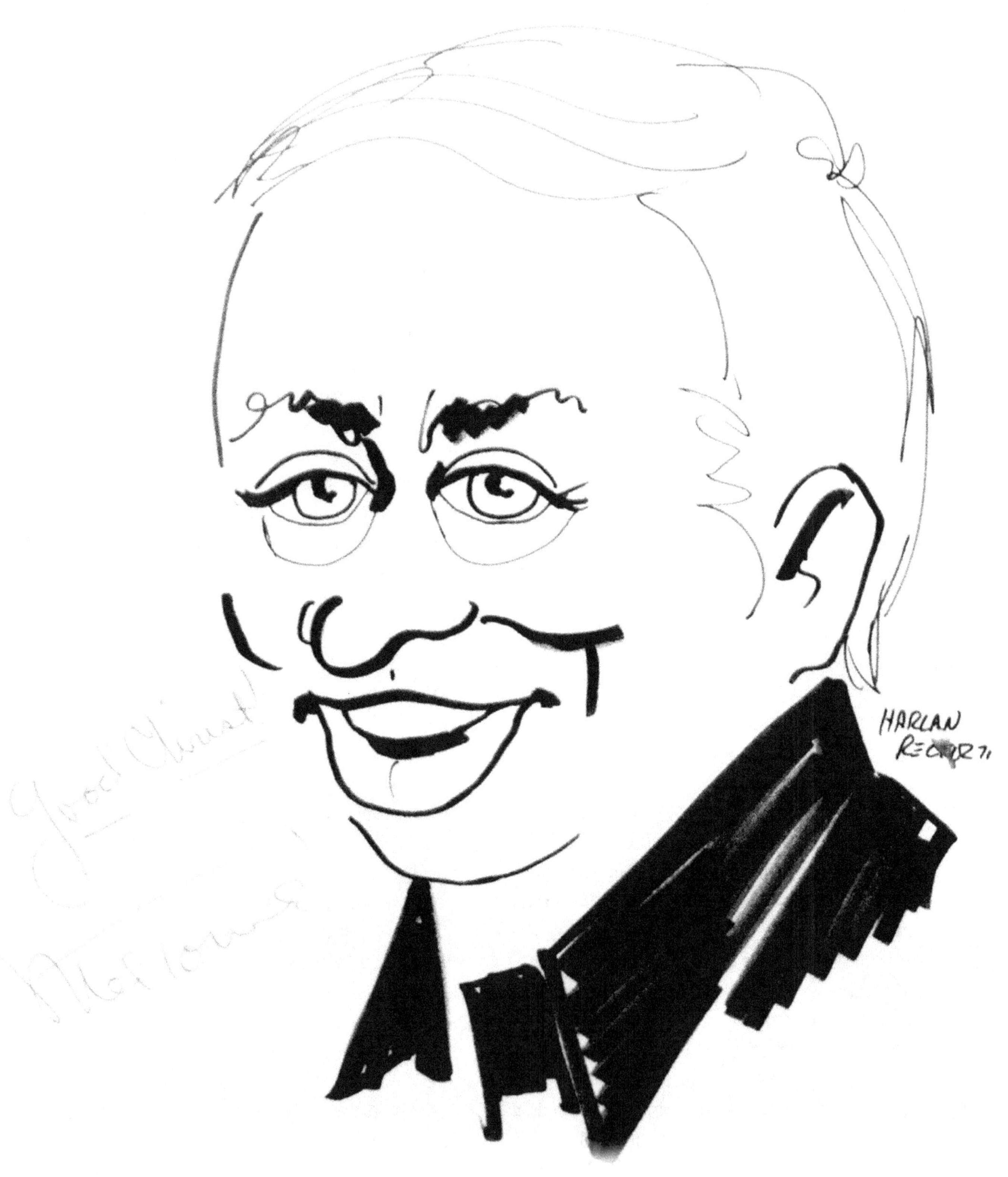

Mel Torme

Mel Torme was one of the most accomplished jazz singers of the 20th Century. As a child prodigy, he sang professionally at age four with the Coon-Sanders Orchestra in Chicago.

Melvin Howard Torma was born on September 13, 1925, in Chicago, Illinois, to Russian Jewish immigrant parents. He later changed his surname to Torme.

Torme began playing drums at the Shakespeare Elementary School, performing in their drum and bugle corps. He said at the time he knew music would be a big part of his life. At age 17, he joined Chico Marx's band as a drummer and singer.

Shortly thereafter, Torme branched out into radio performing and musical arrangement. As a talented and versatile performer, he made his film debut in 1943 in *Higher and Higher* with Frank Sinatra.

In 1945, after being discharged early from the Army for flat feet, Torme formed his own vocal quintet, the Mel-Tones, which was one of the first jazz-influenced vocal groups. The band included notable singers Les Baxter and Ginny O'Connor. They had a number one hit titled *Careless Hands*. A few years later they were fronting Artie Shaw's band and had several hits, including Cole Porter's *What is This Thing Called Love*.

During a performance at New York's Copacabana nightclub, local disc jockey Fred Robbins gave Torme the nickname "The Velvet Fog," recognizing his high tenor voice and his smooth vocal style. Torme disliked the nickname, jokingly rewording it as "this velvet frog voice." However, the nickname stuck for the rest of his career.

In 1949, Torme began recording for Capitol Records. He recorded two of his signature songs, *Again*, by Lionel Newman and Dorcus Cochran, and *Blue Moon*, by Richard Rodgers and Lorenz Hart.

In addition to performing nationally, Torme hosted the radio program *Mel Torme Time*. He also found time to write *The Christmas Song*, which begins with these famous lyrics, "Chestnuts roasting on an open fire."

The years 1955-1957 were prolific for Torme. He recorded seven jazz vocal records and became highly respected among his contemporaries for his well-refined arranging abilities. In the 1960s, Torme ventured into television. He wrote and arranged music for *The Judy Garland Show*, making several guest appearances as well. He was in high demand for other guest appearances as himself, most notably on *Night Court* and *Seinfeld*.

While Torme was involved in many creative endeavors and a wide variety of professions, his first love was singing. In 1982 and 1983, he received Grammy Awards for Best Jazz Vocalist, and in 1999 he was awarded the Grammy Lifetime Achievement Award.

Mel Torme was married four times, had five children plus two step children. He suffered a stroke in 1996, ending his singing career. He died in Los Angeles after another stroke on June 5, 1999. ∎

GREG BARRY

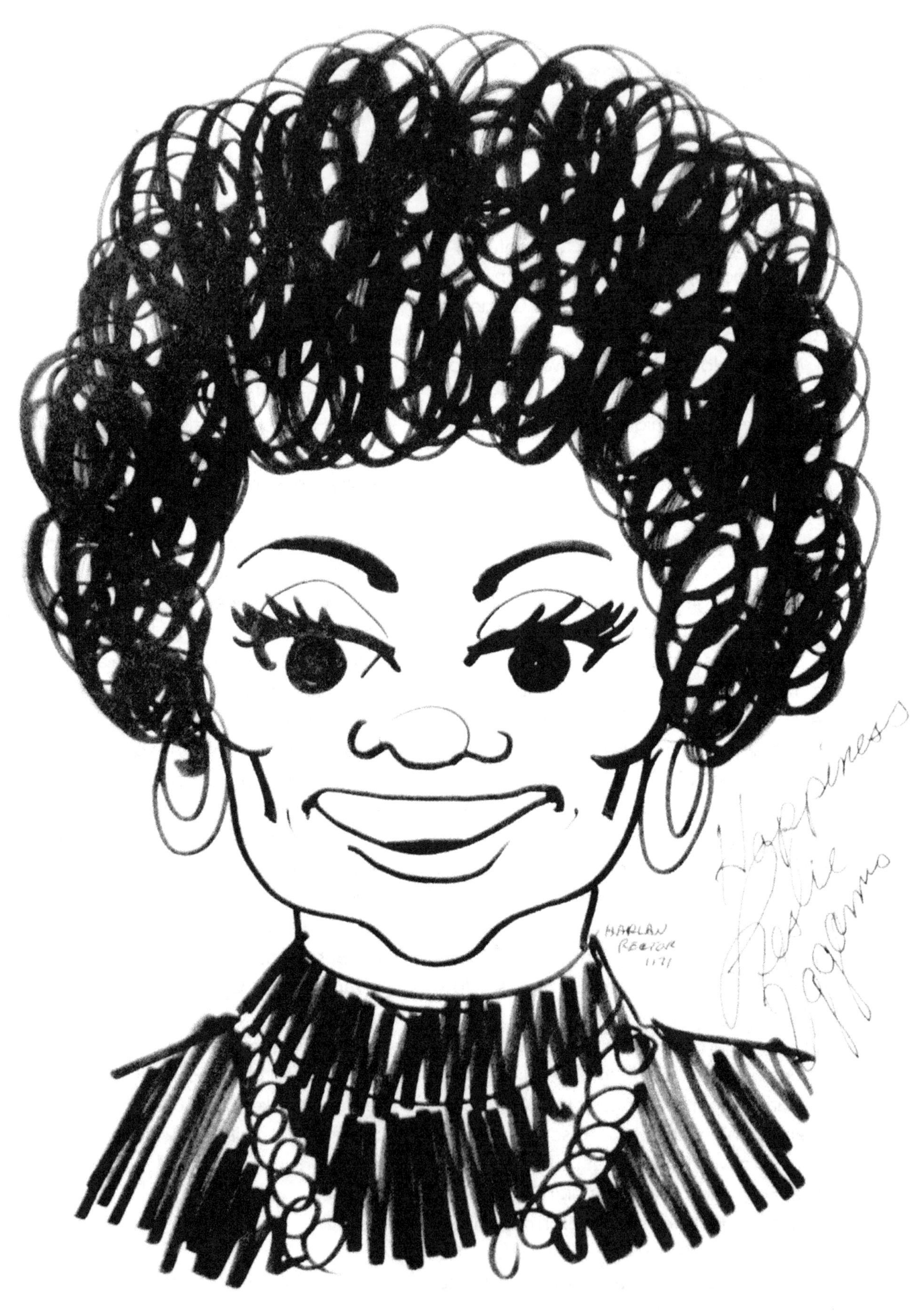
HARLAN
RECTOR
1/71
Happiness
Leslie
Uggams

Leslie Uggams

American actress and singer Leslie Marian Uggams was born May 25, 1943, in Harlem. She was the daughter of Juanita Ernestine (Smith), a Cotton Club chorus girl/dancer, and Harold Coyden Uggams, an elevator operator and maintenance man.

Uggams started show business as a child in 1951, attending the Professional Children's School of New York and Juilliard. She made her professional debut on *Stars and Stardust* and performed on *Arthur Godfrey's Talent Scouts*, but she got her biggest break on *The Lawrence Welk Show*. In 1954, ten-year-old Uggams made a record for MGM, which included a reworking of the song *Santa Baby*. In 1958, a record executive signed her for two records, *One More Sunrise* and *House Built on Sand*, which made *Billboard Magazine's* charts.

In 1969, she appeared in her own television variety show, *The Leslie Uggams Show*, which was the first network variety show to be hosted by a black person since *The Nat King Cole Show* in the 1950s. She had a lead role in the miniseries *Roots*, for which she received an Emmy nomination, and starred in *Backstairs at the White House* for which she was nominated for an Emmy Award for Best Actress.

Uggams also made guest appearances on such popular television shows as Family *Guy* (as herself), *I Spy, Hollywood Squares, The Muppet Show, The Love Boat*, and *Magnum PI*, and played the role of Rose Keefer on *All My Children*. In 1983, she won a Daytime Emmy Award as a host of the NBC game show *Fantasy*.

Her film career includes roles in *Skyjacked, Black Girl*, and *Poor Pretty Eddie*. She later appeared in *Sugar Hill* opposite Wesley Snipes and received renewed notice with her appearances alongside Ryan Reynolds as Blind Al in the MARVEL anti-superhero film *Deadpool* as well as the sequel *Deadpool 2*. She also portrayed Leah Walker, the bipolar mother of Lucious Lyon in the Fox hit series *Empire*.

Stage credits included starring in *Hallelujah, Baby!* after Lena Horne declined the role of Georgina and won the Tony Award for Best Actress in a musical. Other Broadway work included *Blues in the Night, Jerry's Girls, Thoroughly Modern Millie* and many other popular Broadway productions.

As an accomplished singer, Uggams released a series of songs and albums with Atlantic and Columbia Records and was featured on the Supersisters trading card set. ∎

JEFF RECTOR

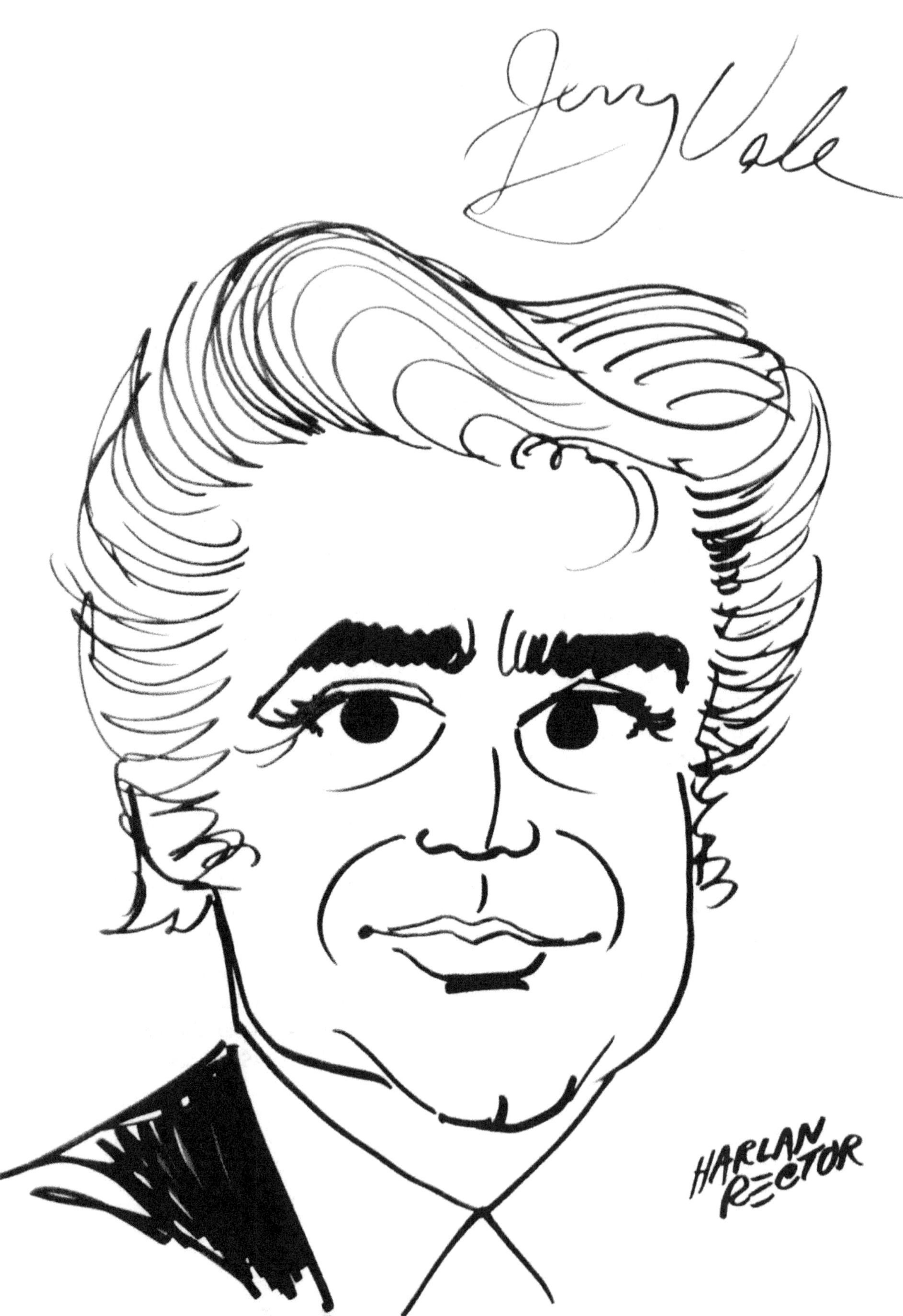

Jerry Vale
HARLAN
RECTOR

Jerry Vale

Romantic balladeer and forever handsome actor Jerry Vale had three hits on the Adult Contemporary charts when he stopped by WJR in the early 1970s.

Genaro Louis Vitaliano was born on July 8, 1930 in The Bronx, New York. His singing career began at age 11, when he got better tips as a shoeshine boy if he sang. By age 15, the high tenor was serenading diners at supper clubs with love songs. He said his crooning was inspired by Perry Como and Bing Crosby. He was featured on *Ted Mack's Amateur Hour* in 1950.

After signing up with Mitch Miller, he had his first hit in 1953 with *You Can Never Give Me Back My Heart*. The 1950s and 1960s saw him selling millions with the chart-topping *You Don't Know Me, And This is My Beloved,* and *Have You Looked into Your Heart*. His Italian versions of *Innamorata (Sweetheart), Volare (I Will Fly),* and *Al Di Là (Beyond),* became classic Italian-American favorites.

The New York Times reported in 1964 that he was the third best-selling male singer, after Tony Bennett and Andy Williams. Many of his more than 50 albums and hundreds of singles sold well. He was popular on television and in clubs throughout the 1970s and 1980s.

His *The Star-Spangled Banner* was the first song inducted into the National Baseball Hall of Fame in Cooperstown, New York. The former stickball player owned the Daytona Beach Admirals minor league team, which he sold to the New York Mets in the late 1980s.

Vale was an honorary pallbearer at the 1998 funeral of his longtime friend Frank Sinatra, who ratcheted-up Vale's live-performance career at the Las Vegas Sands Hotel and Casino with a 22-week, four show a day residency.

Vale was a regular on eponymous shows hosted by Steve Allen, Jack Paar, Johnny Carson, Ed Sullivan, David Letterman, Joey Bishop, Jonathan Winters, Jimmy Dean, Merv Griffin, Howard Stern, and Mike Douglas, as well as on *Hollywood Squares*.

He appeared as himself in *Goodfellas, Casino, The Sopranos,* and *Who's the Boss,* and played a lounge singer in *A Wake in Providence*. Vale's mob movie legacy continued when Stephen Van Zandt (mob consigliere Silvio Dante in *The Sopranos* and guitarist in Bruce Springsteen's E Street Band) portrayed Vale in Martin Scorsese's Oscar-nominated *The Irishman*.

Scorsese lauded Vale as one of the great easy listening voices of his childhood, saying, "It was like a family member in a way; that voice was so familiar and comforting."

In 2000, Richard Grudens released the biography *Jerry Vale: A Singer's Life*.

Vale stopped performing after a stroke in 2002. He died at age 83 on May 18, 2014, at his home in Palm Desert, California. He was married for 55 years to Rita Grapel, a former burlesque dancer. ∎

EDWARD MICKOLUS

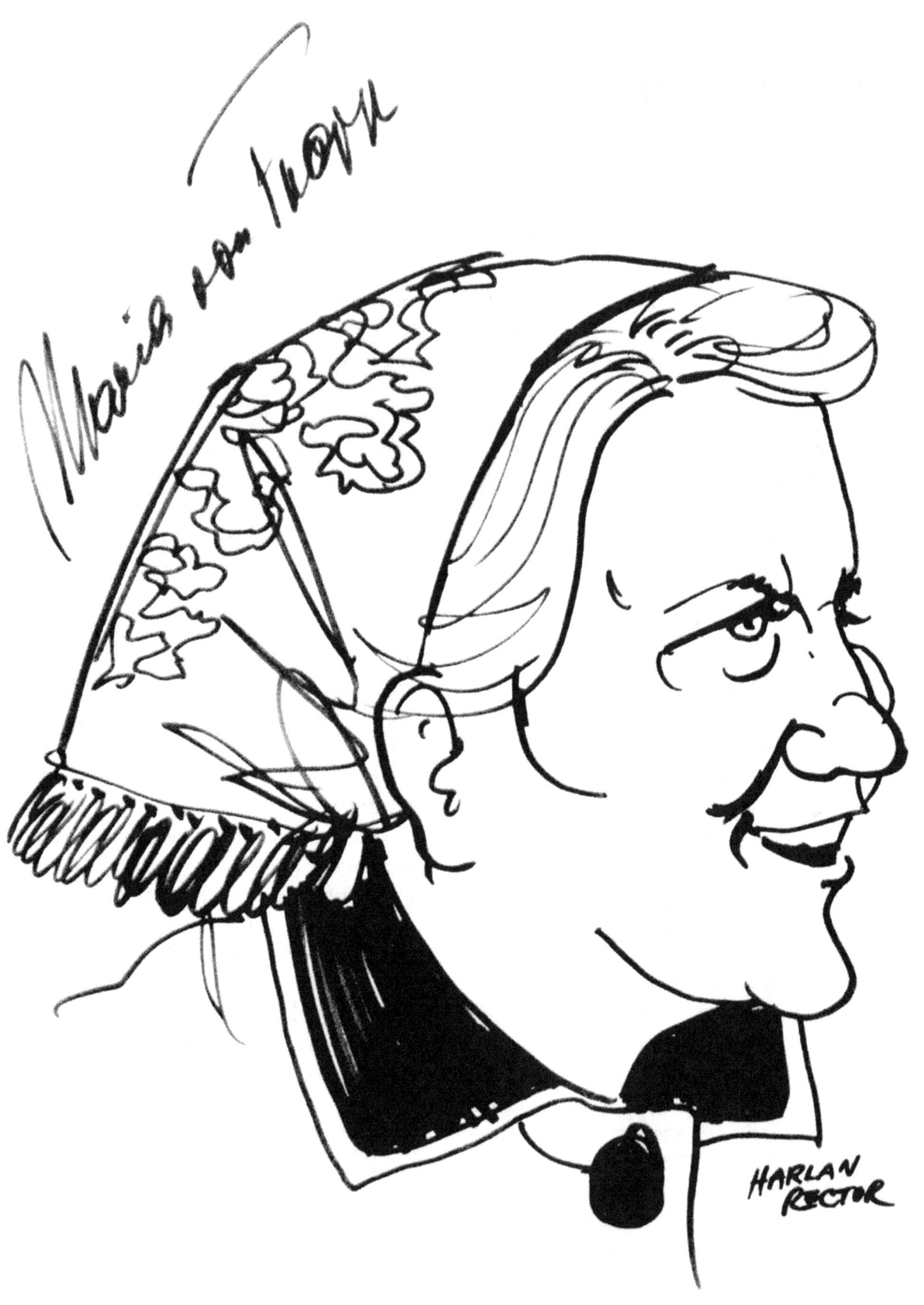

Maria von Trapp
HARLAN
RECTOR

Maria Von Trapp

Maria von Trapp was the stepmother of the von Trapp Family Singers who were internationally recognized as a musical family with a compelling back story.

Maria Augusta Kutschera was born on a train traveling from Tyrol to Vienna, Austria, on January 26, 1905. Only two years old when her mother died, she was sent away by her father to be raised by other relatives. It was an unstable environment in which Maria was regularly mistreated by her Uncle Franz, who had assumed guardianship.

Maria ran away at age 15 after she graduated from high school. She wanted to become a tutor, but instead found work as a tennis umpire. She saved enough money to enter the State Teachers College for Progressive Education in Vienna. After graduating college at 19, she entered Nonnberg Abbey, a Benedictine monastery, to become a nun.

As a teacher at the monastery, Maria was asked by Georg von Trapp, a naval commander and widower, to teach one of his children after his wife Agatha died of scarlet fever. Maria accepted the assignment and eventually taught all seven of the von Trapp children.

Captain von Trapp could sense the joy Maria brought the children and asked her to marry him. Maria was confused, as she had intended to become a nun so she returned to the monastery seeking guidance. She was told, "It's God's will to marry the Captain."

Maria accepted the proposal and learned to love Georg, later realizing she had never loved someone so deeply. They were married on November 26, 1927 and had three children together over the next 12 years.

In 1935, Georg faced financial ruin from a failed bank, so they laid off their servants and moved to the upper floor of their home, renting out the lower level. A Roman Catholic clergyman, Reverend Franz Wasner, agreed to open a chapel in their home and lived there as a guest.

The children often sang during holidays and festivals. After Father Wasner moved in, the children became more professional and organized. After assuming the role of conductor and personal chaplain, the von Trapps soon entered musical contests where their popularity grew.

When Austria was annexed by Germany in 1938, life became more difficult as they witnessed the Nazis' mistreatment of Jews and other Austrian citizens. The family fled Austria when Georg was conscripted into the German navy. They traveled to Italy, then England, and eventually to the United States. They learned their home was used as Heinrich Himmler's headquarters.

The von Trapp family would go on to enjoy great success touring the United States, Canada, and beyond, selling out internationally. The ten singing children toured together for nearly two decades. Their story was brought to the Broadway stage in 1959 where it played for three years. It inspired the film version, starring Julie Andrews and Christopher Plummer, which won five Academy Awards and two Golden Globes—the highest grossing film of 1965.

In the 1940s the family moved to Stowe, Vermont, to establish a music camp and lodge. The children moved on in different directions after their musical careers ended and Maria spent the rest of her life in Morrisville, Vermont, where she died of heart failure on March 28, 1987.◼

GREG BARRY

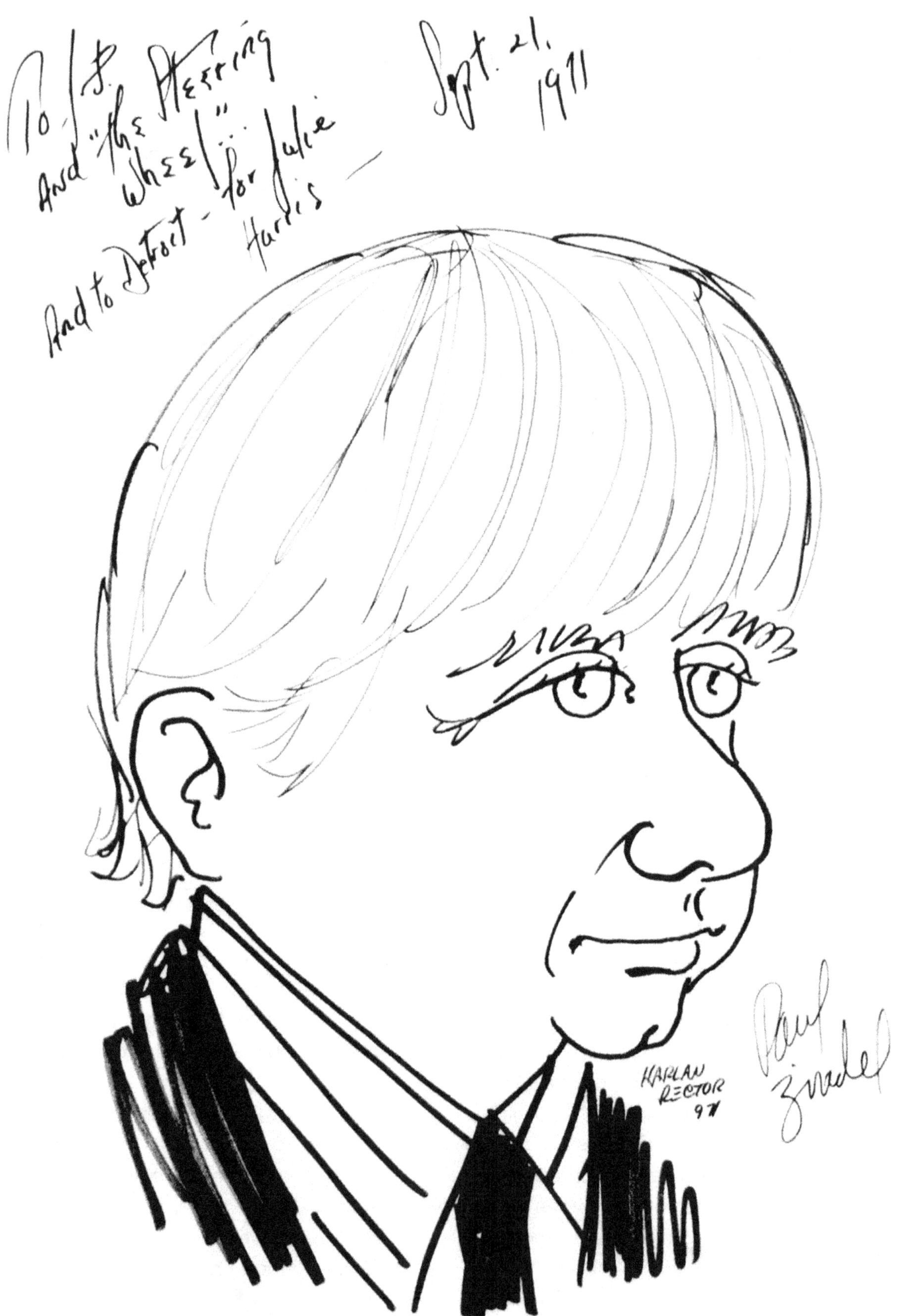
To J. P. Herring
And "The Steering
Wheel"
And to Detroit — for Julie
Harris
Sept. 21,
1977
HARLAN
RECTOR
97
Paul
Zindel

Paul Zindel

Paul Zindel, Jr., was at the top of his game and fame when he visited Detroit. His Pulitzer Prize-winning two-act play, *The Effect of Gamma Rays on Man-in-the-Moon Marigolds*, became a movie in 1972, produced by Paul Newman and starring Joanne Woodward.

Zindel was born on May 15, 1936, on Staten Island, New York. When Paul was two, his father ran off with a mistress. His mother took a series of failed odd jobs to make ends meet, often threatening suicide along the way. Paul grew up in a "house of fear." He day dreamed of worlds that could be, rather than experience the world he grew up in. He escaped the house at age 15, when he was quarantined for 18 months with tuberculosis. He used the hospital time to write his first play. He studied creative writing under his mentor, the playwright Edward Albee.

Upon graduating from Wagner College with a Bachelor's in chemistry and education, and later a Master's in chemistry, he became a technical writer for Allied Chemical. He soon moved on to teach chemistry at Tottenville High School in Staten Island for several years. As a hobby, he wrote such plays as *Dimensions of Peacocks* and *A Dream of Swallows*, which were performed in New York City. With his growing successes, he focused on storytelling, becoming a famous playwright, screenwriter, and author of young adult books.

The prolific Zindel could write for any audience; his output included 53 books (52 of which were for children or teens, many of them autobiographical), eight plays, two short story collections, and eight Hollywood television or movie screenplays. His prolific writing included the screenplays for such titles as *Alice in Wonderland*, *Babes in Toyland*, *Up the Sandbox*, *Runaway Train*, *A Connecticut Yankee in King Arthur's Court*, and *Mame*, starring performers like Keanu Reeves, Barbra Streisand, Lucille Ball, Drew Barrymore, Robert Mitchum, Rebecca DeMornay, Nastassja Kinski, and Jon Voight.

His plays and novels drew upon his difficult teen years, showing how the lives and feelings of adolescents matter. *Marigolds* focused on an abusive, stressed mother and her two daughters, one of whom overcomes her fraught home life via the scientific studies of marigolds.

His first young adult novel sold seven million copies. *The Pigman* examined the betrayed friendship between high school sophomores and a widower whose ceramic pig collection is accidentally smashed during a teen party. *The Pigman* was named the American Library Association's Best Young Adult Book. It is often taught in US schools, but has also appeared on lists for banned books.

His multiple YA series spoke to teens about loneliness, abuse, sex, contraception, abortion, death, love, being left out, friendship, parental pressure, bullying, and truth. He penned hilarious titles, including *My Darling, My Hamburger*; *I Never Loved Your Mind*; *Pardon Me, You're Stepping on My Eyeball!*; *The Undertaker's Gone Bananas*; *Confessions of a Teenage Baboon*; *and Attacks of the Killer Fishsticks*, all books that speak to the emotional underpinnings of teens' concerns.

Zindel died at age 66 in New York City from lung cancer on March 27, 2003. ∎

EDWARD MICKOLUS

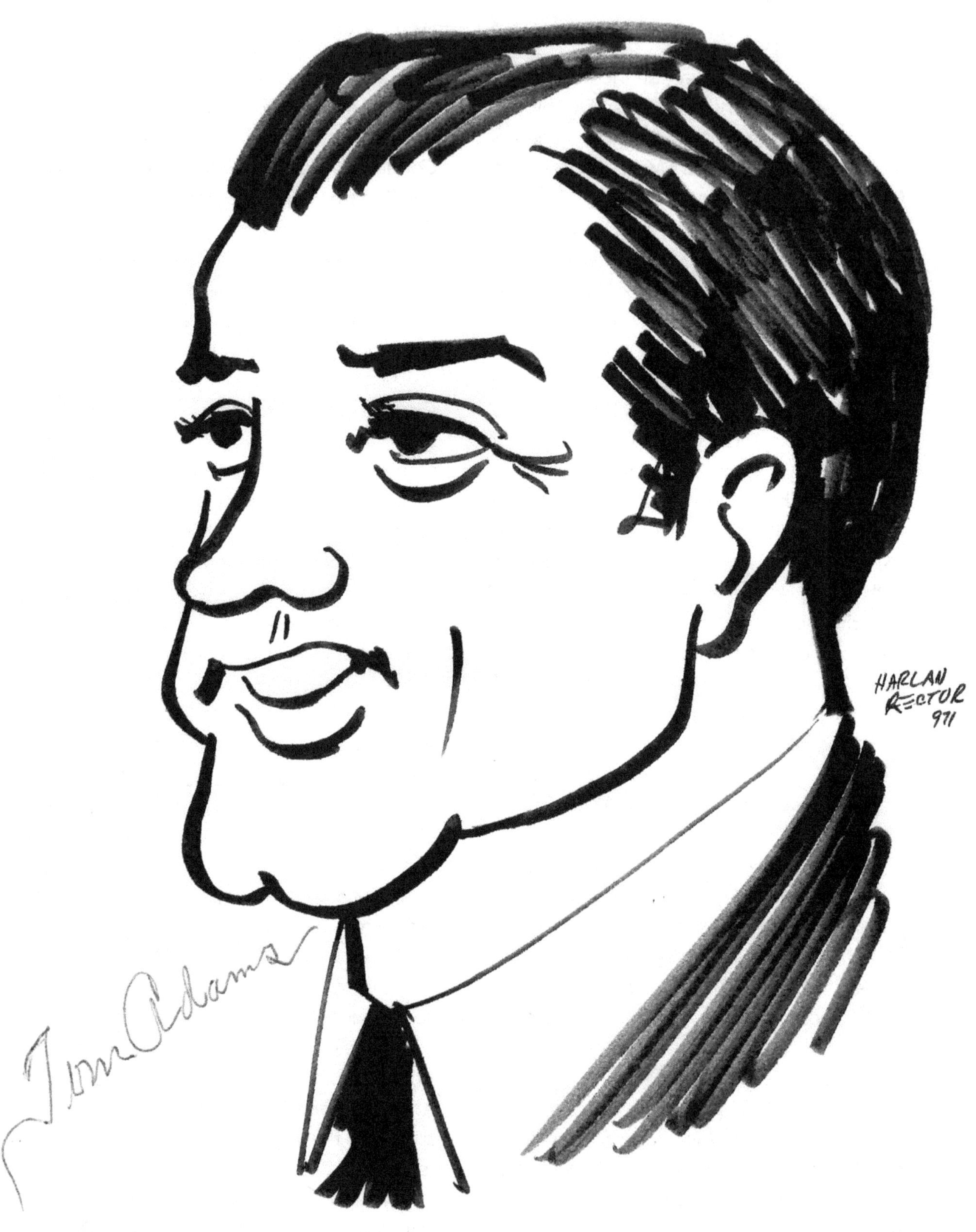

HARLAN
RECTOR
971
Tom Adams

Tom Adams

Thomas B. Adams was raised in Detroit, Michigan, during the Great Depression. There were few benefits of growing up during that time, but one was an appreciation for the little things in life.

Not so little in stature, however, Adams lettered in football and track for three seasons at Wayne State University. For the next four years, he served in the Navy as a fighter pilot during World War II, earning the Distinguished Flying Cross, the Navy Cross, Air Medal, and a Presidential Citation. After his service, Adams, known by most as just Tom, graduated from Wayne State University in 1944.

Tom's career in advertising began as a radio writer at Campbell-Ewald in 1945. As a copywriter, he earned an appreciation for creative people. Art directors and copywriters were beneficiaries of his appreciation. Tom's career was on the rise at Campbell-Ewald, and in 1958 he became President and then, ten years later, Chairman of the Board.

Tom's vision for the company was expansion through the acquisition of clients other than Chevrolet. As the new client list grew, the need for servicing them more efficiently grew as well. Almost on cue, in 1972, The Interpublic Group of Companies proposed a merger with Campbell-Ewald. It became the largest ad agency merger in advertising history. Multiple offices were now operating in New York, Los Angeles, the UK, South Africa, Australia, and Scandinavia.

In 1980, Campbell-Ewald merged with another agency and became Marschalk Campbell Ewald Worldwide, with Tom Adams as its Chairman. He was inducted into The Advertising Hall of Fame upon his retirement in 1984, leaving an incredible legacy of service to his country and community.

Outside of his office, Tom was active in charitable and civic affairs and he was an active alumnus of Wayne State University, particularly sponsoring in their football program. He was so revered at Wayne State that they honored him in 2003 by renaming their football stadium "Tom Adams Field."

I drew this caricature of Tom when he was a guest on the Focus show in September 1971. I have no specific idea why he was there or what he was promoting, but my only thought was, "I owe him a lot, so it better be good."

My experience with Tom over the six years I worked at Campbell-Ewald could fill a book. Looking back, I could have been pink slipped into advertising oblivion more than once were it not for Tom Adams. This one page tribute to my friend, Tom, could not ever be enough. For the rest of my life, his name will be at the top of my gratitude list, and not just because it comes first alphabetically, but of the people whose kindness has been an inspiration in my life.

Thomas B. Adams died in 2005. ◼

HARLAN RECTOR

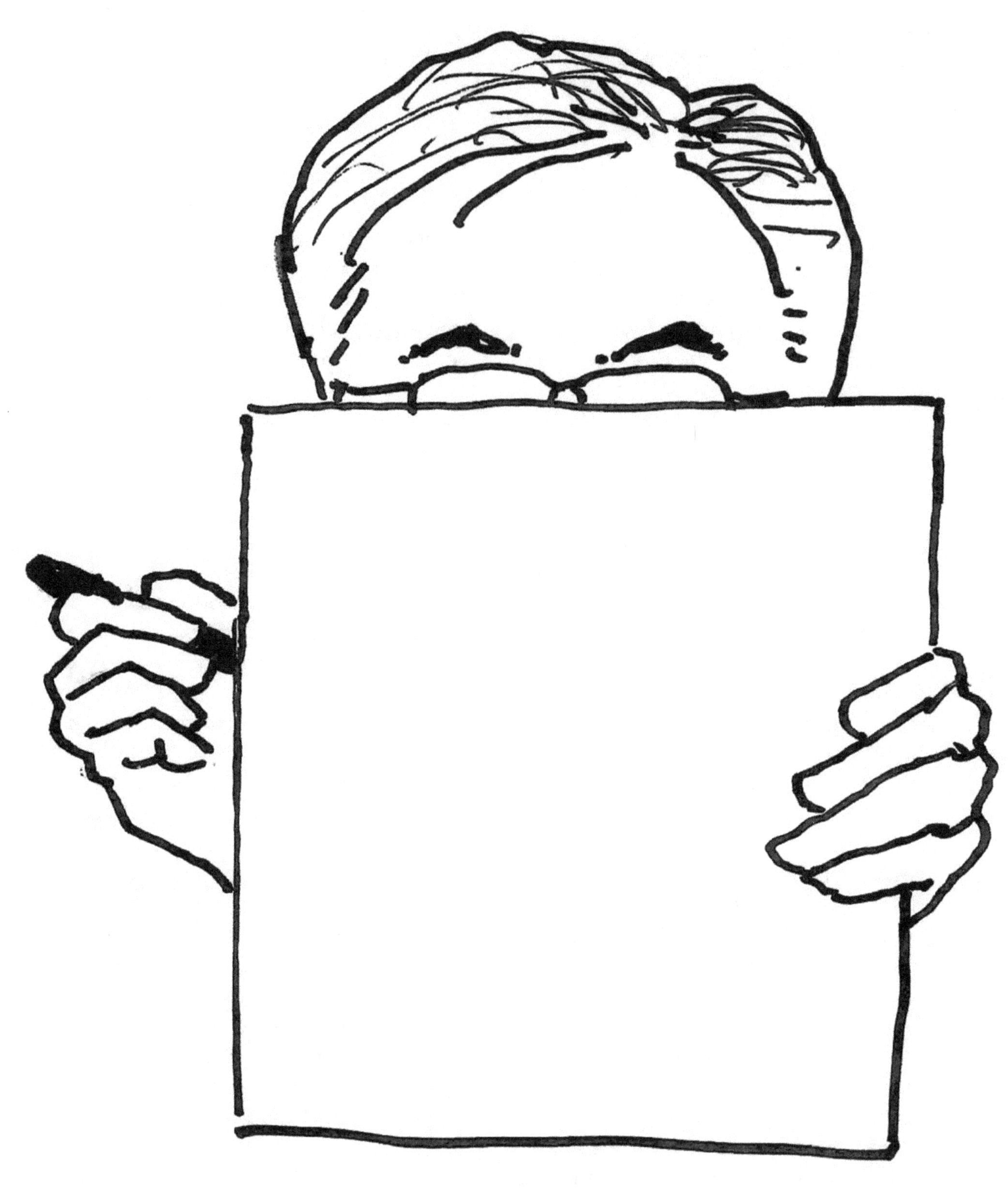

MY SELFIE

Epilogue

It was 1975, we loaded our furniture into a UHaul, our five kids into our station wagon, and moved to Los Angeles. Over the next six years I worked at three ad agencies, a film production company, and freelanced as an art director for a year. Being an advertising art director/producer meant working in a whacky environment which allowed for unorthodox thinking at best and borderline insanity at its worst. It was a colorful life, but it was my black and white time, drawing caricatures with my Sharpie, that created so many precious memories. With the exception of E. G. Marshall and Dom DeLuise, all the caricatures in this book were done while the celebrities were being interviewed on the radio show *Focus* in Detroit.

Long after the radio interviews, I continued drawing caricatures at Hollywood parties and was hired for private parties as well. Once, Michael Landon, 'Little Joe' on the *Bonanza* TV series, hired me to draw caricatures of all the girls at his daughter's private sweet sixteen birthday party at the Beverly Hills Hotel. I always performed wearing a tuxedo out of respect for the occasion. When I met up with Michael at the hotel, and saw him wearing a tuxedo as well, we both laughed. "As an actor," he said, "I'm performing even today—I get to play the father."

While attending an Astrological party hosted by 'The Astrologer to the Stars', Carroll Righter, I drew a caricature of astronaut Buzz Aldrin. He liked the illustration so much he said, "I want to watch you draw Zsa Zsa Gabor!" Now, that was no easy feat. She was like a moving target, talking to everyone, but I managed to draw a good likeness of her. "I want to meet her!" Buzz grabbed her caricature and gave chase. I'd say I was outdone by the second man on the moon.

Working on an ad campaign for Honda, we needed a demo tape of the radio commercial for the client at the presentation. With no money to hire an announcer, I stepped into the booth and read the script, never having done it before. One of the top voiceover women in LA had just finished her session. She was talking with the audio engineer when I began recording but they stopped suddenly when they heard my voice. "Did I do something wrong?" I wondered. No, as it turned out, I was being discovered.

Two voiceover workshops later, I made a demo tape, got an agent and started getting voiceover jobs. I was fired from the big ad agency and on my own. For the first time in my life I was without a steady paycheck. I realized I took my gift of 'art' for granted. Now I had this gift of 'voice' and it changed me from the inside-out. I was told once, "You can't really appreciate your abundance if you don't have gratitude." I turned over my new career to God and placed it squarely in His hands. I went to New York armed with a business card of someone I met back in LA, and a big stack of voiceover demo reels on a Sunday. On Monday, that business card, and a prayer, lead me to the largest agent in NYC. We moved to Connecticut and the rest of my story will be in another book dedicated to God for all His Blessings including, "L.I.G.H.T.", "A Taste of Heaven" and Blue Bell Ice Cream.

When asked if I ever draw my own caricature, I show this picture on the left.■

HARLAN RECTOR

An Artist's Life Before Sharpies

In 1960 I was an art director in St. Louis at Maritz, Inc., a sales promotion firm. It was a colorful change for me after being rescued from an art director job in the yellow page art department of Bell Telephone where everything I did was yellow and black.

All this was during the 'dark ages' of commercial art before there were Sharpies and various colors of Magic Markers.

I was one of seven art directors at the sales promotion company and when we had to prepare larger colorful pieces of art for presentation, we used pastels, the artists' term for colored chalk. Pastels were softer than blackboard chalk making it easier to blend the colors for effect, but also generating more dust residue.

To 'fix' the colored art to the paper, it had to be sprayed with a highly-flamma- ble-rather-toxic mixture somewhat akin to the yet to be invented aerosol spray fixative. To fix the pastel drawings, pictured here, the artist would blow in the small "L" shaped metal tube, similar to a small straw. Some air went down the

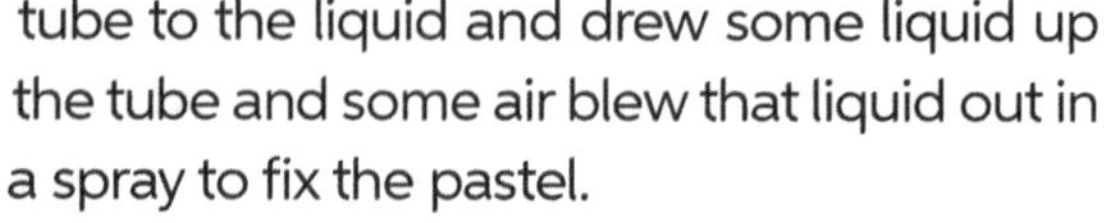

tube to the liquid and drew some liquid up the tube and some air blew that liquid out in a spray to fix the pastel.

In an age where smoking was allowed in the workplace plus breathing some of the vapors, it's a miracle we artists weren't blown to bits or departed before our time from breathing those vapors.

Sharpies and markers in various colors changed forever the artists' way of illustrating layouts for presentation, but too late for me in that job. I left Maritz to begin my career in advertising where the largest layout I had to render was a magazine page for an ad or a storyboard for a television commercial.

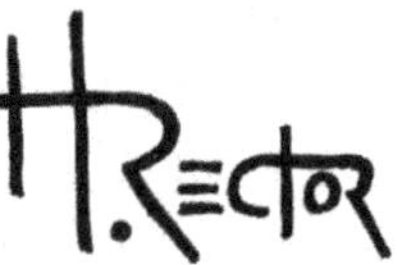

Sharpies, like this actual size drawing, were introduced in 1964 and are being sold today all over the world. I have been using Sharpies since their introduction and this book of caricatures and art is being published on the 50th Anniversary of *Once Upon a Corner in Detroit*.■

HARLAN RECTOR

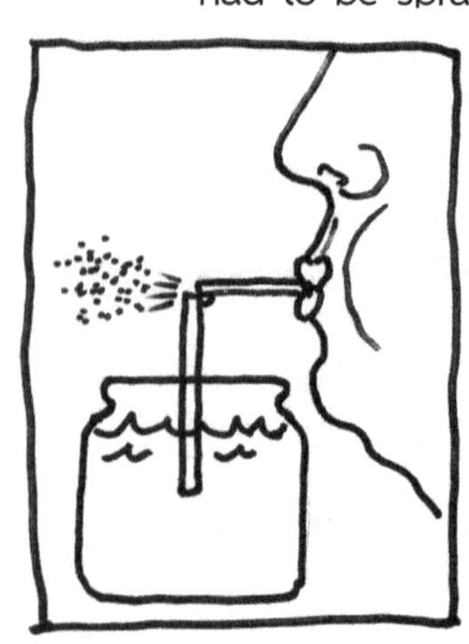

Acknowledgements

Cover Design
Robert Chester Design

Book Design / Production
Cynthia J. Kwitchoff (CJKCREATIVE.COM)

Editing / Proofing
Edward Mickolus   Linda Fields

Biography Writers
Greg Barry   Patricia Daly-Lipe
Johnny Lipe   Linda Fields
Dana Groves   Dorri Hall
Ed Mickolus   Emily Melendez
Jeff Rector   Jerry Rector
Tracy Tripp   Richard Willits

Primary Sources
Wikipedia, IMDb, Personal Knowledge

A
Special
Thanks To

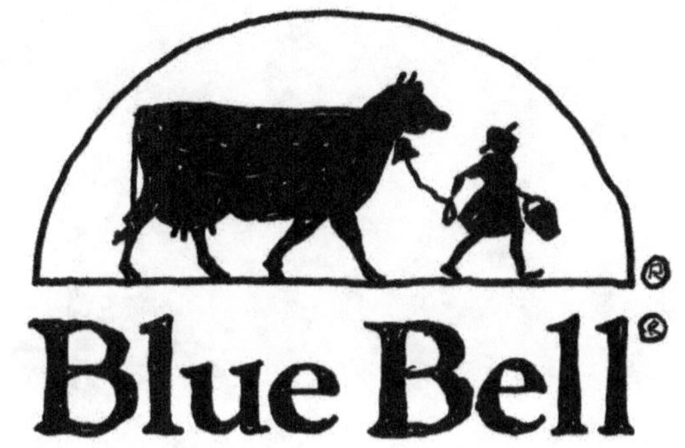

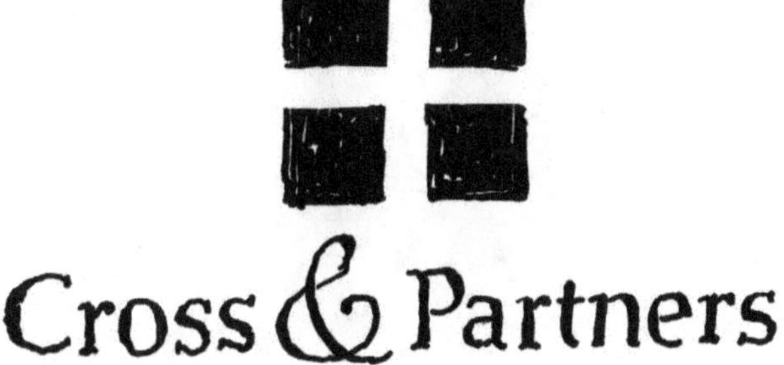

Cross & Partners

H. Rector

www.ingramcontent.com/pod-product-compliance
Lightning Source LLC
Chambersburg PA
CBHW080300030726
47593CB00009B/2557